# LNER STEAM

In 1923, the Great Northern and North Eastern Railways, the famous East Coast route to Scotland, were amalgamated to form the LNER.

During its lifetime the LNER produced the series of famous 'Pacifics' designed by Sir Nigel Gresley, including the world record-breaker *Mallard*.

This masterly account is splendidly illustrated by photographs showing every aspect of steam locomotive design and operation on the LNER.

'Well sustained interest . . . Recommended.'
*Railway Magazine*

'The last fine flowering of the steam age . . . Exhilarating stuff, and excitingly recreated by Mr Nock, the most engaging of railway table-talkers.'
*The Times Literary Supplement*

*Also available in the David & Charles Series*

*The David & Charles Series*

---

# LNER STEAM

---

O. S. NOCK, B Sc, C Eng, FICE,
FI Mech E

UNABRIDGED

PAN BOOKS LTD : LONDON

First published 1969 by David & Charles (Publishers) Ltd.
This edition published 1971 by Pan Books Ltd.,
33 Tothill Street, London, S.W.1.

ISBN 0 330 02680 1

Printed in Great Britain by
Richard Clay (The Chaucer Press), Ltd, Bungay, Suffolk

# CONTENTS

# ILLUSTRATIONS IN PHOTOGRAVURE

**(Photos from the author's collection include the work of the late C. J. Barnard, K. A. C. R. Nunn, E. C. Poultney, R. J. Purvis, W. J. Reynolds, and G. M. Soole.)**

# PREFACE

The London & North Eastern Railway Company had an existence of just twenty-five years, and for the first eighteen of these Sir Nigel Gresley was chief mechanical engineer. His stature eventually became that of a colossus in railway mechanical engineering, as one brilliant success followed another: the 'A3' Super-Pacifics; *Cock o' the North*; the 'Silver Jubilee' service; the 'Coronation'; and eventually the world-shattering speed record of *Mallard*. Then following his untimely death in 1941 came the shock that at least some of those who had been most intimately concerned with the Gresley development did not hold it in the esteem generally recognized. There was bewilderment and resentment at the drastic changes made by Edward Thompson, and the bewilderment was increased when, in turn, Thompson's successor executed a still further *volte-face*.

The story of LNER steam thus has all the elements of drama in it, in the fascinating mixture that it presents of brilliant achievement on the road, the clash of views in the later years, and in the delightful continuance of older traditions and older engine types on the lines of the former constituent companies. My very first book was entitled *The Locomotives of Sir Nigel Gresley*, and in the preparation of the original series of articles which was published in the *Railway Magazine* I had the assistance of Sir Nigel himself, in correcting the proofs of the first three or four instalments right down to the time of his death. The present book naturally contains a good deal of material that appeared in the original, and I am indebted to Mr B. W. C. Cooke, the present Publishing Director, for permission to use it. While the material so gathered, now more than thirty years ago, forms the centrepiece of this present book I have put a good deal of additional 'flesh' on to this basic skeleton. There are chapters dealing with the locomotives of the various constituent companies of the LNER, while the later chapters deal with a period in which I was privileged to see a great deal of LNER engine working at first hand.

The difficult and perplexing period of Edward Thompson's chieftainship was made clearer through his own friendliness to me and my work, and through the candour with which he explained his problems, and the measures he took to meet them. Peppercorn I never met, but the last stages of steam on the East Coast Route were again illuminated for me by my personal friendship with Kenneth J. Cook, who became chief mechanical and electrical engineer of the Eastern and North Eastern Regions of British Railways. My friendship with Cook had begun much earlier, while he was still on the Great Western; and I am glad to be able to set on record the part he played to ensure that steam days ended in a blaze of glory on the East Coast Route.

Many other friends both inside and outside the railway service have helped towards the preparation of this book. Among running superintendents who not only furnished me with footplate passes but also with the guidance of their most senior inspectors, I must particularly mention E. D. Trask, F. H. Petty, L. P. Parker, and G. A. Musgrave, while in later years I have had invaluable help from T. Matthewson-Dick, T. C. B. Miller, and R. H. N. Hardy. Many amateur enthusiasts have helped to fill in the overall picture by sending me numerous logs of train running, and I must thank in particular Messrs R. A. H. Weight, R. I. Nelson, and G. Carpenter. Naturally it has been possible to include no more than a minute fraction of the running data sent to me; but the mass of material available has enabled me to write with greater authority than would otherwise have been possible.

Lastly, as always, I have a special word of gratitude for Olivia my wife. Dealing with the LNER she has been on her home ground, having served the old company at King's Cross for several years, and I only hope that the evident pleasure the typing of the story has given to her will be shared by those who come to read it.

O. S. NOCK

Silver Cedars
High Bannerdown
Batheaston
Bath

# CHAPTER ONE

# *GRESLEY, CHIEF MECHANICAL ENGINEER*

Amalgamation of business concerns, on whatever scale, is inevitably a time of anxiety, frustration, and upheaval; and the grouping of the railways of Great Britain into four large companies, as from January 1st, 1923, was certainly no exception. But there are degrees in everything, and from the outset the Eastern Group – the new London & North Eastern Railway – was supremely fortunate in its top management. The combination of William Whitelaw as chairman of the board and Ralph Wedgwood as chief general manager was a happy one, and their skill in administration and personnel management had felicitous results from end to end of the line. In this book I am, of course, concerned mainly with the department of the chief mechanical engineer, and great interest naturally centred upon the choice of the man to have that vital post.

At the end of 1922, among the constituent companies there were four men of seniority, stature, and unquestioned reputation holding office; A. J. Hill on the Great Eastern, Sir Vincent Raven on the North Eastern, John G. Robinson on the Great Central, and H. N. Gresley on the Great Northern. In Scotland, W. Chalmers had not been very long in office on the North British, and neither he nor Heywood, of the Great North of Scotland, ranked equal in stature to any of the four English engineers just mentioned. Of the four, Robinson had been in office longest, and his reputation as a builder of strong and reliable engines had been greatly enhanced by the choice of the Great Central 2–8–0 as a Ministry of Munitions standard for general service overseas in World War I. Hill and Raven were both nearing the age for retirement, and Robinson himself was 65 years of age at the beginning of 1923. Gresley, on the other hand, was only 48. How Robinson was offered the job and turned it down was told in a letter he himself wrote to *The*

*Railway Gazette* in May 1941, shortly after the death of Sir Nigel Gresley.

Robinson wrote:

It is very gratifying to me to know I was instrumental in recommending Gresley to his position as Chief Mechanical Engineer on the London and North Eastern Railway. It came about when the Chairman, Lord Faringdon, and Mr Whitelaw, were considering the chief officers of the various departments. They sent for me and to my surprise offered the position to me, which I considered was paying me a very great compliment at my age, which was then 65, and in the usual order of things, due for retirement. I thanked them and declined the position, explaining my reasons. However, they would not agree, asked me to 'sleep on it' and in the lounge of the Great Central Hotel after dinner, my old friend Gresley came to see me and informed me that he had heard on the best authority I was going to be appointed Chief and hoped I would accept him as my assistant. I found myself in an invidious position and declined to discuss the question, but I put him at ease, intending that, in the event of my appointment, I would certainly agree to him as my assistant. Gresley then left me apparently happy.

Now for the final interview. I advised the Chairman to appoint a much younger man. I came to the conclusion that to organize four railways into one great railway would take many years to accomplish, to my liking; hence my recommendation to appoint a much younger man. They were disappointed at my decision and asked me if I would *privately* recommend a suitable man. 'Yes,' I replied, and strongly advised the appointment to be given to Mr Gresley, who was the right age. He was sent for and accepted and I am pleased that I have been spared to know of his success and hope his successor, whoever he may be, will follow in his footsteps.

The appointment of Gresley ensured the continuance of the line of development followed on the Great Northern Railway

since 1918, embodying the general use of three-cylinder propulsion, with an arrangement of conjugated valve gear for the
middle cylinder, permitting the use of only two sets of motion
for the three cylinders. But while Gresley developed his own
practice for entirely new designs, no policy of 'scrap and build'
was initiated so far as the other constituent companies were
concerned. A degree of autonomy was granted to the major
works of Stratford, Gorton, Darlington, and Eastfield, so that
while new engines were drafted stage by stage to those areas
the old traditions were allowed to continue so far as the maintenance of existing stock was concerned. Generally speaking,
the locomotives of pre-grouping design were well on top of
their jobs, and Gresley was more than content to let them continue. So far as the Great Northern itself was concerned it is
well known that he had a great affection for the Ivatt large-
boilered 'Atlantics'. In the development of superheating on
those engines he had produced units of outstanding capability,
and although on the basis of nominal tractive effort those GNR
'Atlantics' were among the least powerful of all the pre-
grouping ten-wheeled engines in the LNER group, in performance on the road they were the most puissant of all.

To appreciate fully the line of development of locomotive
practice on the LNER it is necessary at the outset to take a look
at the position on the major constituent railways of the new
group. Although the main development came, somewhat
naturally, from the Great Northern, the other four large
companies all made their contributions, and by the end of the
Gresley régime very little scrapping of 'constituent' engines
had taken place.

# CHAPTER TWO

## THE CONSTITUENTS :
## 1. GREAT CENTRAL

From a revenue-earning point of view the Great Central was not one of the most important constituents of the London & North Eastern Railway. Ever since the construction of the London extension line it had been a continuous fight for traffic, and despite the most enterprising ventures in all phases of railway activity, the results had been disappointing to the shareholders. During this period, however, the engineering progress of the company had been continuous. While the quantity of new locomotives put on the road had not been very great, J. G. Robinson had not been fettered in any way in the production of new designs and at the time of grouping, the Great Central stud was one of the most interesting and best maintained in any part of Great Britain. On the grounds of thermal efficiency the stud as a whole was not very distinguished; but the loads they had to convey for express passenger traffic were not great, and in the very fast services operated between London, Leicester, and Nottingham there were, in 1922, very few locomotive designs in the country which could have worked the service at an appreciably smaller overall coal consumption. The standard of reliability was very high; so was the punctuality of the running, and so far as freight services were concerned one needed to do no more than to point to the selection of the Robinson 2–8–0 mineral engines as the type chosen for service with the ROD in France during World War I, to find ample evidence of the esteem in which Great Central engines were held by the railway world in general. The fact that those engines not only did a splendid job of work in World War I, but were chosen twenty-five years later for an exactly similar role in World War II is further evidence of their solid working reliability.

Two other factors apart from features of engineering design

led to locomotives of the former Great Central Railway playing a considerably bigger part in LNER locomotive affairs in the first years of grouping than those of any other company, other than the Great Northern. With Gresley as chief mechanical engineer it was no more than natural, and logical on the score of merit alone, that Great Northern ideas would predominate; but at first the influence of the Great Central was quite strong. The two factors that contributed to this were, firstly, that Gresley himself felt an undoubted debt of gratitude to J. G. Robinson for his appointment, in the circumstances described in Chapter One. In providing locomotive power for the entire LNER system it was therefore quite natural that Gresley should pay particular attention to Great Central designs when traffic requirements called for a class of locomotive for which there was no Great Northern type immediately available. It was in these circumstances that the Robinson 'Director' class 4–4–0 and the 'A5' 4–6–2 suburban tank were perpetuated in LNER days.

The second factor developed when W. G. P. Maclure was appointed locomotive running superintendent of the Southern Area – Western section. This meant that there was a Great Central man in charge of running, not only over the former Great Central line but also over the Great Northern. Maclure as a good Great Central man was naturally looking for opportunities to display the capabilities of Great Central engines in a wider field, and it was through his influence that, first of all, the four-cylinder 4–6–0s of the 'Lord Faringdon' class, and later 4–4–0s of the 'Director' class had a long-term trial on express passenger working from King's Cross. These trials on the Great Northern line had no connexion whatever with the introduction of new engines of the 'Director' class in Scotland. There, something more powerful than the North British 'Scott' class 4–4–0s was needed for the Edinburgh–Glasgow services, and the 'Director' class of the Great Central provided an ideal short-term answer to the need. Unfortunately the Scottish 'Directors' had not the fine appearance of their Great Central progenitors because the reduced height of the loading gauge over the North British line compelled the use of much shorter chimneys and dome covers of reduced height. The result was not pleasing to those familiar with the exceptionally symmetrical and handsome appearance of the original Great Central engines of the same class. Nevertheless the Scottish 'Directors', with excellent names taken from characters in the Waverley novels, admirably fulfilled the need for enhanced power, and they put in many years of very hard and useful service. The 'A5' 4–6–2 tanks built after grouping were put to work on the Tees-side services of the former NER. They, too, suffered from the use of incongruous boiler mountings, which greatly detracted from their appearance.

The influence of the Great Central, however, was not by any means confined to the construction and usage of Great Central engines beyond their former spheres of activity. From Gorton came that extremely dynamic personality, Robert A. Thom, who eventually became mechanical engineer, Doncaster. If ever there was a live wire it was Thom. Sometimes he was a bit too live for Gresley's liking. He was a most vivid and forceful speaker always bubbling over with ideas and opinions, and in LNER days he fathered through Doncaster works some of the most important developments in locomotive construction carried out during the Gresley era. Of his loquaciousness a good story is told. During one of these periods of development he was summoned to King's Cross to report and discuss how things were going in the works, and as usual he had a great deal to say – so much so that at one stage in the proceedings, Gresley rose from his chair and brought his fist down with a resounding crash on the table with the words: 'damn it all Thom will you shut up, and let me get a word in edgeways!' Despite this, Thom, from the Great Central, was a highly influential and much appreciated member of the Gresley team, and I shall tell later of the practice he successfully fathered in Doncaster works of the casting of all the cylinders, valve chests, and smokebox saddles on several of the major Gresley three-cylinder engine designs in a single monobloc casting. The personality of Thom was eventually perhaps the greatest contribution the Great Central made to the synthesis of ideas and practices that went to make up the Gresley tradition.

The Great Central locomotive headquarters was at Gorton works, but it was at Sheffield that the greatest operational activity was to be seen. Despite the spectacular performance of passenger trains on the London extension, the Great Central was primarily a freight carrier, and the coal traffic dealt with at Wath, and dispatched west, east, and southwards in long trains was at one time enormous. It was on this work that the celebrated 'O4' 2-8-0s earned such a reputation for hard, untiring, reliable work. One could not call them 'dividend-earners', for the Great Central never paid one. But no company had a simpler, or better heavy freight engine. In the north they were well reinforced by Robinson's earliest eight-coupled engines, the 0-8-0s of 1901. These latter engines were rarely seen south of Annesley. On the London extension most of the heavy freights in the last few days of the GCR and in the early grouping years were worked by the large four-cylinder 4-6-0s, which had the reputation of being rather heavy coal burners. Nevertheless, the loads they tackled were at times enormous, and they had to be worked over a route with much grading that could be regarded as quite severe, when it could not be tackled as a hilarious switchback, in express passenger style: tearing down one descent, and charging up the next bank with the impetus gained by the high maximum speeds.

For main-line passenger workings there was a plethora of different designs, of which the majority, whether eight-wheelers or ten-wheelers were used indiscriminately on the fast trains. The various classes of Great Central express engines were:

1. The two-cylinder simple 'Atlantics'.
2. The three-cylinder compound 'Atlantics'.
3. The earlier Robinson 4-6-0s of the 'Immingham' and the '196' classes.
4. The 'Director' class 4-4-0s.
5. The 'Sir Sam Fay' class two-cylinder 4-6-0s.
6. The 'Lord Faringdon' class four-cylinder 4-6-0s.

Leicester shed had nothing more modern than 'Atlantics', and their London workings were exclusively worked by either com-

pound or simple 4–4–2s. On the double-home turns between
Marylebone and Manchester one found 'Directors', 'Fays',
and 'Faringdons' used almost indiscriminately. The London
workings were mostly taken by 'Directors', with 4–6–0s from
the Manchester end. The earlier Robinson 4–6–0s, among the
most beautifully proportioned engines ever to run the rails,
mostly worked north and east of Sheffield. On the through
expresses between Bradford and Marylebone, Lancashire &
Yorkshire engines from Low Moor used to work into Sheffield
Victoria. In the early 1920s, Sheffield was indeed the locomotive spotter's dream of heaven, for a station where only one
railway was involved – except for the odd 'Lanky'. In three
hours' note-taking I once 'bagged' examples of all the express
passenger classes mentioned under headings 1 to 6 above,
together with examples of many freight types:

1. 0–8–0 tender.
2. 2–8–0 (ROD) with small boiler.
3. 2–8–0 large boiler.
4. Four-cylinder 4–6–0 freight.
5. 0–6–0 'Pom-pom'.
6. 4–6–0 'Fish' engine.

All the above were of Robinson design, finished in lined black,
and all immaculate. The party was finished off by a Hughes
rebuilt four-cylinder 4–6–0 of the Lancashire & Yorkshire.

There was much spectacular running, and although the
loads were definitely light in the years before World War I, the
train formations tended to increase considerably in the early
grouping period. During the war itself the Great Central had
managed to avoid the most drastic of decelerations that were
forced upon its larger neighbours. A degree of smartness in the
train workings remained throughout the darkest years of the
war, and above all, these trains alone among the north-going
lines from London retained some form of meal service. It was
only natural that this facility attracted some additional business, and when more normal conditions returned some regular
travellers who had used the Great Central during the war re-

mained. Pre-war schedules were largely restored, and as time
went on loads tended to increase still further; and with no
changes in the types of locomotives available the tasks set to
individual engines and crews became progressively harder. In
fact, some of the finest locomotive work ever done on the Great
Central line took place in the years 1925 to 1935.

In turning to actual performance, one of the most interesting
trains in early grouping days over the Great Central line was
the 6.20 PM from Marylebone to Bradford. This train took the
Wycombe line, and until the year 1936 was booked non-stop
from Marylebone to Leicester, 107·6 miles in 114 minutes.
Slip coaches were detached at both Finmere and Woodford,
and with a load of little less than 300 tons from the start it was
a very stiff proposition for the Leicester 'Atlantics'. Right
down to the year 1936 it was invariably an 'Atlantic' job and I
had the pleasure of recording the locomotive work on a number
of occasions. Taking the Sudbury line at the start, with speed
restrictions over the junctions at Neasden and Northolt and a
stiff climb between these two slacks, it needed very good work
to cover the initial 11·6 miles to Northolt Junction in the
scheduled 17 minutes. This left 94 minutes for the remaining
96 miles on to Leicester. Here again there was little to spare. I
have tabulated details of four runs on this most interesting
train, taken at various times between 1927 and 1936. Three of
these were on the old non-stop timing, while the last one was
made shortly after the abandonment of the slip workings when
the train made intermediate stops at Finmere and Woodford.
The load was lighter from the start, but the intermediate
timings were very sharp and the working was if anything
harder than in the non-stop days. This change in timetable,
however, roughly coincided with the superseding of the 'Atlantics' on this duty by the 'Sandringham' class 4–6–0s, a batch
of which were sent new to Leicester in the spring of 1936.

Turning now to the three non-stop runs, details of which are
tabulated, engine No 5264 on the first of the three had to con-
tend with a very heavy westerly gale which affected the running
considerably once the train was into the open country north of
Princes Risborough. Nevertheless, apart from the permanent

TABLE 1    LNER 6.20 P?

| | Run No<br>Engine GC 4-4-2 No<br>Load tons E/F: to Finmere<br>to Woodford<br>to Leicester | | 1<br>5264<br>276/290<br>239/250<br>202/210 | |
|---|---|---|---|---|
| *Distance<br>miles* | | *Sch.<br>min* | *Actual<br>min   sec* | *Speeds<br>mph* |
| 0·0 | MARYLEBONE | 0 | 0    00 | — |
| 3·0 | Brondesbury | | 6    42 | 40 |
| 5·1 | *Neasden Junction* | 9 | 9    38 | 59/50* |
| — | | | — | 49 |
| 8·8 | South Harrow | | 13    43 | 50 |
| — | | | | 58 |
| 11·6 | Northolt Junction | 17 | 17    05 | 44* |
| 16·1 | Denham | | 22    16 | 60 |
| 18·7 | Gerrards Cross | | 25    10 | 51 |
| 23·0 | Beaconsfield | | 30    05 | 55½ |
| 27·8 | HIGH WYCOMBE | 35 | 34    45 | 66/43* |
| 32·8 | Saunderton | | 41    25 | 45½ |
| 36·0 | PRINCES RISBORO' | 45 | 45    00 | 75 |
| | | | p.w.s. | 50 |
| 41·4 | Haddenham | | 50    03 | — |
| 45·4 | *Ashendon Junction* | | 54    20 | 56 |
| 51·3 | *Grendon Junction* | 60 | 60    28 | 61½ |
| 53·3 | Calvert | | 62    28 | 56/62 |
| 59·0 | FINMERE | 68 | 68    30 | 50 |
| — | | | — | 66 |
| 63·8 | Brackley | | 73    38 | 60 |
| 67·0 | Helmdon | | 77    10 | 53 |
| 70·6 | Culworth | | 80    42 | 64½ |
| 71·8 | *Culworth Junction* | | 81    47 | 70½ |
| 73·6 | WOODFORD | 82 | 83    22 | 67 |
| 76·0 | Charwelton | | 85    48 | 57½ |
| 83·0 | Braunston | | 91    40 | 80½ |
| 87·7 | RUGBY | | 95    51 | 60/68 |
| 91·3 | *Shawell* | | — | 50 |
| 94·5 | Lutterworth | | 102    49 | 60/53 |
| 98·4 | Ashby | | 106    52 | 68 |
| 102·9 | Whetstone | | 110    30 | 81 |
| 106·6 | *Leicester South Goods* | | 113    20 | 72½ |
| 107·6 | LEICESTER | 114 | 114    40 | — |

## MARYLEBONE–LEICESTER

| 2<br>5262<br>285/300<br>248/260<br>211/220 | | 3<br>6090<br>315/340<br>278/300<br>241/260 | | 4<br>5363<br>241/260<br>241/260<br>241/260 | | |
|---|---|---|---|---|---|---|
| *Actual*<br>min  sec | *Speeds*<br>mph | *Actual*<br>min  sec | *Speeds*<br>mph | *Sch.*<br>min | *Actual*<br>min  sec | *Speeds*<br>mph |
| 0  00 | — | 0  00 | — | 0 | 0  00 | — |
| 7  01 | 32 | 7  15 | — | | 6  38 | 32 |
| 9  34 | 63/45* | 10  10 | 50* | 9 | 9  20 | 56 |
| — | | — | | | p.w.s. | 22 |
| 14  23 | 43½ | 15  05 | 43½ | | 16  07 | 43 |
| — | 57 | sigs sev | | | — | 56 |
| 17  41 | 49* | 20  25 | 0 | 17 | 19  45 | 42* |
| 23  05 | 53 | 27  50 | 50 | | 24  58 | 61½ |
| 26  26 | 46 | sigs | 35 | | 27  46 | 55 |
| 31  23 | 57½ | 31  30 | — | | 32  13 | 60 |
| 35  58 | 69/44* | 37  55 | 43 | 35 | 36  48 | 72½/42* |
| 42  39 | 45 | 43  15 | 60/42* | | 43  31 | 47½ |
| 46  23 | 69 | 50  15 | 42 | 45 | 46  56 | 73 |
| | | 54  10 | 63½ | | | |
| 50  43 | 80½ | 58  50 | 74 | | 51  03 | 88 |
| 54  04 | 69 | 62  30 | 63½ | | 54  06 | 78 |
| 59  37 | 64/67 | 68  25 | 57½ | | 59  08 | 67/69 |
| 61  34 | 58/66 | 70  30 | 54/61 | | 60  57 | 65/70 |
| 67  13 | 54 | 76  45 | 47 | 67½ | 66  50 | — |
| — | 69 | — | 62½ | | — | 63 |
| 72  00 | 62 | 82  15 | — | | 7  18 | 57 |
| 75  18 | 57 | 86  00 | 50 | | 10  48 | 54 |
| 78  45 | — | 89  45 | 60 | | 14  13 | 67/62 |
| 79  51 | 72 | 91  00 | 67 | 14 | 15  15 | 76½ |
| 81  24 | 66 | 92  35 | 64½ | 16½ | 17  11 | |
| 83  46 | 60 | 95  00 | 58½ | | 4  52 | 46 |
| 89  42 | 82 | 101  05 | 80½ | | 11  09 | 82 |
| 93  43 | 61/69 | 105  10 | 64/72 | | 15  07 | 63/73 |
| 96  00 | 50½ | — | 57½ | | 18  15 | 56 |
| 100  33 | 60/51 | 111  20 | 66/60 | | 21  31 | 66/61 |
| 104  41 | 67 | 115  00 | 70½ | | 25  08 | 74 |
| 108  23 | 75 | 118  30 | 82 | | 28  27 | 87 |
| 111  57 | — | 121  20 | 75 | | 31  06 | 80½ |
| sigs | — | — | | | — | |
| 114  00 | — | 122  45 | — | 34 | 32  25 | |

restrictions.

way restriction to 50 mph at Haddenham which, coming at a point where speed normally rules very high, cost at least a minute in running, time would have been kept. It was always amusing to see that the Great Central drivers, like their counterparts on the Great Western two-hour Birmingham expresses, always took a liberal view of the speed restriction through High Wycombe. The official limit there was 35 mph, but Great Western and Great Central drivers alike went through at nearly 45 so as to get a good run at the Saunderton bank. Engine 5264 was doing well in the early stages with a sustained speed of 52 mph up the 1 in 254 gradient to Beaconsfield, and 45½ mph up the 1 in 167 to Saunderton. Then the very fast running usually made off the Chiltern Hills was cut short by Haddenham slack after a maximum of only 75 mph. Thus instead of getting a run at the slightly adverse section from the joint line to the joining of the Great Central main line proper at Grendon, the engine was having to work hard against the slightly adverse gradient. Nevertheless, Grendon was passed only half a minute late.

After that comes the negotiation of the undulating main line of the Great Central 'London Extension' with its ruling gradients of 1 in 176, and long stretches at that inclination both uphill and down. Uphill the gradients are not long enough for the speed to fall to an absolute sustained minimum, because drivers used the favourable stretches with skill to gain impetus. From the table it will be seen that the principal uphill minimum speeds were 50 mph at Finmere, 53 at Helmdon, and 50 before Lutterworth, while the downhill speeds on the longer stretches of 1 in 176 descent were 80½ mph at Braunston and 81 below Whetstone. It was always a concluding excitement to observe how rapidly Leicester itself was approached, and the speed was usually maintained at between 70 and 80 mph right up to Leicester South Goods Junction, which was only just a mile from the central station. But for the wind, which was catching the train very badly on the fast downhill sections, there is little doubt that the driver would have brought the train into Leicester on time.

The second run with engine 5262 was considerably slower in

its early stages, and Princes Risborough was passed $1\frac{1}{4}$ minutes late. But after that, with a clear road and fine calm weather, the job was made to look easy. The maximum speed descending from the Chiltern Hills was $80\frac{1}{2}$ mph and very fine uphill work from Grendon, with minimum speeds of 54 mph at Finmere and 57 mph at Helmdon, took the train through Woodford half a minute early. This was the critical point in the run. It was usually possible in favourable conditions to regain a minute, or even two minutes, by hard running from this point, but on this occasion it was not necessary, and the concluding speeds of $50\frac{1}{2}$ mph before Lutterworth and no more than 75 down Whetstone bank would have seen us into Leicester a minute earlier, but for the final check.

The third run was made on the Friday before Whitsun in 1927 with an extra coach on the train and thus an initial load of 340 tons gross behind the tender. The engine, No 6090, was originally built as a three-cylinder simple, but at the time of my run she had been converted to a standard two-cylinder engine. With the heavier load the start out of London was naturally slower than usual, and we then got involved in a whole succession of signal checks. This train followed closely down the joint line behind the 6.10 PM from Paddington to Birkenhead, and at holiday weekends the latter train was usually duplicated. As a result of this we were stopped dead at Northolt Junction and suffered adverse signals in varying degrees right out to High Wycombe. We passed Princes Risborough $9\frac{1}{4}$ minutes late. Having regard to the heavy load being conveyed, it was excellent work to regain half a minute between there and Leicester. Naturally the uphill work was not so fast, and speeds were 47 mph at Finmere and 50 at Helmdon. At Woodford, indeed, we were running $10\frac{1}{2}$ minutes late. But then with the load reduced to 260 tons the driver went as hard as he could for Leicester and regained a clear two minutes. Whether or not we should have been able to keep time with a clear road throughout is doubtful, because the heavy load would naturally have told adversely in the running from Marylebone out to High Wycombe; but it was, nevertheless, an excellent run.

TABLE 2  LNER MARYLEBON

| | 1 |
|---|---|
| Run No | 1 |
| Engine No | 6164 |
| Engine Name | *Earl Beatty* |
| Engine Class | 4–6–0 |
| Load tons E/F | 273/300 |
| Driver | *Chapman (G.)* |

| Distance miles | | Sch. min | Actual min  sec | Speeds mph |
|---|---|---|---|---|
| 0·0 | MARYLEBONE | 0 | 0   00 | — |
| 3·0 | Brondesbury | | 7   15 | — |
| 5·2 | *Neasden Junction* | 9 | 9   40 | 62½ |
| 9·2 | Harrow | 14 | 14   20 | 46½ |
| 11·4 | Pinner | | 16   45 | 61 |
| 13·7 | Northwood | | 19   15 | 51½ |
| 17·2 | Rickmansworth | 23 | 22   50 | 66/40* |
| 19·4 | Chorley Wood | | 26   10 | 38½ |
| 23·6 | Amersham | | 33   10 | 36½ |
| 28·8 | Great Missenden | | 38   40 | 68/50 |
| 33·3 | Wendover | | 43   30 | 68 |
| 38·0 | AYLESBURY | 46 | 47   30 | 74 |
| 44·1 | Quainton Road | 52½ | 53   30 | 53* |
| 46·8 | *Grendon Junction* | | 56   30 | 66 |
| 48·8 | Calvert | | 58   25 | 60/65 |
| 54·5 | FINMERE | | 64   00 | 53 |
| 59·3 | Brackley | | 69   00 | 65 |
| 62·5 | Helmdon | | 72   35 | 52½ |
| 67·4 | *Culworth Junction* | | — | 68 |
| 69·2 | WOODFORD | 77 | 79   00 | 64½ |
| 71·5 | Charwelton | | 81   30 | 54 |
| 78·5 | Braunston | | 87   40 | 76½ |
| 83·2 | RUGBY | | 92   05 | 58/66 |
| 86·8 | *Shawell* | | — | 56 |
| 90·0 | Lutterworth | | 98   40 | 64/60 |
| 93·9 | Ashby | | 102   20 | 71½ |
| 98·4 | Whetstone | | 106   00 | 75 |
| 102·1 | *Leicester South Goods* | | sigs | — |
| 103·1 | LEICESTER | 109 | 111   55 | — |

\* Spee

The last run was made after the slip coaches had been dispensed with, and a load of 260 tons was carried throughout. Things were made difficult in the early stages by the bad permanent way restriction near Wembley Hill; but once on to the

LEICESTER (*via* AYLESBURY)

| 2 5438 Worsley-Taylor 4–4–0 305/330 Rangeley (G.) | | 3 5504 Jutland 4–4–0 279/295 France (N.) | |
|---|---|---|---|
| Actual min sec | Speeds mph | Actual min sec | Speeds mph |
| 0  00 | — | 0  00 | — |
| 7  05 | — | 6  49 | — |
| 9  45 | 64½ | 9  15 | 66½ |
| 14  15 | 45 | 13  22 | 50 |
| 16  40 | 61 | 15  35 | 65½ |
| 19  15 | 57½ | 17  55 | 56 |
| 22  50 | 68/35* | 21  28 | 64/45* |
| 26  45 | 32 | 24  34 | 42 |
| 34  45 | 31¼ | 32  05 | 31 |
| 40  10 | 71½/55 | 37  24 | 74/55 |
| 44  35 | 74 | 41  46 | 74 |
| 48  25 | 75 | 45  20 | 82 |
| 54  15 | 53* | 50  48 | 55* |
| 57  15 | 62½ | 53  43 | 66 |
| 59  15 | 58/62 | 55  33 | 62/69 |
| 65  15 | 50 | 60  52 | 56 |
| 70  20 | 64½ | 65  35 | 69 |
| 74  00 | 51 | 68  57 | 56 |
| 78  50 | 71½ | 73  22 | 75 |
| 80  20 | 66 | 74  52 | 68½ |
| 82  45 | 58½ | 77  00 | 64 |
| 88  40 | 82 | 82  39 | 84 |
| 92  35 | 63½/71½ | 86  26 | 65½/73 |
| 95  50 | 52½ | 89  33 | 54 |
| 99  10 | 64/56 | 92  55 | 62/54 |
| 103  05 | 70½ | 96  50 | 69½ |
| 106  40 | 82 | 100  25 | 76½ |
| — | — | 103  29 | 67 |
| 110  55 | | 104  52 | |

restrictions.

joint line some very hard work was done. Particularly, the ascent of Gerrards Cross bank was magnificent. After falling to 55 mph at Gerrards Cross itself, speed increased up the continuous 1 in 254 gradient to 60 mph at Beaconsfield summit.

Saunderton bank was taken in good style and then we had some tremendous speed on to Ashendon, with a maximum speed of 88 mph. More hard running followed, and when steam was shut off for the Finmere stop speed was still 61 mph up the 1 in 176 gradient.

Time had been slightly improved on to this point, but the very sharp allowance of 16½ minutes start to stop, for the 14·6 miles from Finmere to Woodford proved impracticable, even with such vigorous driving as was indulged in on this occasion. Once again, however, the Woodford–Leicester section provided some recovery, even though the start-to-stop schedule time required an average of 60 mph. With speeds of 82 mph at Braunston, 52 before Lutterworth, a final maximum of 87, and speed still 80 mph (!) at Leicester South Goods Junction the point-to-point time was improved upon by 1½ minutes and the train brought into Leicester slightly ahead of time. I have never seen a finer example of Great Central 'Atlantic' performance than this.

The Aylesbury route was followed by the other two Marylebone–Leicester non-stop expresses, leaving at 3.20 and 4.55 PM. Three runs of my own recording, all with relatively heavy trains, show the high standard of performance required. I have put them in date order, commencing with one on the Thursday before Easter 1927, when I was travelling to Manchester *en route* for Barrow-in-Furness. The 'Lord Faringdon' class four-cylinder 4–6–0s had the reputation of being very free runners downhill; but this trait was not particularly apparent on this run. The uphill work was excellent, with by far the best ascent of the long climb over the Chilterns from Rickmansworth up to Amersham, and in passing Woodford only 2 minutes late there was every chance of clocking into Leicester practically on time. On the other hand, the driver was aware of an excursion train ahead of him, and following the signal checks that eventuated in the approach to Leicester he was badly checked by frequent adverse signals all the way to Sheffield. His relatively moderate running from Woodford may therefore have been by design.

A year later when I was again a passenger on the train we had an extra coach – in fact when I arrived at Marylebone there was talk of adding yet another, and an 'Atlantic' engine was standing ready to act as pilot if this further 'strengthening' of the standard rake proved necessary. In the end we left unassisted behind the 'Director' class 4–4–0 No 5438 *Worsley-Taylor*, and a very competent driver in Rangeley, of Gorton shed. The start out to Rickmansworth was brilliant, equalling that of *Earl Beatty*, despite the heavier load. But the greater tractive power of the six-coupled engine showed to advantage in climbing over the Chilterns, and the 4–4–0, although doing extremely fine work, was falling behind as far as Woodford. After that *Worsley-Taylor* was driven hard, and with top speeds of 82 mph at both Braunston and Whetstone there was a fine recovery, and although there was a loss of 2 minutes on schedule this was no mean performance on a timing originally planned for a five-coach train of less than 200 tons.

The last run was an absolutely brilliant example of what the 'Directors' could do; at a time, moreover, when it was becoming very rare to find engines of Great Central design on crack duties. The start out of London was extremely vigorous, gaining more than a minute on both the previous runs out to Rickmansworth. A somewhat liberal interpretation of the speed limit there enabled the climb to Amersham to be rushed, and then having passed Aylesbury in the very fast time of 45 minutes 20 seconds Driver France put his engine to it in tremendous style over the undulating, though generally rising, length to Woodford. His time of 24 minutes 4 seconds for the 25·1 miles from Quainton Road Junction to Woodford, with 295 tons, puts completely in the shade the corresponding times of 25½ minutes by *Earl Beatty*, and of 26 minutes 5 seconds by *Worsley-Taylor*. Even so, the effort was in no way relaxed subsequently, and the last 34 miles from Woodford into Leicester were covered in the level half-hour, pass to stop. I am glad to have recorded personally so splendid an example of 'Director' performance.

Not many records exist of runs on the London–Manchester 'double-home' turns with the 'Sir Sam Fay' class inside-cylinder 4–6–0s, and none of these showed any significant features. When I was photographing on the line in the years 1922–4 they were frequently on the 3.20 PM down from Marylebone, but I never had occasion to travel behind one of them on that service. All my runs with them were between Manchester and Sheffield, and an interesting example with the pioneer engine is tabulated herewith. I travelled several times on the old 5 PM from Manchester, London Road as far as

TABLE 3

LNER (GC section): MANCHESTER–PENISTONE

Load: 268 tons tare, 285 tons full

Engine: 2-cylinder 4–6–0 No 5423 *Sir Sam Fay*

| Distance miles | | Actual min sec | | Speeds mph |
|---|---|---|---|---|
| 0·0 | MANCHESTER(LONDON ROAD) | 0 | 00 | — |
| 0·8 | Ardwick | 2 | 25 | — |
| 2·7 | Gorton | 5 | 45 | — |
| 3·7 | Fairfield | 7 | 25 | 37½ |
| 5·1 | GUIDE BRIDGE | 9 | 50 | |
| 2·4 | Newton | 5 | 35 | 33½ |
| 3·3 | Godley Junction | 7 | 15 | 36 |
| 4·8 | Mottram | 9 | 35 | 45 |
| 6·9 | Dinting | 12 | 30 | 45 |
| 7·7 | Hadfield | 13 | 40 | 40¼ |
| 10·2 | *Torside* | 18 | 05 | 33½ |
| 12·2 | Crowden | 21 | 30 | 36 |
| | | sig. stop | | — |
| 14·2 | Woodhead | 27 | 00 | — |
| 17·4 | Dunford Bridge | 34 | 25 | 34½ |
| 19·8 | Hazlehead Bridge | 37 | 20 | 67 (max) |
| 23·4 | PENISTONE | 41 | 45 | |

Net time 37 minutes.

Penistone. This line was very heavily utilized by freight trains, and although the paths for the crack London expresses were kept remarkably clear, it was not always so with the lesser lights, and the 5 PM was a Cleethorpes train. On this occasion, however, we got through with only one check, a stop at Woodhead, while a preceding freight was clearing the tunnel section.

This train carried a fair load, and on the continuously adverse opening section, to Guide Bridge, we gradually accelerated to $37\frac{1}{2}$ mph. The gradient is 1 in 173 to Gorton; 1 in 100 onwards to Fairfield, and then easing slightly to 1 in 133. On restarting the gradients are 1 in 92 and 85 to Newton; then 1 in 143 to Godley Junction, by which time we were doing 36 mph. A mile at 1 in 462 brought an acceleration to 45 mph at Mottram, and this was held over the $1\frac{3}{4}$ miles at 1 in 122 and level to Dinting. Then came the long grind at 1 in 100–117 to the western end of Woodhead, $7\frac{1}{4}$ miles of it. Here speed varied between $33\frac{1}{2}$ and 36 mph, until we were checked in the approach to Woodhead. We stood for three-quarters of a minute, and then, as customary, the engine was not pressed on the 1 in 201 gradient in the smoke-laden single-tracked bore of the tunnel. The attained speed at the summit at Dunford Bridge was $34\frac{1}{2}$ mph. The net time was roughly the same as the 37 minutes scheduled for the run of 23·4 miles from Guide Bridge to Penistone.

Mr Robinson's first express passenger design for the Great Central, the 'Sir Alexander' class 4–4–0s of 1901 were so quickly followed by the 'Atlantics' that little detail has been preserved of their early work. In later years when rebuilt with larger boilers and superheaters they rarely appeared in first-class express duty. One evening in August 1934, however, I was fortunate enough to 'catch' one, and I secured a record of a first-class performance. On the 6.20 PM down from Marylebone engines were changed at Leicester, and some hard running was needed to keep the schedule of 25 minutes start to stop for the 23·4 miles on to Nottingham, and of 48 minutes for the sharply graded 38·2 miles on to Sheffield. At that time in the evening an 'Atlantic' was needed at Nottingham, and it was usual to couple it as pilot to the 6.20; and with two engines one often noted some very exciting running between Leicester and Nottingham. We were usually inside 'even time' by Ruddington, 19·0 miles.

Then on the night in question the leading engine from Leicester was the usual Robinson 'Atlantic', but the train engine was a rebuilt 'Sir Alexander', No 6019. As far as Nottingham, to which we flew in traditional style, I imagined that the pilot was carrying the train engine with her; but when

No 6019 continued unassisted it was to make the fastest times
I have ever logged with a steam locomotive up the long ascent
to Annesley. She began well through the steeply graded tunnels
to Basford, attaining 35 mph on 1 in 130; touched 53½ mph in

TABLE 4

LNER (GC section): LEICESTER–SHEFFIELD

Load: 211 tons tare, 225 tons full

Engine: rebuilt 4–4–0 No 6019

Pilot to Nottingham only: 4–4–2 No 6092

| Distance miles | | Sch. min | Actual min sec | | Speeds mph |
|---|---|---|---|---|---|
| 0·0 | LEICESTER | 0 | 0 | 00 | — |
| 2·3 | Belgrave | | 4 | 15 | 44 |
| 5·0 | Rothley | | 7 | 15 | 65½ |
| 7·8 | Quorn | | 9 | 44 | 74½ |
| 9·8 | Loughborough | | 11 | 20 | 79½ |
| 12·8 | *Barnston* | | 13 | 55 | 65 |
| 16·8 | *Gotham Junction* | | 17 | 14 | 79½ |
| 19·0 | Ruddington | | 18 | 57 | 76½ |
| — | | | sigs | | — |
| 23·4 | NOTTINGHAM | 25 | 24 | 38 | |
| 1·6 | Basford | | 4 | 16 | 35 |
| 3·3 | Bulwell | | 6 | 58 | 53½ |
| 5·8 | Hucknall | | 9 | 57 | 49 |
| 9·6 | *Annesley North Junction* | | 14 | 58 | 45½ |
| | | | sigs | | 5 |
| 10·8 | *Kirkby South Junction* | 16 | 17 | 21 | — |
| 17·9 | Pilsley | | 27 | 01 | 60/48½ |
| 20·3 | Heath | 28 | 29 | 36 | 62½ |
| 26·2 | STAVELEY | 33 | 34 | 51 | 74 |
| 28·2 | Eckington | | 36 | 45 | 60½ |
| 30·0 | Killamarsh | | 38 | 26 | 69 |
| 32·1 | Beighton | | 40 | 20 | 63½ |
| 33·2 | Woodhouse | | 41 | 45 | 48 |
| 36·2 | Darnall | | 45 | 43 | 39 |
| 38·2 | SHEFFIELD | 48 | 48 | 38 | |

the slight dip past Bulwell, and then settled down to a steady
45½ mph on the long 1 in 130, that extends for nearly 7 miles.
Then unfortunately we were all but stopped by adverse signals
at Kirkby South Junction. From this point, right on to Sheffield, the line is carried through a colliery area, subject to

temporary restrictions, and although no definite slacks were in operation on the evening in question one could never run so freely as on a line like the London extension.

As will be seen from the accompanying log, the driver regained a minute of the time lost by the signal check, with a maximum speed of 74 mph descending from Heath to Staveley, and a renewed maximum of 69 mph near Killamarsh. There were many slight reductions of speed, particularly from the 63½ mph noted against Beighton in the log to 48 mph over Woodhouse Junction. This gave a restricted start to the final climb of 3¼ miles at 1 in 131–7 to Darnall, where speed fell to 39 mph. The net time of 46½ minutes from Nottingham represented an excellent performance by this relatively small engine. It would have been interesting to see how she would have managed the Leicester–Nottingham 'sprint' unassisted. On the form displayed north of Nottingham, she should have been able to keep that sharp timing. There was indeed a smartness about Great Central working that permeated the whole line from end to end, and made the logging of runs an exhilarating pastime.

# CHAPTER THREE

# THE CONSTITUENTS :
# 2. GREAT EASTERN

The Great Eastern was a remarkable railway. It operated, with the punctuality of chronometers, the heaviest suburban traffic in the world; it conveyed a prodigious amount of goods and minerals into London from East Anglia in general, and in long hauls over the joint line, and then of course there was its excellent service of seaside holiday trains, and the very celebrated boat express trains serving the Continent, via Harwich. The success with which all this was done begins to look all the more remarkable when an analysis is made of the locomotive stock existing in December 1922, and one finds how very few really modern engines the company then possessed. The total was 1,336, and of this 557 were tank engines, 261 indeed of the 0–6–0 type. The main-line goods engines were all 0–6–0s, 272 of the Worsdell standard design of 1883, and 90 of the larger series first introduced by Holden in 1900. Of A. J. Hill's fine 0–6–2 tanks, of which such swarms were at work as LNER class 'N7' in later years, only 12 existed in December 1922.

But the Great Eastern, in the locomotive department as everywhere else in its organization, had a priceless asset in its magnificent sense of 'pride in the job', and in the cherishing of old and proud traditions. When F. V. Russell completely reorganized the London suburban services after World War I, and provided on the Chingford and Enfield lines alone from Liverpool Street departures every *two minutes* in the rush hours, he did not call for vast capital expenditure in the way of new motive power, and other facilities. If he *had* done, it would have been turned down flat, and he would probably have gone off the job! Instead, he organized it to the last detail with the existing 0–6–0 tank engines, and the mechanical signalling and Sykes 'Lock and Block' apparatus installed when the station was enlarged in 1895. Each of these smartly worked suburban trains consisted of 16 four-wheeled coaches. The engines were the class later designated 'J69' by the LNER.

About the density of traffic at Liverpool Street there is an amusing story to be told. The general manager at that time was the very distinguished American railwayman Sir Henry Thornton, who prior to his appointment in 1914 had been president of the Long Island Railroad. Now the 'Long Island' was little more than a suburban network, albeit one carrying a heavy traffic, and there were not a few eyebrows raised when its president was appointed to manage an English trunk line like the Great Eastern. Thornton succeeded brilliantly; he did some sterling work for transport during the war and collected a knighthood in the process. Then one day in 1922 *The New York Times* ran a feature story on the Long Island Railroad; it is to be feared that this was in a somewhat boastful vein. Sir Henry Thornton saw this, and wrote a letter to that newspaper, which, for measured and modest phraseology in such circumstances, must remain a classic for all time. He wrote:

> I notice in your issue of June 4th, 1922, some figures relating to passenger traffic handled on American railways, with particular reference to passengers passing through Flatbush Avenue Station in Brooklyn. The volume of business handled by the Long Island Railroad reflects much credit upon its management, which has earned the admiration of the railway industry. However, although the Long Island handles 32,893,995 passengers in Flatbush Avenue which leads you to suspect that these figures represent perhaps the largest passenger business in any station in the world, I would humbly direct attention to the fact that the Great Eastern Railway, at its Liverpool Street Station (London), handles annually 76,136,823 passengers.

Hill's 0–6–2 tank, introduced in 1915, was designed on the experience gained over many years with the standard Holden 0–6–0s. Only twelve of them were built in Great Eastern days, but by the time of the grouping the class was thoroughly proved in heavy suburban traffic and ready for adoption as a standard. Naturally there was some doubt as to whether the

LNER would use it; but as it turned out Gresley accepted it in its entirety, and the class was multiplied exceedingly. With this one design alone the Great Eastern made a notable contribution to the motive power stud of the LNER. It is interesting and thoroughly typical of Gresley that although he had a very successful suburban tank engine of his own in the Great Northern 'N2', he accepted the 'N7' for Great Eastern needs. Engines of the 'N7' class were subsequently built as follows:

| | | |
|---|---|---|
| In 1923–4: | at Stratford works | 10 |
| In 1925: | at Gorton works | 10 |
| In 1925/6: | at R. Stephenson & Co | 20 |
| In 1926/7/8: | at Gorton works | 30 |
| In 1927: | at W. Beardmore & Co | 20 |
| In 1927/8: | at Doncaster works | 32 |

The Great Eastern had no very striking contribution to make in the way of freight engine power. Much of its traffic centred around the class of business that has almost entirely passed away from railways today, namely the small individual load, often not amounting to a full wagon, picked up at country stations, and worked at modest speed to some equally rural destination. It is true that a large amount of coal for the eastern districts of London came south by the GN & GE joint line, but the tonnage of individual trains was not to be compared with that on the Great Northern main line. The Great Eastern, like the Midland and the London & North Western found ample employment for a large number of small 0–6–0 tender engines of the late Victorian vintage. The really powerful superheater 0–6–0s of class 'J20', with a nominal tractive effort of 29,044 lb, were, in 1922, few in numbers; only 25 of them were at work in December 1922, and unlike the 'N7' tanks the class was not multiplied.

The main-line express engines were a splendid lot, yet even so of relatively modest dimensions. Unlike some other constituents of the LNER, and notably the Great Central and North Eastern, they were of few classes, thus:

| | |
|---|---|
| 4–6–0 '1500' class (LNER 'B12') | total 70 |
| 4–4–0 'Claud Hamilton' (LNER 'D14' & '15') | total 111 |
| 4–4–0 'Super-Claud' (Introduced March 1923) | total Nil |
| 4–4–0 Rebuilt 'T19' (LNER 'D13') | total 58 |

The 'Super-Claud', essentially a Great Eastern design, but not introduced until March 1923, would probably have been multiplied considerably, had grouping not taken place, by rebuilding more of the original non-superheated 'Claud Hamilton' class as boilers became due for renewal; but in the event the supply of further motive power for the Great Eastern lines went in a different direction, as will be told later. The '1500' class was a very sound design, capable of quite extraordinary work on the road; yet I have always felt that its outstanding success was due to Stratford traditions, as much as to the inherent qualities of the design itself. It had certain features of a superficial nature that would have made it unpopular on other railways, particularly the inordinate distance between the shovelling plate and the firebox door. Instead of being able to pick up the charge, and swing round to place it in the firebox in one movement, the fireman had to take a step intermediately. Yet by the Great Eastern men these engines were successfully and enthusiastically fired on turns requiring some of the heaviest coal consumption in the country at that time. The Hook and Antwerp Continental boat expresses used to average about 60 lb of coal per mile between Liverpool Street and Parkeston Quay.

After grouping, with Gresley quickly appreciating the great and proud tradition of individual achievement that existed at Stratford, there was little change to be seen on the Great Eastern line for several years. Gresley was the last person to trample upon, or try to eliminate such strong traits as existed, however they might differ from his own ideas. There was no swamping of Stratford with Great Northern practice, and apart from painting engines in the new apple-green livery there was no change.

Engine performance in express passenger service was of a different character from that of the Great Central. The time-table called for an intermediate service of heavy trains. The booked speeds gave a comfortable margin in reserve with the winter service, when train-loads rarely exceeded 400 tons on the principal trains to Cambridge, Norwich, and Yarmouth; but in the summer, particularly on Saturdays, loads up to 500 tons were not uncommon. Many a time I have spent such a day with a lineside photographic pass at Brentwood, and watched the holiday trains following each other 'nose to tail': thirteen-, fourteen-, and fifteen-coach trains packed with perspiring humanity; one engine only to each, blasting their way up the bank, through that picturesque cutting, which was then no more than double-tracked. Save for an occasional rebuilt 'T19' 4-4-0 on some secondary duty, these holiday trains were hauled by engines of two types only: the '1500' class 4-6-0s, and the non-superheater 'Claud Hamiltons'. Some of these crowded trains showed evidence of having been strengthened at the last minute, because two or three non-corridor six-wheelers were interposed between the engine and the bogie, corridor train-set.

In recent years some very spectacular work was done by the 'Britannia' class 'Pacifics' between Ipswich and Norwich, in both directions of running; but in the last days of the GER, and for some years after grouping all the finest work was done on the London side of Ipswich. With locomotives of such moderate tractive power as the '1500' class 4-6-0s, and loads regularly over 400 tons, the sharp intermediate gradients very much ruled the performance. There was a world of difference between the task of working 400 tons with a 64-ton 4-6-0 having a nominal tractive effort of 21,969 lb, and that of working 300 tons with a 'Pacific' having a nominal tractive effort of 30,000 lb. The gradients need some careful consideration before I refer to any individual runs.

The Colchester main line begins with the sharp rise at 1 in 70 for two-thirds of a mile, to Bethnal Green, and then, characteristically, what could provide a fine swinging start to the long rise to Ingrave summit, a stretch of 3 miles falling at 1 in 350 from Bethnal Green station, is spoiled by the need to reduce speed to 30 mph through Stratford. Then follows the long gradual rise to Harold Wood, on gradients varying between 1 in 380 and 1 in 435 followed by the Brentwood bank proper: $2\frac{1}{4}$ miles at 1 in 103 followed by a mile of 1 in 85-155 to the summit. Fast running conditions downhill through Ingatestone were checked by the restriction to 40 mph through Chelms-

ford, and the line is a succession of sharp undulations onwards
to Colchester, where there was another 40 mph slack. Both
these regular restrictions were followed by sections of adverse
grading. For the Continental boat trains the worst slack of all
was at Manningtree, to 20 mph, whereas the East Anglian
expresses, making their first stop at Ipswich, could go through
at full speed. With these restrictions, and steep, though short
gradients following them, the schedules laid down assume
their true degree of difficulty, and are not merely a case of comparing minutes with miles.

I had a typical run myself on the 12.25 PM express, details of

TABLE 5

LNER 12.25 PM LIVERPOOL STREET–IPSWICH

Load: 407 tons tare, 435 tons full

Engine: class 'B12' 4–6–0 No 8535

| Distance miles | | Sch. min | Actual min sec | | Speeds mph |
|---|---|---|---|---|---|
| 0·0 | LIVERPOOL STREET | 0 | 0 | 00 | — |
| 1·1 | Bethnal Green | | 3 | 20 | — |
| 3·0 | *Bow Junction* | | 6 | 40 | 46 |
| 4·0 | Stratford | 8 | 8 | 05 | 40* |
| 7·3 | Ilford | | 12 | 20 | 50 |
| 10·0 | Chadwell Heath | 16 | 15 | 27 | 52 |
| 12·4 | Romford | | 18 | 15 | 53 |
| 15·0 | Harold Wood | | 21 | 20 | 50½ |
| 18·2 | Brentwood | | 26 | 10 | 30 |
| 19·3 | *Ingrave Box* | | 28 | 35 | 25¾ |
| 20·2 | SHENFIELD | 30 | 30 | 10 | 50 |
| 23·6 | Ingatestone | | 33 | 40 | 64½ |
| | | | p.w.s. | | 40 |
| 29·7 | CHELMSFORD | 40 | 40 | 30 | — |
| 32·1 | *New Hall Box* | | 44 | 20 | 43½ |
| 38·6 | Witham | 50 | 51 | 35 | 62 |
| 44·1 | *Hill House Box* | | 57 | 40 | 45 |
| 51·7 | COLCHESTER | 66 | 66 | 15 | 62½ |
| 54·1 | *Parsons Heath* | | 69 | 05 | 43 |
| 59·5 | MANNINGTREE | 75 | 75 | 15 | 69 |
| 63·2 | Bentley | | 79 | 10 | 53 |
| — | *Belstead* | | — | | 38 |
| 68·0 | *Halifax Junction* | | 85 | 15 | 60 |
| 68·7 | IPSWICH | 88 | 86 | 35 | |

Net time: 84½ minutes. * Speed restriction.

which are tabulated herewith. This train had a somewhat easier timing than the boat trains, which were booked to pass Manningtree in 70 minutes. But the load was a heavy one, and the engine put up some excellent performance. We got through Bethnal Green in fine style, and then after the Stratford slack this small engine did some fine uphill work on the long rise to Harold Wood, sustaining 50–53 mph all the way. Brentwood bank took its toll, bringing us down to $25\frac{3}{4}$ mph, and the approach to Chelmsford was made even slower than usual by a long slowing for relaying work. On the undulating stretch that followed speed varied between 45 and 62 mph, and Colchester was passed practically on time, despite a full 2 minutes lost by the relaying check. We went through Manningtree in grand

TABLE 6

8.30 PM LIVERPOOL STREET–PARKESTON QUAY

Load: 388 tons tare, 415 tons full

Engine: class 'B12' 4–6–0 No 1566

| Distance miles | | Sch. min | Actual min sec | | Speeds mph |
|---|---|---|---|---|---|
| 0·0 | LIVERPOOL STREET | 0 | 0 | 00 | — |
| 1·0 | Bethnal Green | | 3 | 25 | — |
| 4·0 | Stratford | 8 | 7 | 50 | 35* |
| 7·3 | Ilford | | 11 | 55 | — |
| 10·0 | Chadwell Heath | 15 | 14 | 50 | 55 |
| 12·4 | Romford | | 17 | 25 | 54 |
| 15·0 | Harold Wood | | 20 | 15 | 55 |
| — | | | sigs | | — |
| 18·2 | Brentwood | | 24 | 25 | — |
| 19·3 | *Ingrave Box* | | 26 | 25 | 27 |
| 20·2 | Shenfield | 28 | 27 | 40 | — |
| 23·6 | Ingatestone | | 31 | 00 | $71\frac{1}{2}$(max) |
| 29·7 | CHELMSFORD | 38 | 36 | 30 | 55* |
| 32·1 | *New Hall Box* | | 39 | 00 | — |
| 38·6 | Witham | 48 | 45 | 35 | 66 |
| 44·1 | *Hill House Box* | | 51 | 00 | 54/70 |
| 51·7 | COLCHESTER | 61 | 58 | 25 | 50* |
| 54·1 | *Parsons Heath Box* | | 61 | 10 | 45 |
| 59·5 | MANNINGTREE | 70 | 67 | 20 | 25* |
| 65·1 | Wrabness | | 75 | 20 | |
| 68·9 | PARKESTON QUAY | 82 | 80 | 15 | |

Net time: $79\frac{1}{2}$ minutes.    * Speed restrictions.

style at 69 mph and with time now comfortably in hand speed
was allowed to fall to 38 mph up the 2 miles at 1 in 157 to
Belstead summit, and Ipswich was reached 1½ minutes early.

As showing something of the maximum of which these
engines were capable Mr Cecil J. Allen recorded from the footplate a magnificent run on the Hook of Holland boat express
with engine No 1566, and a gross load of 415 tons. This run is
also tabulated. These boat trains were worked by a small, but
very expert and enthusiastic link of enginemen, and on this
occasion the crew was Driver Chapman and Fireman Dale.
The immediate start out of Liverpool Street was fractionally
slower than mine on the 12.25 PM train, but after that there
was no comparison. Speed was sustained at 55 mph past
Romford, and although there was a momentary signal check
at Brentwood, the climb of the bank was so fine that Shenfield
was passed in the record time of 27 minutes 40 seconds. From
then onwards the running followed the same pattern as that on
the 12.25 with slightly higher speeds at all points. The outcome was a gain of nearly 2 minutes on this most difficult
schedule. The engine was worked extremely hard to achieve
the very fast initial time to Chelmsford; but the general performance was typical of work regularly achieved by these
engines in the last years of the Great Eastern Railway, and in
the early years of grouping.

The Great Eastern, if not contributing any outstanding
design, certainly brought a tradition of fine workmanship and
superb maintenance into the LNER group. How else, one could
well ask, could engines of such proportions as the '1500' class
regularly perform such work as that demanded by the night
Continental expresses. The 'N7' tank was in the same tradition: a splendid little workhorse of a locomotive, which
Gresley was glad enough to adopt as a standard.

# CHAPTER FOUR

# THE CONSTITUENTS:
# 3. NORTH EASTERN

At the time of the grouping the locomotive department of the
North Eastern Railway, under the strong management of Sir
Vincent Raven, was firmly set on a policy of three-cylinder
propulsion for all except the smallest engines. Since the year
1911 six major designs had been produced, and, with the
exception of the giant 'Pacifics' of 1922, all passed for quantity
production. These classes were:

'D'  4–4–4 fast passenger tank.
'S3'  4–6–0 express goods and mixed traffic.
'T3'  0–8–0 heavy mineral.
'Y'  4–6–2 short-distance mineral tank.
'Z'  4–4–2 main-line express passenger.

By the time of grouping only two of the Raven express passenger 'Pacifics' had been built, and only three more were added
afterwards.

Unlike the Gresley development on the Great Northern
Railway, all these three-cylinder classes on the NER had separate sets of valve gear for each cylinder, using the Stephenson
link motion with a traditional arrangement of short-lap valves,
and consequently short travel. By contemporary standards all
these North Eastern designs were thoroughly successful, and
the 'Z' 'Atlantics', the flagships of the fleet, were free-running
and regularly made speeds of 75–80 mph on level track, with a
train like the 8.49 PM 'flyer' from Darlington to York, booked
to cover the 44·1 miles in 43 minutes start to stop. The older
North Eastern engines, both passenger and freight, had all
been maintained in good condition, and the two-cylinder
'Atlantics' of class 'V' and the larger 4–4–0s of classes 'R' and

'R1' could always be relied upon for sound, and sometimes very fast work. Furthermore, under Sir Vincent Raven, a policy of superheating older engines had been systematically carried out, and the Worsdell 4–4–0s of classes 'F', 'G', 'M', and 'Q' had all been superheated.

Although attention was naturally concentrated on the working of the main-line passenger services, the revenue derived therefrom was very small compared to that resulting from the mineral traffic. This does not take any account of the work done by the considerable stud of 4–6–0 mixed-traffic engines. Nevertheless, it is, of course, the performance in express passenger services that can make or mar the reputation of a school of locomotive design, and the work of the 'Z' 'Atlantics', whether in lightly-loaded high-speed running, or in heavy weight haulage on the East Coast expresses, proved an ample justification of the precepts and practice of Sir Vincent Raven. His culminating design, the great 'Pacific' of 1922, never really got a chance. It was tested against its Gresley counterpart between King's Cross and Doncaster in the summer of 1923. Since it proved somewhat heavier on coal, Gresley was justified in recommending the standardization of his own 'Pacific' in preference to that of Sir Vincent Raven.

Taken all round, the North Eastern was not a particularly fast running line in 1922–3. The East Coast expresses were liberally timed throughout between York and Edinburgh, and although loads were often in excess of 400 tons, both two-cylinder and three-cylinder 'Atlantics' had no difficulty in working them punctually. The big 'R1' class 4–4–0s worked mainly from Leeds, taking the morning Leeds–Glasgow express as far as Newcastle, together with certain turns to Scarborough. The secondary lines in East Yorkshire – Leeds to Hull, Leeds to Bridlington, Hull to Scarborough, and so on – were worked mainly by the rebuilt and superheated 4–4–0s of classes 'F', 'G', 'M', and 'Q'. Some of the 'J' class 4–2–2 singles were still at work in 1919 and 1920, and the first time I ever rode on an engine's footplate was on No 1522, a 'J' 4–2–2, while she was doing pilot work at Bridlington in 1919. Not only the 'J' class, but the still older 2–4–0 express engines of the 'Tennant' and '901' classes were on passenger service well into the grouping era.

Although there were many engines on the active list of the NER that would almost have been classified as antiques, they all had work eminently within their capacity. The '901' class, for example, worked three-coach trains over the severe gradient of the Darlington–Tebay–Penrith line with complete success, and on the network of secondary routes in the East Riding the 'F', 'G', and 'Q' class 4–4–0s were well on top of their respective jobs. To a connoisseur of locomotives the North Eastern of those days was a fascinating line. Every passenger engine one saw was beautifully clean, in the handsome pale green livery, and the main-line 'Atlantics' were always immaculate. The North Eastern men were intensely proud of their railway and their engines, and it must be added that they had no particular respect for their allies to north and south. This attitude was to have certain repercussions in later years when a degree of inter-working of engines and trains was instituted.

The LNER inherited its dynamometer car from the North Eastern. In 1901 the locomotive engineers of other major British railways had taken great interest in the building of Churchward's new dynamometer car. In 1903 Wilson Worsdell had borrowed it to test his great new 'Atlantic' No 532, the first of the 'V' class and H. A. Ivatt of the Great Northern had taken advantage of its journey north to put it behind his pioneer large-boilered 'Atlantic' No 251. In the 1905–10 decade both Crewe and Horwich built modern dynamometer cars, but Wilson Worsdell's was most closely modelled upon the Great Western car, and was indeed an almost exact copy of it. There is a faint twist of irony in that the copy and not the original should have been preserved, and awarded a place of honour in the National Museum of Transport at Clapham. It so befell, however, that the Worsdell car came to record the most spectacular piece of high-speed running ever achieved with steam – the world record of *Mallard* in July 1938 – and on that account alone the ex-North Eastern car is deserving of immortality.

In North Eastern days, in the charge of that great locomotive

personality Inspector Weatherburn, the Worsdell dynamometer car recorded some interesting work, though the
results might not have been altogether to the liking of Wilson
Worsdell himself. Tests carried out on East Coast expresses
between Newcastle and York proved that W. M. Smith's four-
cylinder compound 'Atlantics' were better engines than the
'V' class, the load ratio established being 1·00:1·28:1·45 for
the 'R' class 4–4–0, the 'V' 'Atlantic' and the '4CC' 'Atlantic'.
A number of interesting tests was carried out with other North
Eastern engines, but by far the most significant work done
with this dynamometer car was after the grouping. Gresley
was delighted to have the car among the various items of
equipment for which he became responsible in 1923, and like
any engineer who had locomotives in the blood he could not
resist running competitive trials at a very early stage in grouping history; just as Riddles did later, on a national scale, in
1948. In the trials of 1923 and 1924 North Eastern engines
were prominently involved.

The 'Pacific' trials, between Doncaster and King's Cross,
were a fairly close-run thing. The North Eastern engine
No 2400 was manned by a crew of the highest calibre in Driver
Tom Blades and Fireman Charles Fisher of Gateshead. Blades
was a great deal more than the 'senior driver' at that shed. He
had fired to Bob Nicholson on the 'M' class 4–4–0 in the concluding stages of the 'Race to the North' in 1895. Charlie
Fisher became a locomotive inspector at York, and I enjoyed
many trips in his company. They did some excellent work on
the GN main line in 1923, and a fine example of this is tabulated
herewith. The overall results are shown in the accompanying
table, and it will be seen that by a narrow margin they favoured
the Great Northern engine, none other than the historic 4472
*Flying Scotsman*. At that time, however, the engine was numbered 1472, and had not then been named. Furthermore, her
superiority over No 2400 was achieved with the original valve
gear. The extent to which this was improved is described in
Chapter Seven of this book. Had the North Eastern engine
been run against No 4472 as she was from 1928 onwards the
result would have been overwhelmingly in favour of the

| | | | 1472 GNR | | 2400 NER | |
|---|---|---|---|---|---|---|
| Engine No Design Load, tons (E/F) | | | | | | |
| Doncaster–Grantham | | | 453/485 | | 453/485 | |
| Grantham—King's Cross | | | 483/520 | | 483/520 | |
| Distance miles | | Sch. min | Actual min sec | Speeds mph | Actual min sec | Speeds mph |
| 0·0 | DONCASTER | | 0    00 | — | 0    00 | — |
| 4·6 | Rossington | | 7    36 | 50½ | 7    07 | 53 |
| 6·5 | Milepost 149½ | | 9    55 | 45 | 9    11 | 51½ |
| 12·0 | Ranskill | | 15    41 | 63 | 14    24 | 68 |
| | | | — | — | sigs | |
| 17·4 | RETFORD | 21 | 21    27 | — | 20    26 | — |
| 4·6 | Milepost 134 | | 8    25 | 39½ | 8    05 | 41½ |
| 11·2 | Crow Park | | 14    58 | 75 | 14    25 | 74 |
| 18·5 | NEWARK | 21 | 21    23 | 64 | 21    17 | — |
| 23·2 | Claypole | | 26    04 | 58 | 7    29 | 53 |
| 27·1 | Hougham | | 30    17 | 53 | 11    39 | 56 |
| 28·9 | Barkston | | 32    32 | 42½* | 13    43 | 50* |
| 33·1 | GRANTHAM | 38 | 38    30 | — | 19    25 | — |
| 5·5 | Stoke Box (Mp 100) | | 12    02 | 35 | 10    01 | 43½ |
| 8·4 | Corby | | 15    23 | 65 | 13    05 | 65 |
| 13·3 | Little Bytham | | 19    36 | 74 | 17    12 | 76½ |
| 16·9 | Essendine | | 22    25 | 77 | 19    55 | 79 |
| 20·7 | Tallington | | 25    31 | 74 | 22    56 | 74½ |
| 29·1 | PETERBOROUGH | 33 | 34    00 | — | 31    27 | — |
| 3·8 | Yaxley | | 6    33 | 53 | 6    39 | 51½ |
| 7·0 | Holme | | 9    47 | 63 | 9    55 | 62½ |
| 12·9 | Abbots Ripton | | 15    45 | 50½ | 16    00 | 47½ |
| 17·5 | HUNTINGDON | 20 | 20    36 | 68 | 20    50 | 73 |
| 20·4 | Offord | | 23    10 | 68 | 23    16 | 73 |
| 24·7 | St Neots | | 27    18 | 56 | 27    04 | 60 |
| 28·9 | Tempsford | | 31    31 | 63 | 31    03 | 65½ |
| 32·3 | Sandy | | 34    51 | 58 | 34    13 | 62½ |
| 35·3 | Biggleswade | | 37    51 | 60 | 37    03 | 63 |
| 39·3 | Arlesey | | 42    19 | 57 | 41    13 | 61 |
| 44·5 | HITCHIN | 48 | 48    07 | 47½ | 46    34 | 51 |
| 47·8 | Stevenage | | 52    46 | 42 | 50    55 | 44½ |
| 51·4 | Knebworth | | 57    06 | 49 | 55    04 | 51 |
| | | | sigs | 36 | — | |
| 58·7 | HATFIELD | 64 | 66    41 | 56 | 62    04 | 71 |
| 63·7 | Potters Bar | | 72    43 | 49½ | 66    51 | 61 |
| 67·3 | New Barnet | | 75    40 | 65 | 69    58 | 74½ |
| | | | p.w.s. | 44 | p.w.s. | slight |
| 71·4 | Wood Green | | 81    16 | 60 | 73    35 | 73½ |
| 73·9 | Finsbury Park | | 83    47 | — | 75    38 | 68½ |
| 76·4 | KING'S CROSS | 84 | 87    37 | — | 79    24 | — |

* Minimum speed at Peascliffe Tunnel.

Gresley design. It was of course not a straight case of Walschaerts *versus* Stephenson's valve gear. It was the detail design of the gear that made all the difference.

TABLE 8

LNER PACIFIC ENGINE TRIALS

Average results for all tests: June and July 1923

| Engine No<br>Section | 1472<br>GN | 2400<br>NE |
|---|---|---|
| Average speed mph | 53·7 | 53·0 |
| Actual 1,000 ton miles (train only) | 73·11 | 76·5 |
| Average db horsepower | 663 | 673 |
| Superheat deg F | 547 | 574 |
| Boiler pressure psi | 164 | 197 |
| Steam-chest pressure psi | 118 | 106 |
| Cut-off, per cent | 40 | 40 |
| Water: gallons per mile | 38·3 | 40·4 |
| lb per dhp-hr | 31·0 | 31·7 |
| Coal: lb per mile (inclusive) | 52·6 | 58·7 |
| lb per mile (exclusive of lighting up) | 48·6 | 54·4 |
| lb per dhp-hr | 3·94 | 4·29 |
| lb per sq ft of grate area per hr | 65·2 | 68·9 |
| Evaporation: Feed water, temperature deg F | 61·0 | 61·6 |
| lb of water per lb of coal | 7·47 | 7·7 |
| gallons of water per hour used | 2081 | 2153 |

Very little was known of the 'Atlantics' trials of 1923, between Newcastle and Edinburgh, until K. J. Cook, formerly of the GWR, when chief mechanical and electrical engineer of the Eastern and North Eastern Regions of British Railways, permitted me to examine the dynamometer car records existing at Darlington. The competitors were a North Eastern 'Z', No 735, a North British 'Atlantic', No 878 *Hazeldean*, and a Great Northern large 'Atlantic', of the variety with 20-in cylinders and piston-valves, No 1447. To clear the North British loading gauge this latter engine had to have the height of her chimney and boiler mountings reduced. Whether any adjustment to the draughting was made to compensate for the reduced height of chimney I do not know. If not, her steaming could have been affected adversely, and as the performance was somewhat below the best standards of the class there may be

TABLE 9

LNER ATLANTIC ENGINES

Results of the tests: 1923

| Railway Engine No | GNR 1447 | NER 733 | NBR 878 |
|---|---|---|---|
| Average load, tons tare | | | |
|     Service trains | 307 | 311 | 345 |
|     Special trains | 406 | 406 | 406 |
| Average speed mph* | | | |
|     Service trains | 49·3 | 49·0 | 48·8 |
|     Special trains | 46·0 | 47·2 | 47·5 |
| Average dhp | | | |
|     Service trains | 393 | 391 | 529 |
|     Special trains | 527 | 529 | 525 |
| Average steam-chest pressure psi | | | |
|     Special trains | 97 | 132 | 138 |
| Average cut-off | | | |
|     Special trains, per cent | 40 | 42 | 38 |
| Coal per dhp hr, lb | | | |
|     Service trains | 5·08 | 4·45 | 4·12 |
|     Special trains | 4·42 | 3·63 | 4·15 |
| Average superheat temp. in deg F | 624 | 577 | 520 |
| Evaporation lb of water per lb of coal | 7·2 | 8·6 | 8·2 |

\* Inclusive of various checks on most runs.

PERFORMANCE ON COCKSBURNSPATH BANK

| Railway Engine No | GNR 1447 | NER 733 | NBR 878 |
|---|---|---|---|
| Load tons | 406·5 | 406·5 | 366 |
| Average boiler pressure psi | 162 | 175 | 175 |
| Steam chest pressure psi | 140 | 147 | 138 |
| Average cut-off, per cent | 40 | 56 | 52 |
| Speed on bank mph | | | |
|     at foot | 47·5 | 50·5 | 44·0 |
|     minimum | 20 | 22·5 | 21·5 |
| Drawbar pull tons | | | |
|     at foot | 2·45 | 2·20 | 2·35 |
|     maximum actual | 4·75 | 4·80 | 4·70 |
|     maximum corrected for gradient | 5·92 | 6·08 | 5·97 |

some point in this. Certainly the driver who went north with No 1447 was no faintheart. He was none other than Albert Pibworth, of King's Cross, who put up such a grand show under difficulties with the Gresley 'Pacific' No 4474 in the 1925 Interchange Trials with the Great Western between Paddington and Plymouth.

Too great a significance should not be attached to the results obtained with the three designs of 'Atlantic', as tabulated herewith, except that they give the complete lie to the suggestion, sometimes made by persons who ought to have known better, that the North British 'Atlantics' were inordinately heavy coal burners. All three designs showed themselves capable of doing the job comfortably, on a coal consumption that was normal for good, first-line express passenger engines of that period. Basic rates of 4 to $4\frac{1}{2}$ lb of coal per drawbar horsepower hour were normal on all lines except the Great Western, and the considerably lower rates customary with engines like the 'Saints', 'Stars', and 'Castles' would not have been possible save for special measures taken to regulate the grades of fuel used on top-link duties, and to train the drivers and firemen concerned. The LNER figures of 4 to $4\frac{1}{2}$ lb per dhp-hour were paralleled by the best LNWR and Midland figures of the day, though engines of Lancashire and Yorkshire and of Caledonian design did not show up so well in tests made at about the same period.

North Eastern locomotives in general did not give such favourable results in a further series of tests made between Newcastle and Edinburgh in 1924. Gresley was anxious to demonstrate the inherent advantages of three-cylinder propulsion, and in the North Eastern 'Atlantics' of classes 'V1' and 'Z' he had two types that were superficially identical save that one had two cylinders and the other three. On both the steam distribution was by the Stephenson link motion; both classes had the same boiler, and a roughly similar nominal tractive effort. The two classes seemed ideal for a direct comparison. The 'Z' class engine put up a performance much the same as that registered by the sister engine in the 1923 trials, but the 'V1' did very poorly so far as basic economy was concerned. The test trains were run punctually, but on a disproportionately heavy consumption of coal up to a maximum of 6 lb per dhp-hour. Of course the results suited Gresley's argument admirably. They were a triumph for the three-cylinder system. But no matter how many cylinders, a design that needed over 6 lb of coal per dhp-hour to work trains at the moderate speeds scheduled for the tests would now appear to be materially wrong in certain details. It is probable from the experience gained elsewhere that a simple rearrangement of the valve gear would have reduced the coal consumption to less than 4 lb per dhp-hour.

It is a pity that these tests provide the only record of the coal consumption of the 'V' and 'V1' 'Atlantics'. They were magnificently impressive engines, and immensely strong in getting away with a load. I always remember the remark of a Great Northern fireman working one of the King's Cross–Newcastle double-home turns when the rostered 'Pacific' failed *en route*, and they had to run the train unassisted with an Ivatt 'Atlantic' from Grantham to York. In his own words: '. . . one of those North Eastern "700" class [a 'V1'] coupled on ahead of us at York, and she just about lifted us and the train from there to Newcastle'. Despite the introduction of many new 'Pacifics' the North Eastern 'Atlantics', both 'Vs' and 'Zs' continued on main-line work until the mid-1920s.

So far as individual performances were concerned nearly all my best runs were with 'Z' class 'Atlantics', though I was not able to catch one of those occasions when they were handling really heavy loads. The first one tabulated was on the 1.55 PM out of York, and was a most exhilarating effort by engine No 710. The start, round the curves to Poppleton Junction, was never very brisk, but once into the 'straight' we went ahead in grand style. Beyond Alne, on dead level track, we attained 69½ mph; there was a slight falling off on the faint rise to Sessay, and then a maximum of 72 on the level through Thirsk. The rise at 1 in 626 to Northallerton was cleared at 66½ mph, and a maximum of 73¼ mph at Wiske Moor troughs preceded another slight fall in speed on the rise to Eryholme. By this time we had covered 29·2 miles of level and slightly rising track at an average speed of 68·7 mph, and this fine run

was rounded off by a top speed of 75 mph across the Tees viaduct at Croft Spa. Adverse signals pulled us up dead at the
platform end at Darlington, but the net start-to-stop time from
York to a normal stop in the station was no more than 43½
minutes.

In the reverse direction engine No 2163 put up a characteristic performance on the 8.49 PM up 'Flyer'. This run was
logged by the late R. J. Purves. There was a rather close time-

TABLE 10

1.55 PM YORK–DARLINGTON

Load: 10 coaches, 292 tons tare, 315 tons full

Engine: class 'Z' 4–4–2 No 710

| Distance miles | | Actual min    sec | Speeds mph |
|---|---|---|---|
| 0·0 | YORK | 0    00 | |
| 1·6 | *Poppleton Junction** | 3    54 | |
| 5·5 | Beningbrough | 8    22 | 61 |
| 9·7 | Tollerton | 12    18 | 66 |
| 11·2 | Alne | 13    38 | 67½ |
| 13·4 | Raskelf | 15    34 | 69½ |
| 16·1 | Pilmoor | 17    58 | 68 |
| 18·0 | Sessay | 19    40 | 67 |
| 22·2 | THIRSK | 23    18 | 72 |
| 26·5 | Otterington | 27    00 | 69 |
| 30·0 | NORTHALLERTON | 30    02 | 66½ |
| 33·7 | Danby Wiske | 33    20 | 73¼ |
| 38·9 | *Eryholme Junction* | 37    46 | 67 |
| 41·5 | Croft Spa | 39    59 | 75 |
| | | sig. stop | |
| 44·1 | DARLINGTON | 49    30 | |

Net time: 43½ minutes.     * Now Skelton.

table margin between this train and the up 'second mail' at
York, and it became customary to start easily from Darlington,
and give the engines their head after Northallerton. There was
often some very fast running at the York end, clearly shown on
the run tabulated, with speeds of over 80 mph sustained on
dead level track. I never had the opportunity of logging this
train myself; but one afternoon, when I was travelling by
the 2.5 PM from Edinburgh to King's Cross two 'Zs' were

provided to work a train of 475 tons, and they kept the sectional times of the 8.49 PM 'Flyer' as far as Alne, passing Thirsk in 22½ minutes, and Alne in 31 minutes 53 seconds. Maximum speed was 73½ mph, and after passing Alne the engines were eased down, and York was reached in 43 minutes 54 seconds against a schedule, for that train, of 47 minutes.

TABLE 11

8.49 PM DARLINGTON–YORK

Load: 7 coaches, 211 tons tare, 220 tons full

Engine: class 'Z' 4–4–2 No 2163

| Distance miles | | Sch. min | Actual min | sec | Speeds* mph |
|---|---|---|---|---|---|
| 0·0 | DARLINGTON | 0 | 0 | 00 | |
| 2·6 | Croft Spa | | 4 | 55 | 31·8 |
| 5·2 | *Eryholme Junction* | | 7 | 50 | 54·5 |
| 10·4 | Danby Wiske | | 12 | 50 | 62·4 |
| 14·1 | NORTHALLERTON | 15 | 16 | 15 | 65·0 |
| 17·6 | Otterington | | 19 | 15 | 70·0 |
| 21·9 | THIRSK | 23 | 22 | 45 | 73·7 |
| 26·1 | Sessay | | 26 | 09 | 74·2 |
| 28·0 | Pilmoor | | 27 | 38 | 76·7 |
| 30·7 | Raskelf | | 29 | 40 | 79·6 |
| 32·9 | Alne | 32 | 31 | 17 | 81·7 |
| 38·6 | Beningbrough | | 35 | 28 | 81·6 |
| 41·0 | *Skelton Bridge* | | 37 | 16 | 80·0 |
| 42·5 | *Poppleton Junction* | | 38 | 35 | 68·5 |
| | | | sigs | | |
| 44·1 | YORK | 43 | 42 | 55 | |

\* Average speeds from point to point.

One of the best runs I had with a 'V' class engine was on the Saturday 1.34 PM down from York in 1934. Here again there were some very close timetable margins, as this train left York immediately in the wake of the non-stop 'Flying Scotsman', and just ahead of the 10.5 AM from King's Cross. All the way we were running block and block behind the 'non-stop', frequently sighting adverse signals from her, while our running was further handicapped by two permanent way checks. There was some good going intermediately, though anything harder would have been of no avail due to the close proximity of the train in front. The run finished with a good sprint down the bank from Chester-le-Street, but further checks brought us in $2\frac{3}{4}$ minutes late.

TABLE 12

1.34 PM YORK–NEWCASTLE

Load: 9 coaches, 283 tons tare, 305 tons full

Engine: class 'V' 4–4–2 No 649

| Distance miles | | Sch. min | Actual min sec | Speeds mph |
|---|---|---|---|---|
| 0·0 | YORK | 0 | 0 00 | |
| — | | | sigs | |
| 1·6 | *Poppleton Junction* | | 4 53 | |
| 5·5 | Beningbrough | | 9 33 | $58\frac{1}{2}$ |
| 11·2 | Alne | | 15 00 | 65 |
| 16·1 | Pilmoor | | 19 41 | 61 |
| 22·2 | Thirsk | 26 | 25 38 | 65 |
| 30·0 | NORTHALLERTON | $33\frac{1}{2}$ | 33 16 | 58 |
| 33·7 | Danby Wiske | | 36 58 | $65\frac{1}{2}$ |
| 38·9 | *Eryholme Junction* | | 42 00 | 60/63 |
| — | | | sigs | |
| 44·1 | DARLINGTON | 48 | 49 40 | 30 |
| 48·0 | *Milepost 48* | | 55 08 | 51 |
| — | | | p.w.s. | 25 |
| 49·5 | Aycliffe | | 57 45 | — |
| 57·0 | Ferryhill | | 67 13 | $64\frac{1}{2}$ |
| — | | | p.w.s. | 35 |
| 66·1 | DURHAM | 74 | 78 12 | — |
| 70·0 | Plawsworth | | 82 40 | 60 |
| — | | | p.w.s. | 45 |
| 71·9 | Chester-le-Street | | 84 45 | $62\frac{1}{2}$ |
| 76·3 | Lamesley | | 88 47 | $72\frac{1}{2}$ |
| — | | | slight check | |
| 79·5 | *King Edward Bridge Junction* | | 92 28 | |
| — | | | sigs | |
| 80·1 | NEWCASTLE | 92 | 94 42 | |

Net time: $87\frac{1}{2}$ minutes.

On the north main line I had, on another occasion, a good run to Berwick with the same train. This time we had a 'Z' for a 350-ton load, and were completely unchecked. The start out of Newcastle was, by tradition, never very fast, and the attained speed of $38\frac{1}{2}$ mph up the 1 in 200 gradient to Forest Hall was succeeded by no more than moderate speeds over the slight undulations to the summit point near Cramlington. After that we went splendidly, steadily gaining on schedule time. The climb of Longhoughton bank with its 4 miles at 1 in 170 was good, and the engine ran freely on the gradual descent to the seashore at Beal. The final climb, 4 miles at 1 in 190 to the summit point on the cliffs a mile beyond Scremerston, was rushed at a minimum speed of exactly 50 mph.

TABLE 13

NEWCASTLE–BERWICK

Load: 10 coaches, 320 tons tare, 350 tons full

Engine: class 'Z' 4-4-2 No 733

| Distance miles | | Sch. min | Actual min sec | | Speeds mph |
|---|---|---|---|---|---|
| 0·0 | NEWCASTLE | 0 | 0 | 00 | |
| 1·7 | Heaton | | 4 | 47 | |
| 5·0 | Forest Hall | | 10 | 15 | 38½ |
| 7·7 | Annitsford | | 13 | 49 | 53 |
| 9·9 | Cramlington | | 16 | 28 | 47½ |
| 13·9 | Stannington | | 20 | 32 | 68 |
| 16·6 | MORPETH | 25 | 23 | 20 | slack |
| 20·2 | Longhirst | | 27 | 49 | 58 |
| 28·5 | Acklington | | 36 | 17 | 67 |
| 31·9 | Warkworth | | 39 | 31 | 60/65 |
| 34·8 | ALNMOUTH | 45 | 42 | 20 | 54* |
| 39·4 | Little Mill | | 48 | 16 | 41 |
| 43·0 | Christon Bank | | 52 | 30 | 64 |
| 46·0 | Chathill | | 55 | 08 | 71½ |
| 51·6 | BELFORD | 63 | 60 | 18 | 63½ |
| 58·6 | Beal | | 66 | 17 | 76½ |
| 60·8 | Goswick | | 68 | 10 | 69 |
| 63·5 | Scremerston | | 70 | 54 | 50 (min) |
| 65·7 | Tweedmouth | | 73 | 31 | 55 |
| 66·9 | BERWICK | 80 | 75 | 35 | |

* Speed restriction.

I must mention also an excellent run on the down 'Aberdonian' sleeping-car express made at the August Bank Holiday weekend in 1935. I was travelling north to make my first footplate journey on the giant 2-8-2s of the 'P2' class, described later in this book, and on a hot summer's night I did not sleep well. In any case I had to rouse early to ride the engine from

Edinburgh northwards. I was awake when we stopped at New-castle, and noted the time of the restart. Then I dozed off again, and did not note any further times till we passed Berwick, in the good time of 73¾ minutes. We had a big load of 515 tons, and I discovered on arrival in Edinburgh our engines were a 'V' class 'Atlantic' No 1794 and a class 'R' 4–4–0 No 2025. Despite a permanent way check just north of Berwick they covered the remaining 57½ miles to Edinburgh in 66¼ minutes with a time of 37 minutes 53 seconds for the 38·2 miles from Grantshouse to Portobello.

# CHAPTER FIVE

## THE CONSTITUENTS:
## 4. NORTH BRITISH

It is remarkable that the North British Railway, so complicated to operate by reason of its many branches and other minor routes, should have presented a relatively simple problem so far as motive power was concerned. In its few major engine classes it resembled the Great Eastern, just as the North Eastern at the opposite extreme resembled the Great Central. The North British had no more than five modern superheater engine classes: the Reid 'Atlantics'; the 4–4–os of the 'Scott' and 'Glen' classes; the 4–4–2 suburban tanks and the very powerful o–6–o goods. So far as the LNER locomotive stud is concerned it is only these five classes that need consideration.

There were 22 'Atlantics', and at the time of grouping they were used exclusively on the Waverley route to Carlisle, and between Edinburgh and Aberdeen. The workings southwards to Newcastle were experiments only. On the Waverley route, over the very long and difficult inclines, on gradients of up to 1 in 70 and much curvature the maximum tare load permitted to an unassisted 'Atlantic' was 290 tons. At the time of grouping there were two day and two night services to St Pancras, and these rarely exceeded the 290-ton limit and so obviated the use of bank engines. The introduction of third-class sleeping-cars on the principal night trains changed things completely and not long afterwards some Gresley 'Pacifics' were allocated to the Waverley route. Within their load limit the Reid 'Atlantics' worked the route most competently. There was no opportunity for fast running, and those engines seemed to excel in hard slogging uphill on those most severe gradients.

On the Aberdeen route, north of Edinburgh the actual gradients were in places just as severe as on the Waverley route, only much shorter. In many cases the steepest pitches could be rushed, though in the southbound direction the stiff climbs out of Aberdeen itself, out of Stonehaven, and out of Montrose had, with most trains, to be tackled from a standing start. This was the reason for the difference in maximum tonnage allowed to the 'Atlantics' on the northbound and on the southbound run. Northbound the limit was 370 tons; southbound it was 340. Difference or not these were mighty big tonnages for 'Atlantic' engines over such a route; but as on the Waverley they ran the trains with the punctuality of chronometers. Cecil J. Allen, whose extensive travels over all railways in Great Britain made him a very experienced observer, once remarked that the North British was the most punctual line in the country.

On the Edinburgh–Aberdeen route engines were always changed at Dundee, and the workings were such that the 'Atlantics' stationed at Edinburgh (Haymarket) and Dundee (Tay Bridge) could make two return trips in the day's work. I have not got the exact times that then prevailed but a typical Haymarket diagram was:

|  |  |
|---|---|
| *Depart* | |
| *approx.* | |
| 10 AM | Edinburgh to Dundee |
| 2.30 PM | Dundee to Edinburgh |
| 6.15 PM | Edinburgh to Dundee |
| 9.30 PM | Dundee to Edinburgh |

The daily mileage (revenue earning) was 237, and the final trip was the sharply booked King's Cross sleeper – later named 'The Aberdonian' – which made the run non-stop. All the other turns involved intermediate stops. Similar workings operated north of Dundee, with slightly greater daily mileages of 284. As far as I can recall the 'Atlantics' were divided between Dundee, Haymarket, and Carlisle Canal shed. I don't remember that any were ever stationed at Aberdeen – at any rate in the early 1920s.

The Reid superheater 4–4–0s collectively were really excellent engines. They represented a parallel development to the far-famed Caledonian 'Dunalastairs', being descended from the same parent, the Drummond '476' class 4–4–0 of 1876, built specially for the inauguration in that year of through express services to St Pancras over the Waverley route. The 'Scotts' were the North British equivalent of the Caledonian 'Dunalastair IV' superheater class. The former engines had an excellent front-end design, and the unusual provision of 9-in diameter piston-valves. They were strong, reliable, and free-running engines, mostly used on the inter-city services between Edinburgh and Glasgow, and on the Glasgow through portions of Aberdeen trains which the 'Scotts' worked as far as Kirkcaldy. There the Edinburgh and Glasgow sections were combined. On the Edinburgh and Glasgow services many of the trains were quite heavy, loading to over 300 tons, and making intermediate stops. In later years they were much used for assisting 'Atlantics' on the Aberdeen route; but in 1922–3, in the rare cases where the loads of the principal expresses exceeded the 'Atlantic' limit, 4-4-0s of earlier vintage were used for assisting.

The smaller-wheeled version of the superheater 'Scott', the 'Glens', were an altogether outstanding class. They were introduced primarily for the West Highland line, and in hard, slogging mountain climbing on lengthy gradients of 1 in 60, they were the most successful engines ever put on to that line. Their maximum load was 190 tons tare, as compared to the 220 tons allowed to the ex-GNR 'Moguls' of class 'K2' that were put on to the West Highland line after grouping. Those load limits were in exact proportion to the nominal tractive efforts of the two classes; but in frequent travelling over the line I found that the 'Glens' were consistently faster on the banks with their maximum load than the 'K2's were with their maximum of 220 tons. Moreover, the 'Glens' were notably immune from slipping. They would take a maximum load train up a 1 in 60 gradient at 25 to 26 mph. Like the 'Scotts' they had 9-in diameter piston-valves, and with an excellent design of the Stephenson link motion they were very free running. In their heyday one had to speak in whispers of the maximum speeds they attained on favourable stretches of the West Highland line, because there was an overall speed limit of 40 mph throughout from Craigendoran to Mallaig. Now I can reveal that I frequently clocked them at well over 50 mph, and once registered a sustained 66 mph over Rannoch Moor! It is altogether fitting that one of these really splendid 4–4–os, the *Glen Douglas*, should have been preserved, and housed in the Glasgow Museum of Transport with other celebrated Scottish locomotives.

The Reid superheater 4–4–2 suburban tank was a natural off-shoot of the NBR 4–4–0 family. It was yet another handsome and successful design, though it came to be superseded on the most arduous local duties earlier than other North British classes. After grouping a batch of the very successful Gresley 0–6–2 tank engines of Great Northern origin (LNER class 'N2') was built new for service in Scotland, and these engines were undoubtedly superior to the Reid 4–4–2s in rapidly accelerating between stops, and taking heavy trains. Nevertheless the Reid engines had many years of useful work still ahead of them. Like all North British engines they were massively built, with strong frames and generous bearing surfaces; and their freedom from trouble and relatively low maintenance costs ensured their longevity.

The last North British design to be specially mentioned is the Reid superheater 0–6–0 goods engines (LNER class 'J37'). These were the heavy freight equivalent of the 'Scott' and 'Glen' class 4–4–os, and they were equally successful. Despite their small driving wheels, only 4 ft 3 in diameter, they had a fine turn of speed. They worked some passenger trains on the Mallaig extension of the West Highland line, and frequently exceeded the 40-mph speed limit for the line. I always think they were among the most handsome 0–6–os ever built. Many engineers who built 4–4–os of much grace and beauty seemed to 'lose interest' where appearances were concerned, when it came to the freight equivalents. But Reid, like J. G. Robinson with his very graceful 'Pom-Poms' on the Great Central, excelled in his production of a powerful 0–6–0. Like the superheater 'Scotts' and the 'Glens', the whole stud of 'J37' 0–6–os passed into British Railways ownership in 1948.

Apart from the provision of a stud of hard-working, reliable engines operating over a high proportion of the Scottish mileage of the LNER the North British made an indirect contribution of some importance. The chairman, the great William White-law, who became the first chairman of the LNER, was a lover of all the practical aspects of railways, and largely at his insti-gation the North British became involved in three separate sets of locomotive interchange trials. There was one set in which an 'intermediate' 4–4–0 – the non-superheated forerunner of the celebrated 'Glen' class – was pitted against a Highland 4–6–0 of the 'Castle' class; a second set, when a North British 'Atlantic', in non-superheated condition, made a return trip from Carlisle to Preston in competition with an LNWR 'Ex-periment' class 4–6–0, and finally there was a series of heavy freight engine trials on Glenfarg bank, when the NBR acted as hosts to visiting engines from the Great Western and the North Eastern.

It has been shown on many occasions that drivers in isolated interchange trials have little time to familiarize themselves with the different conditions, and personalities often play a pre-dominant part. A driver who is not readily adaptable to change will put up a poor show; another who has the temperament for a big occasion will put up a performance that is unrepresenta-tive on the credit side. So it certainly proved to be on two out of the three trials in which the North British was involved. The 'Atlantic' that ran from Carlisle to Preston and back did not have her regular driver, and of the man who did participate it was once said that he was not fit to drive a horse and cart, let alone an express train! The freight engine trials were influ-enced in a different way, and it was these that had some effect upon future motive-power provision in the North Eastern Area of the LNER. The North British authorities were anxious to consider the possibilities of improved freight train operation on their heavily graded sections by use of eight-coupled en-gines, and comparative tests were arranged between a Great Western '28XX' class 2–8–0, and one of the new North Eastern three-cylinder 0–8–0s of class 'T3' (later LNER 'Q7').

The human element entered into this set of tests through the dynamic personality of the North Eastern dynamometer car inspector, J. J. Weatherburn, who took the North Eastern engine and dynamometer car up to Perth prepared to 'lick the

proverbial pants' off the Great Western. Tests with the latter
engine were conducted in January 1921 working between
Bridge of Earn and Glenfarg, a distance of 6¾ miles, six of
which are inclined continuously at 1 in 75. On the first trip the
start-to-stop run was made in 33 minutes with a load of 590
tons; but on a subsequent run, when the load was increased to
686 tons the engine stalled on the bank through slipping.
Weather conditions were certainly bad, with snow falling
throughout, and the dry sanding gear of the Great Western
became completely choked with snow and entirely inoperative.

The North Eastern 0–8–0 No 903 was tested on Sunday,
August 28th, 1921, in the presence of a large number of senior
officers of all three railways, and Mr Whitelaw himself. Three
runs were made, and on the first, with a load of 617 tons those
on the footplate were clearly keeping something in reserve. The
start-to-stop time was 35½ minutes. Then the load was increased to 702 tons, and Weatherburn and his men began to
show their hand. A magnificent climb was made, in 30 minutes
start to stop. On this run the engine was worked in 75 per cent
cut-off to the first tunnel, and 65 per cent thereafter, with regulator full open throughout. Finally the load was made up to
the enormous total of 755 tons. The engine was worked 'flat-
out' from start to finish – full regulator and 75 per cent cut-
off – and made the run in 33 minutes, the same time that the
Great Western engine had made with 590 tons. As it turned
out grouping was imminent, and the North British took no
steps to develop an eight-coupled design; but so far as the
North Eastern was concerned the supreme competence of the
'T3' engine in such severe conditions was enough to show that
no engines of greater power would be needed for the freight
traffic for many years to come, and it was not until more than
twenty years later that any freight engines other than of North
Eastern design were drafted into the area.

In the course of travelling in Scotland during the early
years of grouping I had many opportunities of observing the
performance of North British engines, and in turning through
my old notebooks I cannot find a single occasion on which any
time was lost. Any odd minutes dropped intermediately due

TABLE I.

| Run No | I |
|---|---|
| Train | 12.45 PM |
| Engine No 4–4–2 No | 9869 |
| Engine Name | Bonnie Dundee |
| Pilot engine No | — |
| Load tons E/F | 333/355 |

| Distance miles | | Actual min sec | Speeds mph |
|---|---|---|---|
| 0·0 | ABERDEEN | 0 00 | — |
| 4·8 | Cove Bay | 10 43 | 36/30½ |
| 7·1 | *Milepost 234* | 14 52 | 36 |
| 11·6 | Muchalls | 19 47 | 64 |
| 16·2 | STONEHAVEN | 25 00 | |
| 2·6 | *Dunnottar Box* | 7 17 | 30/36½ |
| 5·5 | Carmont | 12 17 | 33 |
| 11·2 | Fordoun | 18 17 | 65 |
| 14·5 | LAURENCEKIRK | 23 15 | |
| 19·8 | Craigo | 7 33 | 69½ |
| 21·9 | *Kinnaber Junction* | 9 53 | 25 |
| 24·5 | MONTROSE | 13 40 | |
| 2·1 | *Usan Box* | 5 32 | 30 |
| 4·9 | Lunan Bay | 10 14 | 35/51 |
| 7·5 | Inverkeilor | 12 49 | 68 |
| | | , p.w.s. | 25 |
| 10·7 | Letham Grange | 16 49 | — |
| 13·7 | ARBROATH | 21 35 | — |
| 1·8 | Elliott Junction | 3 51 | |
| 6·1 | Carnoustie | 9 20 | 58 |
| 13·0 | Broughty Ferry | 16 15 | 60 |
| 17·0 | DUNDEE | 22 05 | — |

\* Rebuilt Holmes 4–4–0 class 'D31'

to adverse signals, or to temporary engineering restrictions
were always recovered, usually before the very next stopping
station. 'Atlantics' figured in all my journeys on the Waverley
route and on the East Coast main line north of Edinburgh.
Because most of my journeys were made in the height of the
summer, and at weekends into the bargain, I encountered
some very heavy loads, with consequent double-heading; indeed, one could not expect any engine short of a Gresley 2–8–2

BERDEEN–DUNDEE

| 2<br>7.35 PM<br>9902<br>*Highland Chief*<br>9769\*<br>434/470 | | 3<br>7.35 PM<br>9869<br>*Bonnie Dundee*<br>9413†<br>523/565 | |
|---|---|---|---|
| *Actual*<br>min   sec | *Speeds*<br>*mph* | *Actual*<br>min   sec | *Speeds*<br>*mph* |
| 0   00 | — | 0   00 | — |
| 9   30 | 39/35 | 9   33 | 41/35 |
| 13   15 | — | 13   11 | 41 |
| 18.   20 | 64½ | 18   05 | 64½ |
| 24   00 | | 23   42 | |
| 5   40 | 30/42 | 6   39 | 38½ |
| 10   00 | 37 | 11   13 | 34½ |
| sigs | 68/45 | — | |
| 16   10 | 53 | 17   20 | 62½ |
| 20   15 | 49 | 20   41 | 52 |
| — | 69 | 26   23 | 62½ |
| 28   15 | 37 | 29   10 | |
| 32   00 | | 33   40 | |
| 5   20 | 30 | 4   53 | 32½ |
| 10   05 | 34½ | 9   28 | 38½ |
| 12   40 | 68 | 12   11 | — |
| — | 56 | p.w.s. | 45 |
| 16   15 | 63½ | 16   54 | 62½ |
| 20   40 | | 21   15 | |
| 3   25 | | 3   27 | |
| 9   00 | 56 | 8   25 | 60 |
| 16   35 | 60 | 14   59 | 64½ |
| 22   30 | | 21   05 | |

Superheated 'Scott' class: *Caleb Balderstone.*

to tackle 560 tons unassisted out of Aberdeen, as I noted one evening on the 7.35 PM up King's Cross 'sleeper'.

I have tabulated details of three journeys of my own recording between Aberdeen and Dundee. Two of these were on the sleeper, while the third was on the 12.45 PM out of Aberdeen, with very nearly the maximum load for an unpiloted 'Atlantic'. On this latter occasion I rode on the footplate. It was a steady performance admirably displaying the reliability of these

TABLE 1

| Run No<br>Engine 4–4–2 No<br>Engine Name<br>Pilot engine No<br>Load tons E/F | 1<br>9875<br>*Midlothian*<br><br>364/390 | |
|---|---|---|
| Distance<br>miles | Actual<br>min    sec | Speeds<br>mph |
| 0·0   DUNDEE | 0    00 | |
| 2·7   *Tay Bridge South Box* | 7    55 | 37½ |
| 4·6   St Fort | 10    35 | 62/52 |
| 8·3   Leuchars Junction | 14    35 | 60½ |
| 11·6   Dairsie | 18    35 | 44½ |
| 14·6   Cupar | 22    05 | 55½ |
| 16·9   Springfield | 25    10 | 39 |
| 20·1   Ladybank Junction | 29    35 | 50½ |
| 24·3   *Lochmuir* | 37    05 | 28½ |
| 25·9   Markinch | 39    25 | 63 |
| —   | p.w.s. | |
| 28·5   Thornton | 41    55 | 35 |
| —   *Milepost 29* | — | 34 |
| 33·3   KIRKCALDY | 48    15 | 66 |
| 39·0   Burntisland | 54    20 | 45* |
| 41·8   Aberdour | 58    15 | — |
| 43·2   *Dalgetty* | 61    10 | 28½ |
| 46·0   INVERKEITHING | 64    45 | 60/35* |
| 48·0   *Forth Bridge North* | 68    35 | 23 |
| 52·7   Turnhouse | 75    30 | 61½ |
| 58·0   Haymarket | 81    10 | — |
| 59·2   EDINBURGH WAVERLEY | 84    00 | |

\* Speed restrictions

'Atlantic' engines on the heavy banks. Although driven very hard on all the inclines there was never the slightest tendency to slip. Out of Stonehaven the engine was worked in 53 per cent cut-off, while on the 1 in 88 gradient from Montrose up to the Usan crossing the cut-off was continually in 60 per cent with regulator three-quarters full open. The attained speed of 30 mph on this gradient was the outstanding feature of the run. As usual speed was restricted to around 60 mph on the dead level stretch along the coast between Arbroath and Dundee.

UNDEE–EDINBURGH

| 2 9877 *Liddesdale* 9427† 434/475 | | 3 9510 *The Lord Provost* 9427† 511/550 | |
|---|---|---|---|
| *Actual* min   sec | *Speeds* mph | *Actual* min   sec | *Speeds* mph |
| 0   00 | — | 0   00 | — |
| 7   05 | — | 7   05 | — |
| 9   40 | 65 | 9   45 | 57 |
| 13   40 | 62 | 13   38 | 63 |
| 17   40 | 45 | 17   22 | 50½ |
| 21   00 | 57½ | 20   27 | 61 |
| 23   40 | 48 | 23   12 | 47½ |
| 27   35 | 60 | 26   52 | 58½ |
| 34   05 | 33¼ | 32   30 | 35 |
| 35   55 | — | 34   40 | 60 |
|  | 60 | p.w.s. |  |
| 38   50 | — | 38   32 | 20 |
|  | 35½ | — | 32 |
| 45   45 | 64½ | 46   19 | 63½ |
| 52   20 | 35* | 53   20 | 20* |
| 56   25 | 48/37½ | 57   48 | 45½/39 |
| 58   35 | 39 | 59   50 | 39 |
| 62   05 | 60/45* | 63   27 | 54/40* |
| 65   45 | 28 | 67   50 | 23½ |
| 72   10 | 65 | 74   42 | 63½ |
| 78   20 | — | 80   35 |  |
| sig stop |  |  |  |
| 82   40 | — | 83   55 |  |

Superheated 'Scott' class: *Lord Glenvarloch.*

On the second run, *Highland Chief* was assisted by a small Holmes rebuilt 4–4–0, and the two engines dealt very competently with a 470-ton load. If one divided this in the proportions of 290 tons to the 'Atlantic' and 180 tons to the 4–4–0 they still each had a respectable tonnage to handle over this difficult road. Their finest effort was the start from Stonehaven, attaining 30 mph up the initial 1 in 92–107 to Dunnottar, accelerating rapidly to 42 mph on the three-quarters of a mile at 1 in 423 that follows, and clearing the last 1½ miles to Carmont summit, on 1 in 102, at 37 mph. It will be seen that in starting out of Montrose the unassisted *Bonnie Dundee* was almost as fast.

The last run of the three was a remarkable performance, again with *Bonnie Dundee*, and a superheated 'Scott' 4–4–0, on a 565-ton train. This run was made on Easter Monday 1934, which accounts for the exceptional loading. Except in starting out of Stonehaven *Bonnie Dundee* and *Caleb Balderstone* together made the fastest times of all three runs. I travelled in the leading coach, and can certainly testify that they made plenty of noise about it! But what remains so vividly in mind is the confidence with which both drivers flailed their engines from the moment they got the 'right-away' from each station stop. As I had seen for myself from the footplate of *Bonnie Dundee* there was no gentle nursing, when the regulator was first opened; they had 'the lot' from the word 'go'. This was typical of all North British working, and exhilarating it certainly was to observe, and to hear!

I did not continue on the footplate south of Dundee on the 12.45 PM, but in company with my two runs on the 'sleeper' I have included a third logged by Mr Cecil J. Allen on the same train, with an unpiloted 'Atlantic' and a very heavy load of 390 tons. This engine was within six tons of the maximum permitted south of Dundee; but her driver and fireman went for it in characteristic style, and did remarkably well to lose only a single minute on schedule time. This was amply accounted for by the permanent way check at Thornton. In later years a very serious colliery subsidence developed at this point and seriously affected the running of all trains; but this run was made shortly after grouping, and the check was no more than a normal temporary engineering restriction. On the second run in the table, made in 1928, we went through Thornton at full speed.

There were slight speed restrictions at Leuchars, Cupar, and Ladybank, which did not affect a run like that of *Midlothian*, on which the speed was barely above the 60 mph laid down in each case; but the driver went somewhat harder round the curves at Burntisland and Inverkeithing than the 25-mph limits laid down, and thereby gained some impetus for the heavy grades

that follow. The major uphill efforts were grand, namely the
$28\frac{1}{2}$ mph at Lochmuir, after $3\frac{1}{4}$ miles of 1 in 111–95–105;
$28\frac{1}{2}$ mph again at Dalgetty, after 3 miles at 1 in 100–108–100;
and finally 23 mph entering upon the Forth Bridge after 2 miles
of 1 in 70 up from Inverkeithing. The engine concerned, No
9875 *Midlothian*, was the last of her class to be withdrawn, in
December 1937, and when she was subsequently returned to
traffic it was hoped, and generally understood, that she was to
be preserved. She continued in service until the outbreak of
war in September 1939, after which she became a victim of
wartime conditions.

On the second run in the table *Liddesdale*, assisted by a
superheated 'Scott' No 9427 *Lord Glenvarloch*, continued the
good work by *Highland Chief* and his pilot from Aberdeen.
This run was made at night, and I did not secure all the detail
I should have liked of the fine start across the Tay Bridge. The
two engines naturally had the advantage over the heavily
loaded *Midlothian* on all the uphill sections, and they were
leading by $3\frac{1}{4}$ minutes at Turnhouse. The net time was about
$80\frac{1}{2}$ minutes. On the last run, the removal of a four-wheeled
van reduced the load on the Easter Monday trip to 550 tons,
and *Lord Glenvarloch* was again the assistant engine, this time
with No 9510 *The Lord Provost*. After almost exactly dead-
heating with the previous run through Leuchars this third
run began to draw ahead until experiencing the full severity of
the Thornton subsidence check. This was followed by a much
more rigorous observance of the slack at Burntisland, not to
mention that over the villainous little S-curve in the middle
of Kinghorn tunnel. Until I rode on the footplate I had been
unaware of the existence of this latter; but by 1934, with
'Pacifics' in regular service over the route, and the 'P2' 2–8–2s
under construction, a much closer watch was being kept upon
all speed restrictions.

*The Lord Provost* and *Lord Glenvarloch* together made a very
fine climb past Aberdour to Dalgetty, but the back-breaking
ascent from Inverkeithing up to the Forth Bridge took its toll,
and we fell to $23\frac{1}{2}$ mph. The schedule had been eased out by
2 minutes by the time this run was made allowing 85 instead of

83 minutes, partly as a concession to the Thornton subsidence, but also to provide for running slowly through to the east end of Waverley station, instead of as previously stopping short of the central scissors crossing in the middle of the main up platform. Taken all round these six individual engine performances are thoroughly typical of the North British at the period. The mere fact that four out of the six required two engines did not signify there was any lack of hard work on the footplate. One had only to listen to the exhausts to realize that!

# CHAPTER SIX

# *HERITAGE FROM THE GREAT NORTHERN*

In October 1911, the date of Gresley's appointment as loco-motive superintendent of the GNR, it was not in express passenger motive power that the greatest need lay. A marked trend towards faster goods services all over the country was evident; the GNR was in the forefront of this movement, but strangely enough the company did not possess any engine really suitable for the traffic. In consequence every available passenger tender engine was pressed into service, and 'Atlantics', 4–4–0s, Stirling 2–4–0s and even 'singles' could be observed working freight trains. It was this boom in fast goods traffic that began to break down the old principle of 'one driver, one engine', for the fullest use had to be made of locomotives such as the large 'Atlantics', most of which included a fair proportion of fast goods mileage in their regular rosters. But the use of other types could be regarded only as a temporary measure pending the construction of suitable engines. Such was the Great Northern's need that for the first ten years of Gresley's chieftainship at Doncaster all new engines turned out were intended for freight service.

The first new types to appear were two classes of o–6–o superheater goods, one with 5 ft 2 in coupled wheels, and the second with 5 ft 8 in. Both did good work, but a o–6–o locomotive is not ideal for duties needing speeds of 60 mph or more, no matter how well aligned the road may be. In preparing a new design to meet contemporary needs, therefore, Gresley followed the general trend of British practice at the time for mixed-traffic work, and chose the 'Mogul' wheel arrangement. Since the advent in 1899–1901 of the imported 2–6–0s on the Midland, Great Central, and Great Northern Railways, the 'Mogul' was in many quarters looked upon as an undesirable Yankee intrusion. By the year 1912, however, its popularity had been firmly assured by Churchward's '43XX' class on the Great Western and the new Great Northern engines appeared almost contemporaneously with 2-6-0s on the Brighton, Caledonian, and Glasgow & South Western; not many years later another example appeared on the SE & CR. Gresley's engine was described by the *Railway Magazine* of the day as 'a No 1 class 0-6-0 with the addition of a pony truck'; but actually the new type was a far greater departure, and as the parents of a large and successful family of engines the 'Moguls' of 1912 are worthy of special attention.

Ten of the type were built, and numbered 1630 to 1639. Their leading dimensions were: cylinders 20 ins by 26 ins, coupled wheels 5 ft 8 in diameter, total heating surface 1,420 sq ft, grate area 24·5 sq ft, working pressure 170 psi. The principal feature was the front end; Walschaerts valve gear was used, working 10-in diameter piston-valves. The valve setting was carefully arranged so as to give a large exhaust opening when the engine was running well linked-up. Apart from the outside Walschaerts gear and the high raised running-plate their appearance was thoroughly Great Northern, and the footplate arrangements were unaltered from standard practice since Stirling days. Of these latter, the characteristic feature was the pull-out type of regulator, working in a horizontal plate.

The 'Moguls' of 1912 were not unduly long in showing what they could do; they worked the fast night goods to Doncaster, a 'lodging' turn, and a great variety of mixed-traffic jobs, including express passenger trains at times of pressure. In the early days of World War I they were often requisitioned for ambulance train workings. If there was a weakness in their design it lay in the boiler, which in proportion to the cylinder dimensions was on the small side by Great Northern standards; the next batch which came out in 1914 had boilers 5 ft 6 in diameter, instead of 4 ft 8 in, though the cylinders remained the same. Engine No 1640 was the pioneer of a series numbering 75 engines; on the LNER their designation was class 'K2', but on the GNR they formed class 'E1'. As wartime train-loads increased and schedules were eased out, they were sometimes to be seen on regular express passenger turns, but usually there was far too much in the way of fast goods, munition, and troop trains for them to be spared as deputies for the 'Atlantics'. Indeed, they never seemed quite at home on express working, but as fast freight engines they were second to none at the time of construction.

Enhanced locomotive power was needed for other classes of freight service too. The coal traffic between Peterborough and London had already grown to large dimensions, so much so that the Ivatt '401' class 0–8–0s, though satisfactory engines in themselves, were being worked at near their full capacity. Gresley's new design of 1913, the '456' class of 2–8–0s was a logical development both of the previous 0–8–0s and the '1630' class 'Moguls' designed for the heaviest freight service. The pony truck, in addition to supporting a heavy and powerful front end, provided a degree of flexibility in the vehicle that is especially valuable for freight working on a route like the GNR main line, with its frequent diversions from fast to slow road and vice versa.

As motive power units the '456' class (LNER class 'O1') proved as good as their ample dimensions suggest. Their cylinders were 21 ins by 28 ins and in combination with 4 ft 8 in coupled wheels and a working pressure of 170 psi gave the class a nominal tractive effort of 31,000 lb at 85 per cent of the working pressure. The boiler was the largest Doncaster had produced up to that time, the barrel being 15 ft 5 ins long, and 5 ft 6 ins diameter, and the heating surface of the tubes alone was 1,922 sq ft. Unlike the first 'Moguls' these 2–8–0s were fitted with Robinson superheaters; a high degree of superheat was evidently aimed at, for the heating surface provided, 570 sq ft, was unusually large for that period. The grate area of these engines was 27 sq ft; adhesion weight $67\frac{1}{2}$ tons; the total weight of engine and tender in working order $119\frac{1}{4}$ tons. Equipment included 10-in diameter piston-valves, as in the 'Moguls', and the Weir feedwater heater and feed pump. In outward appearance the engines remained faithful to Great Northern traditions, and the Stirling type of regulator handle still featured among the footplate fittings. Thus in the short space of three years Gresley had produced four eminently good designs, three of which, the '71' class 0-6-0s, the '1640' class 'Moguls', and the 2-8-0s were suitable for extensive building if the need arose. Actually they were used merely to meet the immediate requirements of the moment, while still more successful designs were being worked out.

By the beginning of 1915 immediate needs had been met, and Great Northern locomotive history was just entering an interesting transition stage. All over the country new locomotive types were being produced. On all hands superheating was being hailed as the final and conclusive answer to the exponents of compounding, yet on the GNR nothing very much seemed to be happening, outwardly at any rate, in the realm of express passenger power. Elsewhere one of the most strongly marked trends of the time was the introduction of multi-cylindered single-expansion locomotives. By 1914, the Great Western had practically standardized the four-cylinder system for crack express engines; the LNWR 'Claughtons' were out and doing good work, while the Great Northern's own historic partner, the North Eastern, had already turned out a considerable variety of three-cylinder simple designs.

Throughout the Gresley régime close study of contemporary practice, both at home and overseas, was applied to design at Doncaster works, and in the early years of his chieftainship it was not surprising, in view of what was taking place elsewhere in the country, that Gresley made some experiments with multi-cylindered locomotives. The first step was the complete rebuilding in 1915 of 'Atlantic' No 279, as a four-cylinder simple; this engine was one of the standard Ivatt '251' class, having two cylinders 18¾-in diameter by 24-in stroke. As rebuilt the engine was provided with four cylinders 15-in diameter by 26-in stroke – a 40 per cent increase in cylinder volume – and the boiler was modified by the fitting of a twenty-four-element Robinson superheater (instead of the previous eighteen-element one) affording 427 sq ft of heating surface. This heating surface was the same as that of the original Ivatt superheater 'Atlantics' of the 1452–1461 series. No 279 was fitted with the Walschaerts valve gear, but only two sets were provided, the valves of the inside-cylinders being actuated by rocking shafts driven off the tail rods of the outside-cylinder valve spindles. This rebuilding increased the weight of No 279 from the original $65\frac{1}{2}$ tons to $73\frac{1}{2}$ tons. As rebuilt No 279 was, in nominal tractive effort, the most powerful express engine on the GNR though curiously enough she never came into the limelight to the same extent as the ordinary '251' class. In her second rebuild, in 1938, as a two-cylinder engine with Walschaerts valve gear, she still remained unique among the 'Atlantics'. As then running No 3279 (GNR No 279) had two cylinders 20-in by 26-in diameter, but she was not the first GNR 'Atlantic' to be so equipped. In 1917 the four-cylinder compound No 1300, built by the Vulcan Foundry Co Ltd, was converted into a two-cylinder simple by Gresley, and a pair of standard 20-in by 26-in cylinders as used on the 'K1' and 'K2' 2-6-0s, was fitted. The original boiler, after twelve years of continuous service in express traffic, was retained and modified for superheated steam; a twenty-two-element super-heater was fitted, having a heating surface of 280 sq ft. The working pressure was reduced from the 200 psi of the original compound to 170 psi. No 1300, as converted, was nominally more powerful than the standard superheated 'Atlantics' of the '251' class, and for a time during the early months of 1918 she was working on the 5.30 PM Newcastle express from King's Cross. With a nightly load of over 400 tons, and an allowance of 125 minutes to cover the 105·5 miles from King's Cross to Grantham, it was a difficult turn. Another Gresley conversion was that of the Ivatt four-cylinder compound 'Atlantic' No 1421 into a standard superheater '251' in 1920.

It was not until May 1918, three years after Gresley's in-teresting experimental rebuilding of No 279, that the next multi-cylindered engine appeared on the GNR; this was the first three-cylindered 2-8-0 No 461. The suitability of three-cylinder propulsion for heavy freight working had already been demonstrated on the North Eastern Railway, where Wilson Worsdell's class 'X' 4-8-0 tanks were operating successfully in the Erimus hump yard. The system equally had advantages in such duties as the haulage of the Peterborough–London coal trains, in which a locomotive might have to start from rest against a 1 in 200 gradient. A more even crank effort is obtained with a three-cylinder engine, having its cranks set at 120 degrees to each other, than with the two-cylinder arrangement in which the cranks are at right-angles to each other, and a smoother start is possible; it was not so much a matter of power as the way in which that power is applied to the drawbar.

No 461 carried a boiler identical with that of the '456' class, but the two 21-in by 28-in cylinders were replaced by three cylinders 18 ins by 26 ins arranged in line and driving the second pair of coupled wheels. The connecting-rods were thus much shorter than in the earlier engines, and the cylinders were steeply inclined. But at the time of its construction the outstanding feature of No 461 was the valve gear. All previous three-cylinder simple locomotives built in this country – Robinson's Great Central 0-8-4 humping tanks, his one three-cylinder simple 'Atlantic' No 1090 and the various North Eastern types – used three sets of valve gear. By an ingenious mechanism, however, Gresley eliminated one set of valve motion. As applied to No 461 the details were rather different from that subsequently standardized; it was necessary to place the valve casing for the inside-cylinder in a different transverse plane from that of the two outside-cylinders; this disposition involved the use of vertical levers in the derived valve motion, and made the layout of the gear rather more complicated. Another novel feature of this engine later became standard on all the largest LNER locomotives; this was the vertical-screw reversing gear. The adjustment of cut-off was facilitated by the inclusion of ball bearings in the screw mounting.

No 461 was put to work on the Peterborough–London coal trains and very soon showed a certain superiority over the '456' class, particularly in starting. In the haulage of a heavy coal train weighing 1,300 tons gross behind the tender, a cut-off of 45 per cent, with regulator something below one-half open, was needed to maintain an average speed of 22½ mph over the 15 miles from Huntingdon to Sandy, on a typical journey. In getting away, and on the 1 in 200 banks, as much as 60 per cent cut-off was customary. But in spite of the successful working of No 461, building of the '456' class two-cylinder 2–8–0s continued.

The next three-cylinder engine was another advance upon former practice, and its advent was surrounded by just enough secrecy to set going a flood of rumours. Soon after the armistice of November 1918, the news got about that a 'super' main-line locomotive was under construction at Doncaster; everything pointed to a 'Prairie' at least, if not a 'Pacific', and then, early in 1920, No 1000 came out, the first of the three-cylinder 'Moguls'. This remarkable engine created quite a stir at the time by reason of her boiler; up till then a diameter of 5 ft 6 ins had been regarded as the maximum conveniently possible within the British loading gauge, whereas the boiler of the Gresley three-cylinder Mogul was 6-ft diameter over the smallest ring, and accommodated 217 tubes of $1\frac{3}{4}$-in outside diameter. The other leading boiler dimensions were: heating surface, tubes, 1,719 sq ft, firebox 182 sq ft, thirty-two-element superheater, 407 sq ft. The grate area was 28 sq ft, and the working pressure was 180 psi – the latter a slight advance upon previous Gresley practice.

There were further features of interest in the front end, for not only was the cylinder volume far in excess of that of any eight-wheel engine then at work on any other British railway, but there was also an alteration in the arrangement of the valve gear. The three cylinders were $18\frac{1}{2}$-in diameter by 26-in stroke, and by inclining the central cylinder at a much steeper angle than the outside ones it was possible so to arrange the valves that the simple horizontal rocking lever mechanism subsequently standardized, could be used for actuating the piston-valve of the inside cylinder. This was found to be a great improvement upon the layout of the gear used on the 2–8–0 engine No 461. Another detail destined to become standard practice on the LNER which made its first appearance on No 1000 was the provision of twin regulator handles, one on each side of the cab; the handle on the fireman's side was often of great value when a locomotive was being manoeuvred in a busy yard. The outward appearance of the cab remained faithful to Great Northern traditions, though in later days, of course, only a tiny minority of ten in the great regiment of 'K3' 'Moguls' possessed that outward sign of true Doncaster lineage. The original engines, though intended mainly for fast goods working, came into the limelight during the coal strike of 1921 when they tackled express passenger trains loading up to 20 bogie vehicles on the fastest schedules then operating between King's Cross and Doncaster, and showed themselves capable of 75 mph on stretches like that from Stoke summit down to Peterborough.

In the meantime much progress was being made in the modernization of existing types. Quite apart from the superheating of the '251' class 'Atlantics', to which special reference is made later, the performance of a number of Ivatt types was improved. Larger boilers, with superheaters, were fitted to some of the 4–4–0 express locomotives; a number of the small 'Atlantics' and the 0–8–0 goods engines were also superheated, and one of the most interesting conversions was that applied to the Ivatt 0–8–2 tanks. After their departure from the London suburban district these engines were transferred to Colwick for use in the coal and goods marshalling yards; there they were engaged on purely local traffic. But the superheating of some of this class enabled them to work heavy coal trains between Colwick and the New England yard, Peterborough, a run of 47 miles. The saturated 0–8–2s were unable to undertake this turn as the tanks carried insufficient water to supply their consumption which was greater than that of the superheated engines. The fitting of superheaters to low-speed short-haul engines was not, however, inaugurated on these 0–8–2 tanks. In 1913 a new 0–6–0 shunting tank locomotive of Gresley's own design was put into service; the first of this class, No 157, used saturated steam, but a later one, No 167 (put into service in 1914), was superheated. The respective leading dimensions were: cylinders $18\frac{1}{2}$ ins by 26 ins; wheels 4 ft 8 in diameter; working pressure 175 and 170 psi; total heating surface 980 and 932·5 sq ft, the latter including 171 sq ft provided by the superheater; grate area 17·8 sq ft; weight in working order, including 1,500 gallons of water and 3 tons of coal, $56\frac{1}{2}$ tons. These original engines later became LNER class 'J51'. They were the forerunners of the numerous standard 0-6-0 shunting tanks of the LNER, which were classed 'J50', and were generally similar to the engine of 1913, except that the boiler was larger, 4 ft 5 in diameter against 4 ft 2 in in the original engine, with a total heating surface of 1,119 sq ft; the grate area, however, was slightly less at 16¼ sq ft. With a larger coal bunker to hold 4¾ tons, the 'J50' was slightly heavier, weighing 58 tons. It was not superheated.

In 1913 Gresley designed his twin-tube superheater. There were thirty-four flue tubes, 4-in external diameter, each element being in two flue tubes. By this arrangement greater evaporation and superheating areas were obtained; the saturated header was located above the level of the flue tubes, and the superheated header below. How successful this layout proved in practice was shown in one of Gresley's last designs for the GNR, one that stands out from the general line of continuity in practice displayed in the locomotives built by him up to that time, and subsequently. The superheated 0-6-2 passenger tanks, the first of which was turned out in January 1921, were just a simple straightforward two-cylinder job, well suited to the pressing needs of the London suburban traffic. What appeared to be the exceptionally high-line pitch of their boilers was rather an illusion caused by the severe restrictions of the Metropolitan loading gauge which cut the height of the engines working over the widened lines to 12 ft 7 ins, and made it necessary to use unusually squat boiler mountings. The leading dimensions of the class were as follows: cylinders 19-in diameter by 26-in stroke; coupled wheels 5 ft 8 in diameter; total heating surface 1,205 sq ft, of which the seventeen-element superheater contributed 207 sq ft; grate area, 19 sq ft; working pressure 170 psi; weight in working order, 70¼ tons, including 2,000 gallons of water and 4 tons of coal. Such preliminary experience as was necessary had already been obtained by the superheating of one of the numerous Ivatt 0-6-2 tanks (LNER class 'N1') No 1598, and the new locomotives, which were a logical development of Ivatt's design, were drafted to the most arduous suburban duties the moment they were broken in.

Sixty of these engines, later LNER class 'N2', were turned out very rapidly, ten from Doncaster, and fifty by the North British Locomotive Co Ltd, the original numbers being 1606–15 (Doncaster) and 1721–70. Further examples, without condensing apparatus, were built after grouping for suburban service around Glasgow and Edinburgh. They were not only powerful engines for their size, but also speedy. Before the days of the 'Pacifics' they were sometimes requisitioned to pilot main-line expresses out to Potters Bar; while their hill-climbing feats over the tremendous gradients of the High Barnet branch, though a commonplace in later days, were exceptional when they first came out. Up the $2\frac{1}{2}$ miles at 1 in 59–63 from Finsbury Park, for example, with the trains that passed a number of stations, speeds usually rose to 30 mph, or so, with loads of 160 tons.

The first of a new batch of three-cylinder 2–8–0s came out in 1921; they differed from No 461 in having the alteration to the derived valve gear that had proved so satisfactory in the '1000' class 'Moguls'. No 477 was the first of the new series, later LNER class 'O2', in which the principal dimensional changes from No 461 were an increase in boiler pressure from 170 to 180 psi, and the enlargement of the cylinders from 18 to $18\frac{1}{2}$-in diameter. The cylinder disposition was almost identical with that of the '1000' class, the inside cylinder being steeply inclined so that the three steam-chests could be arranged in line. That design became the standard heavy freight engine of the LNER, until the advent of the Thompson 'O1' class.

While these new types were being introduced, an important modification to the large 'Atlantics' was being applied one by one to the whole class. The ten superheater engines built by Ivatt, Nos 1452–1461, showed a definite though not very great superiority over the saturated variety, particularly in uphill work, but their work fell considerably short of the feats to which we later became accustomed. They were the victims of a mistaken conception of superheating. Ivatt attempted to exploit the principle purely for the reduction of boiler maintenance, reducing the working pressure from the 175 psi of the saturated engines to 150 psi, so that although the cylinders were increased in diameter from $18\frac{3}{4}$ ins to 20 ins the power of the engines was barely altered. There were steaming troubles too – a thing almost unheard of with the '251's of later days, or with the original non-superheater engines. When a start was made with the superheating of the original Ivatt 'Atlantics' bolder measures were taken, the boiler pressure being retained practically at the former figure of 175 psi. The process of transformation was gradual, for many of the engines at first retained their slide-valves, while others were fitted with new 8-in diameter piston-valves. The first engines to be equipped were provided with twenty-four-element superheaters, having the same amount of heating surface – 427 sq ft – as Nos 1452–61 and the four-cylinder engine No 279. In 1919, however, No 1403 was fitted with a thirty-two-element superheater, having 568 sq ft of heating surface. This variety later became standard for the whole class, and those engines which for a time had twenty-four-element superheaters were subsequently modified. By no means all of them were fitted with piston-valves, however; the slide-valve engines, which retained their $18\frac{3}{4}$-in cylinders, were in their later days mostly to be found on the Great Central section. Credit for the wonderful work of the '251' class is usually bestowed in its entirety upon Ivatt, but the modifications that transformed them from a type of moderate and at times indifferent performance into some of the most capable engines of their size and weight that have ever run on British metals were carried out during the Gresley régime.

It is interesting to try to analyse why they were so good. The basic design of the boiler was certainly first class, and they were very easy to fire. In later years there were occasions when crews who had never worked them before stepped on in an emergency, and proceeded to make a well-nigh phenomenal run. The grate was level at the back, and then from about half-way forward sloped down towards the front. If a fireman kept the back corners well packed the action of the engine itself 'jiggered' the coal forward to maintain an ideal firebed. The periodic swaying from side to side of the rear end may have been disconcerting to the privileged stranger on the footplate, but it made things easier for the fireman, providing he could

keep his feet! The trailing axle had some side-play without any
centring spring control. The engines were easy on the track,
and excellent riders, as vehicles.

I had not been regularly footplating for many years when I
made my first trips on these engines. It was no gradual introduction either. The 'Queen of Scots' Pullman was one of the
fastest trains on the line in the early 1930s, and it was on one of
these trips that I clocked my first instance of a maximum speed
of 90 mph. I was discussing the results with an old friend, a
locomotive engineer of long experience, and when I mentioned
the very rough riding – from my point of view – he kindly suggested that I would perhaps not know what rough riding really
was. But when I went on to tell how on one engine the coal had
been shaken down off the tender until the footplate was ankle-
deep in Yorkshire hards, his tune changed, and his rather
patronizing smile faded. I can remember to this day how he
remarked, quietly and seriously: 'If it brought the coal down
like that it *must* have been rough!' But so far as running and
free steaming I have rarely known the like of that engine.

Many engines have had splendid steaming boilers, but still
would not run freely. The Great Northern 'Atlantics' had an
excellent front end, with short direct steam passages, and
beautifully streamlined ports. But what put the finishing touch
on their performance was, I am sure, the very high degree of
superheat. The heating surface of their superheaters was
568 sq ft, which was greater than that of the earliest Gresley
'Pacifics' to be described in the next chapter. The high degree
of superheat would have given the steam itself extreme fluidity,
so that great volumes could be put through the relatively small
cylinders without any choking effect. I think it is most significant that all the large-boilered 'Atlantics' eventually had the
thirty-two-element superheaters, while not all of them were
rebuilt with piston-valves. Those retaining the original slide-
valves were doing some absolutely first-class work in the mid-
1930s.

The piston-valves were 8-in diameter, with very large ports,
and it was the engines thus fitted that did the most outstanding
work. Their running on the Pullman trains is referred to at

some length in a later chapter of this book, and it is at this stage enough to say that although at Maclure's instigation a long sustained trial of Great Central engines was made on those trains, by the early 1930s the Great Northern 'Atlantics' were left in sole possession. Maclure used the four-cylinder 'Lord Faringdon' class 4–6–0s, and the 'Directors', and when the Sheffield Pullman was first put on, the 'Sir Sam Fay' class 4–6 os. The 'Atlantics' had the field to themselves when the substantial accelerations of 1932 took place.

Reverting to the last days of the Great Northern Railway, and to the early years of grouping, the East Coast main line south of York witnessed what has so frequently happened elsewhere, following the introduction of larger and more powerful locomotives. The traffic people began to pile on the tons, and then one day one of the new engines is not available, and one of the older and smaller engines is faced with what might be considered an overwhelming task. On the Great Northern there were running traditions as proud as any to be found in the country at that time, and instances were recorded, particularly on the 10.51 AM up from Doncaster, of 'Atlantics' taking tremendous loads without assistance. Certainly there were regulations about piloting of 'Atlantics' on the difficult start out of King's Cross, and sometimes the pilots were carried to Peterborough, or even to Grantham; but when these 'Atlantic' engines were shown capable of handling 500-ton trains on the 'Pacific' timings it was significant of the extent to which they could be opened up in emergency.

At this stage I will mention three runs only, all between Peterborough and King's Cross, on all of which magnificent work was done. The first two, with engines 1454 and 1452, were in normal working, while the third was an experience during the coal strike period of 1921 when the combination at Doncaster of certain Leeds expresses with others from Newcastle was producing some gargantuan loads. I have not tabulated the runs in full detail but have calculated certain very significant quantities from the performance.

These runs do not represent, by a long way, the utmost the large-boilered 'Atlantics' could do. In the years 1921–4, rather, they provided no more than a glimpse of what was to come.

TABLE 16

PETERBOROUGH – KING'S CROSS: 76·4 miles

| Engine No | 1454 | 1452 | 290 |
|---|---|---|---|
| Load tons full | 440 | 490 | 600 |
| Total time min | 87* | 84¾ | 92½ |
| Average speed | | | |
| Holme to Arlesey, 32·4 miles | 60·6 | 57·8 | 55·1 |
| Average dhp | 754 | 756 | 832 |
| DB pull as percentage of | | | |
| nominal TE | 26·9 | 28·5 | 32·7 |

* 83 minutes net.

This chapter opened with a reference to the very first loco-motives for which Gresley was responsible – two varieties of 0–6–0 superheater goods. He used the 0–6–0 type as something of a stopgap measure in 1926 when new engines for inter-mediate goods service were required for general service all over the LNER system. They did not follow any of the consti-tuent 0–6–0 designs, but carried a boiler of enlarged capacity, which was afterwards used very successfully on the 'D49' class of three-cylinder 4–4–0. There were two varieties of these inside-cylinder 0–6–0s; the 'J38', with 4 ft 8 in diameter coupled wheels, and the 'J39' with 5 ft 2 in. The boilers had a total heating surface of 1,644 sq ft and a grate area of 26 sq ft. The cylinders of both classes were 20-in diameter by 26-in stroke, and the boiler pressure was 180 psi. The 35 engines of the 'J38' class were used in Scotland, while the 289 engines of class 'J39' were to be seen in most parts of the LNER, except on the former GNR main line.

# CHAPTER SEVEN

# THE 'PACIFICS' AND THEIR DEVELOPMENT

The locomotive history of the Great Northern Railway as an individual concern closed in spectacular fashion with the completion of the first two 'Pacific' engines, 1470 and 1471. These behemoths fitly concluded a remarkable locomotive lineage turned out of Doncaster works between 1867 and 1922; their superiority over the '251' class, both in mere size and tractive power, was in just about the same ratio as that of the first Ivatt 'Atlantic' No 990, over the Stirling eight-footers. Yet the trend of development had been so clearly marked in the past that the proportions of the new engines were no surprise. In view of the success of the '251's it was hardly likely that the Wootten firebox would be abandoned, and nothing less than six-coupled wheels would have been adequate to cope with the increasing East Coast loads. The girth of the boiler could be anticipated from the 6-ft boilers fitted to the '1000' class 'Moguls'; three-cylinder propulsion, with derived motion for the inside-cylinder, was almost a certainty, and the only thing that remained in doubt was the wheel arrangement. A 2-6-2 was actually contemplated at one time; the design of pony truck used on the 'Moguls' had already proved suitable for high-speed running, but as the design took shape a leading bogie was decided upon, and No 1470 *Great Northern* was the result.

Many problems beset the designer who puts on the road a machine that embodies such bold advances upon previous practice, if he is to produce a thoroughly sound job from the railway point of view; the country had already witnessed the spectacle of a great engine so limited in her sphere of activity as to be more of a liability than an asset to her owners. The length of the new 'Pacific' was one of the problems in design, for although the Great Northern main line boasts one of the finest alignments in the country, matters are not so favourable to a

long engine in the immediate neighbourhood of King's Cross.
By the use of heat-treated nickel–chrome steel having a tensile
strength some 50 per cent greater than ordinary mild steel it
was possible to make the connecting- and coupling-rods much
lighter than usual, and thus the effect of the unbalanced forces
due to the reciprocating mechanism were reduced. The fine
riding qualities of the class, which had to be sampled on the
footplate to be fully appreciated, were due to the springing
arrangement to be seen on the sole survivor, which was arrived
at only after trials of several different layouts; uncompensated
plate springs are used for all three pairs of coupled wheels.

The leading dimensions of No 1470 are well known, but are
included for reference purposes: three cylinders 20-in diameter
by 26-in stroke; coupled wheels 6 ft 8 in diameter; total heating
surface 3,455 sq ft; grate area $41\frac{1}{4}$ sq ft; working pressure
180 psi; total weight of engine and tender in working order,
with 8 tons of coal and 5,000 gallons of water, $148\frac{3}{4}$ tons. The
unusually large grate area of $41\frac{1}{4}$ sq ft caused some shaking of
heads by people who thought the fireman's burden was becoming overwhelming, but in actual fact the Gresley 'Pacifics'
were not difficult to fire; the accurate wrist-work needed to
shoot the coal into the back corners of the grate called for
knack rather than brute force.

The new engines were not long in showing what they could
do. On Sunday, September 3rd, 1922, a special test run was
made with No 1471, then unnamed, on which a train of twenty
vehicles weighing 610 tons behind the tender was worked over
the 105·5 miles from King's Cross to Grantham in 122 minutes. The highlights of this performance were a time of 23
minutes from Hitchin to Huntingdon, an average speed of
70 mph, and a fine climb to Stoke with an average speed of
45 mph up the final three miles from Corby. In ordinary service the 'Pacifics' were not called upon to perform anything
like such strenuous work as this. During the late autumn and
winter of 1922 they were usually on the 4 PM and 5.40 PM
trains from King's Cross. The former, in deference to its traditionally heavy load, was then allowed no less than 101 minutes to Peterborough, but the 5.40 PM with an average load of

500 tons and 87 minutes allowed for the King's Cross–Peterborough run, was a stiff proposition in those days. The results
obtained from Nos 1470 and 1471 were sufficiently good for a
further ten 'Pacifics' to be ordered before the Great Northern
became merged in the LNER group, but the first of the new
series – the famous No 4472 – was not turned out of Doncaster
works till January 1923. But by this time the supremacy of the
1470s was being challenged, and from within the same group
too; the first of Sir Vincent Raven's still larger 'Pacifics' had
just been turned out at Darlington works, and although differing radically from the Great Northern design, had about the
same tractive effort.

My first personal experience of the Gresley 'Pacifics' was in
June 1923, when I travelled from King's Cross to Doncaster
behind No 1473. For quite a trivial reason I decided to my
lasting regret to go by the 4 PM instead of the 5.40 PM; that
very day the 5.40 was worked by No 2400, a North Eastern
'Pacific' afterwards named *City of Newcastle* in one of a series
of trials in competition with Great Northern type 'Pacifics'.
These are referred to in Chapter Four in which detailed
results of the performance of the Great Northern and North
Eastern 'Pacifics' are tabulated.

Then, in the autumn of 1923, the first of the Great Western
Railway 4-6-0 'Castle' locomotives appeared. The tractive
effort of this new class, 31,625 lb, gave them a lead of nearly
2,000 lb over both the LNER varieties of 4-6-2, and substan-
tiated a claim that the GWR 'Castles' were the most powerful
express locomotives in the country. It can well be imagined
that the LNER refused to accept such a claim without question,
though Doncaster was not the prime mover in suggesting a
scientific trial, with subsequent interchange of results. That
suggestion, as I have told elsewhere, came from Paddington.
Unfortunately, from the engineering standpoint, the 'challenge'
was taken up with such gusto that technical achievement became rather lost in a welter of partisanship. Railway enthusiasts,
and indeed the general public, had in some measure been prepared for this event. At the British Empire Exhibition at
Wembley in 1924, No 4472, named *Flying Scotsman* specially

for the exhibition, and No 4073, *Caerphilly Castle*, stood on adjacent stands. It seemed as if the two types were fated to try conclusions sooner or later.

The chance actually came, after a week of trial running, from April 27th to May 2nd, 1925, and between Paddington and Plymouth the GWR staged some spectacular performances. Engine No 4074 *Caldicot Castle* in charge of a driver who was to the GWR of that time what Bill Sparshatt became to the LNER in more recent times, twice within the week brought in 'The Limited' a quarter of an hour before time. Feats such as these were bound to confuse the issue, and placed the competing LNER engine No 4474, whose driver had been instructed to run to schedule, at a disadvantage. The West of England main line between Reading and Plymouth is an exceptionally awkward road for a stranger, and to be practically on time at Plymouth on their very first trip with the down 'Limited' was a masterly piece of locomotive handling by the LNER crew. What is more, the coal consumption was only 50 lb per mile, which, even allowing for the higher calorific value of Welsh coal, was very little above the normal 'Pacific' figure. In the hectic excitement of what was generally regarded as a purely sporting contest, however, such considerations counted for little with the general public and the popular Press.

But there is no disguising the fact that the LNER was beaten on its own road. The locomotive principally concerned was No 2545 which, since named *Diamond Jubilee*, was a hurriedly picked second string after the first choice, No 4475, had failed with a hot box. To the chagrin of her supporters No 2545 struck a particularly bad patch and failed to rise even to normal 'Pacific' standards. The reason was to be found in one of the hundred-and-one minor ailments that can, on any railway, jaundice locomotive performance; but that such trouble should have developed in the company's chosen representative during so critical a week was a piece of extremely bad luck. The Great Western engine – No 4079 *Pendennis Castle* – certainly took the wind out of the LNER sails. On trip after trip she lifted her 475-ton trains through Finsbury Park in less than 6 minutes, and on the fastest run was through Hatfield in 23 minutes 25 seconds. After that short cut-offs and light steaming sufficed for speeds of average East Coast quality, and brought her trains into Peterborough and Doncaster well before time on each journey. Full details of the times and speeds made on the test runs were published in the *Railway Magazine* for July and August 1925.

The immediate results of the exchange, details of the running, and certain technical items were published by the companies concerned soon after the event. Controversy raged around the merits and demerits of the two types for many months afterwards, but much of this centred upon the differences in boiler and firebox. Each was of outstanding design peculiarly suitable for its own class of fuel and service. It is true that the Great Western engine did very well on Yorkshire coal, but a close examination of the logs of her running shows that most of the sparkle and brilliance of her work took place at the beginning of the journeys; there was never quite the same dash about the Grantham–Doncaster stage as was so noticeable between King's Cross and Peterborough, and one wonders what might have happened had *Pendennis Castle* essayed the later 'Pacific' duty of working through from London to Edinburgh.

The essential difference between the two types lay in the front end – long-travel versus short-travel valves. In a general way it was known that long-travel valves made for economical running and higher speeds, but few if any definite figures have been published to show exactly where the difference lies. With short-travel valves both the admission and exhaust ports were never more than partly open when a locomotive was running well linked up, and the earlier the point of cut-off was brought the smaller those openings became. Narrow valve openings severely throttle the steam both at admission and exhaust, and hamper an engine severely; an investigation into the cylinder and valve performance of one of the Midland compounds – generally accepted as a most efficient class – showed that when running at 68 mph 35 per cent of the total energy of the steam put through the cylinders was spent in getting through the admission and exhaust ports. By increasing the length of valve-travel the movement of the valves could be so arranged that the full width of the exhaust ports was available even when the engine was linked up to mid-gear. For many years British locomotive engineers were inclined to look askance at the long travels of the GWR on account of the extra wear on valves and liners consequent upon higher valve speeds. But in many ways the term 'long-travel' valves was a misnomer; they should, strictly speaking, have been called long-lap valves, for when an engine was linked right up and running at 70 mph the actual travel of the valves might well be *less* than that of a locomotive fitted with short-lap valves and needing to be worked at comparatively long cut-offs.

After the exchange tests of 1925, the first trial of long-travel valves was made on the LNER. In 1926 the valve gear of No 4477 *Gay Crusader* was modified so as to give longer laps and a freer exhaust. As many as possible of the existing parts of the gear were used in carrying out this experimental rearrangement, which thoroughly justified itself. No 4477 proved decidedly more economical than the standard 'Pacifics'. This success prompted a re-design of the gear, in which the lap was increased from the original $1\frac{1}{4}$ in to $1\frac{5}{8}$ in; this was tried out early in 1927 on No 2555 *Centenary*. Trials between this engine and No 2559 with short-travel valves showed that the altered gear reduced the coal consumption from roughly 50 to 38–39 lb per train mile; and from that time onward the whole stud, one by one, had their valve gear altered to the *Centenary* arrangement.

The more economical working of the engine was an important factor that contributed much to the feasibility of the London–Edinburgh non-stop running of the 'Flying Scotsman', which was inaugurated on May 1st, 1928. Engine No 4472 *Flying Scotsman* was transferred from Doncaster shed, where she had been stationed ever since her construction, to King's Cross specially for this working, and with No 4476 *Royal Lancer* bore the brunt of the non-stop running throughout the summer. The timing of $8\frac{1}{4}$ hours involved very easy locomotive work, and for that reason was subjected to some disparagement; but the standard of punctuality was set high and the experience gained in this, particularly with the lubri-

TABLE 17   TABLES OF VALVE SETTING (FORWARD GEAR)

For Gresley 'A1' Pacifics with three 20-in × 26-in cylinders and 8-in piston-valves

Original setting, Lead 3/16 in, steam lap 1½ ins, exhaust lap −¼ in (negative)

| Cylinder | Nominal cut-off per cent | Valve opening in | | Cut-off per cent | | Exhaust opens per cent | | Exhaust port opening above full port in | | Exhaust closes per cent | |
|---|---|---|---|---|---|---|---|---|---|---|---|
| | | F | B | F | B | F | B | F | B | F | B |
| Outside | 25 | 19/64 | 19/64 | 25·9 | 24 | 63·4 | 60·8 | 1/16 | 1/16 | 75·5 | 77 |
| Centre | 25 | 5/16 | 5/16 | 25·9 | 24·3 | 64·9 | 59·9 | 1/16 | 1/16 | 75·7 | 79·4 |
| Outside | 65 | 31/32 | 1 | 67 | 62·9 | 85·7 | 83·3 | 25/23 | 23/32 | 90·8 | 92·3 |
| Centre | 65 | 29/32 | 1 | 64·2 | 62·2 | 87 | 85 | | 21/32 | 92·3 | 92·7 |
| Later standard setting. Lead ⅛ in, steam lap 1⅝ in, exhaust lap 1⅝ in = line and line | | | | | | | | | | | |
| Outside | 15 | 12/64 | 13/64 | 14·4 | 15·6 | 65·6 | 65·1 | 5/64 | 4/64 | 65·1 | 65·6 |
| Inside | 15 | 12/64 | 14/64 | 15·3 | 16·5 | 65·9 | 65·3 | 6/64 | 4/64 | 65·3 | 65·9 |
| Outside | 25 | 19/64 | 20/64 | 24·3 | 25·9 | 72·8 | 71·6 | 12/64 | 11/64 | 71·6 | 72·8 |
| Inside | 25 | 18/64 | 23/64 | 24·7 | 25·7 | 73 | 71·1 | 15/64 | 10/64 | 71·1 | 73 |
| Outside | 65 | 1 3/16 | 1 1/4 | 67·3 | 63·9 | 89·9 | 88·2 | 1 1/8 | 1 1/16 | 88·2 | 89·9 |
| Inside | 65 | 1 1/8 | 1 5/16 | 64·9 | 63·7 | 90·6 | 89·9 | 1 3/16 | 1 | 89·9 | 90·6 |

cation in the greatest feat of locomotive endurance attempted up to that time in this country, paved the way for the more remarkable developments of later years. As to the performance of the 'A1's, my own log-books reveal run after run of great merit. There is one of Sparshatt's characteristic feats, for example, with engine 4472 on the up 'Flying Scotsman'; with a load of 565 tons gross behind the tender he ran from Darlington to a signal stop at Poppleton Junction 42·5 miles, in 40 minutes 18 seconds, start to stop, speed averaging exactly 72 mph for the 27 miles from Northallerton to milepost 3. That was in 1933, and on the last lap of another run on the same train a few weeks later, with another noted King's Cross driver, the late Harry Gutteridge, engine 4474 *Victor Wild*, worked a load of 520 tons through Finsbury Park in 102 minutes 52 seconds from Grantham, 103·0 miles; but for a signal stop at Belle Isle the terminus would have been reached in about 107½ minutes. Schedule was 114 minutes.

Then, on a most unlikely occasion at the close of 1935 – a miserable winter's evening of thin drizzling rain – the late W. Payne, yet another well-known King's Cross driver, made some glorious running with No 2552 *Sansovino*. On the up 'Scotsman', loading to 520 tons behind the tender, we were inside 'even time' from the Grantham start as early as Werrington Junction; did the 27 miles from Huntingdon in 24 minutes 31 seconds and were through Hatfield, 87·8 miles, in 86¾ minutes, against 91 minutes then scheduled. Adverse signals delayed us badly at Potters Bar; otherwise we should have reached King's Cross in 104 minutes for the 105·5 miles from Grantham. Booked time, 111 minutes.

On the footplate I witnessed an interesting example of the ease with which the 'A1's handled 500-ton loads on the East Coast timings of 1935. No 4476 *Royal Lancer* was the engine, in charge of the crew that made such astonishing records on *Silver Link*'s *première* in September 1935 – Driver Taylor and Fireman Luty, of King's Cross shed. A delay at Offord had made the 1.20 PM 'Scotsman' 10 minutes late into Grantham, and it is from this point that the run is tabulated on page 80. The timing of 92 minutes for the 82·7 miles from Grantham to

York was not unduly difficult, and there were then drivers in the link who would have attempted to wipe off all the lateness on this one section. On the other hand, such energy was some-times offset later in the journey by a need to nurse the engine on the usually stiff passage from York to Darlington, especially as in this case, when the wind was on the quarter. Taylor was content with the recovery of six minutes, for six minutes he certainly had 'in the bag' on passing Chaloners Whin Junction, though adverse signals robbed him of just over a minute in approaching York. As a result of this gentler treatment *Royal Lancer* was in first-class form over the North Eastern line, and Northallerton was passed only three minutes behind time. As regards the actual working of the engine, it will be seen that Taylor never used less than 25 per cent cut-off, though it was only in making the very fine start out of York that full regu-lator was used for any length of time.

After 1937 the work of the streamlined engines rather stole the thunder of the 'A1's and of the 'A3's too, for that matter. A journey I enjoyed on the 10.5 AM down 'Junior Scotsman' in the late summer of 1937 did, however, show better than any-thing I had hitherto recorded what an 'A1' could do over the Grantham–York section. With 'A4'-hauled trains before and behind him in the morning procession from King's Cross, the driver of 'A1' No 2581 *Neil Gow* was evidently determined to do some thunder-stealing on his own account. With a gross load of 535 tons we were through Newark in exactly 15 minutes at 80 mph; sustained 74 across the Trent Valley right to Crow Park, and with a minimum of 56 mph at Markham and a top speed of 79 at Grove Park passed Retford in 31 minutes 32 seconds. Continuing in tremendous style, Black Carr Junc-tion was passed in 44 minutes 13 seconds, at 75 mph, after which we had to make a special stop at Doncaster. In spite of this delay, which cost us fully 10 minutes in running, we passed Chaloners Whin Junction in 86 minutes 29 seconds, and would have made York in 90 minutes but for concluding delays. The very fast net time of 80 minutes from Grantham represented, however, a gain to engine of no more than three minutes on the strenuous booking then in force. Leveson, of

TABLE 18  LNER 3.16 PM
Engine: class 'A1' 4–6–2
Load: 483 tons tare,
Driver: Taylor; Fireman:

| Distance miles | | Schedule min | Actual | |
|---|---|---|---|---|
| | | | min | sec |
| 0·0 | GRANTHAM | 0 | 0 | 00 |
| 4·2 | Barkston | | 6 | 29 |
| 9·9 | Claypole | | 11 | 27 |
| 14·6 | NEWARK | 15 | 15 | 23 |
| 21·9 | Crow Park | | 21 | 49 |
| 28·2 | *Markham Box* | | 28 | 40 |
| 33·1 | RETFORD | 35 | 33 | 32 |
| 38·4 | Ranskill | | 38 | 30 |
| 44·0 | *Milepost 149½* | | 44 | 00 |
| 47·7 | *Black Carr Junction* | | 47 | 43 |
| 50·5 | DONCASTER | 53 | 50 | 28 |
| 54·7 | *Shaftholme Junction* | 58 | 54 | 38 |
| 60·5 | Balne | | 60 | 07 |
| 67·5 | *Brayton Junction* | | 66 | 55 |
| 68·9 | SELBY | 74 | 68 | 40 |
| 73·0 | Riccall | | 74 | 30 |
| 80·7 | *Chaloners Whin Junction* | | 82 | 43 |
| | | | | sigs |
| 82·7 | YORK | 92 | 87 | 25† |
| 0·0 | | 0 | 0 | 00 |
| 1·6 | *Poppleton Junction* | | 3 | 46 |
| 5·5 | Beningbrough | | 8 | 30 |
| 11·2 | Alne | | 13 | 58 |
| 18·0 | Sessay | | 20 | 22 |
| 22·2 | THIRSK | 25 | 24 | 23 |
| 30·0 | NORTHALLERTON | 33 | 31 | 45 |
| | | | | p.w.s. |
| 38·9 | *Eryholme Junction* | | 43 | 32 |
| 41·5 | Croft Spa | | 46 | 13 |
| | | | | sigs |
| 44·1 | DARLINGTON | 48 | 50 | 40‡ |

\* Severe service slack.     † Net time:

# GRANTHAM–DARLINGTON
No 4476 *Royal Lancer*
515 tons full
Duty (King's Cross shed)

| Speeds mph | Regulator | Cut-off per cent | Pressure, psi | |
|---|---|---|---|---|
| | | | Boiler | Steam-Chest |
| — | Full | 65 | — | — |
| 60 | $\frac{5}{8}$ | 25 | 170 | 135 |
| 75 | $\frac{3}{8}$ | 25 | | |
| 72 | $\frac{3}{4}$ | 25 | 175 | 140 |
| 66 | $\frac{7}{8}$ | 25 | 170 | 150 |
| 50 | $\frac{1}{2}$ | 25 | 170 | 120 |
| 68 | Shut | 25 | 170 | — |
| 60 | $\frac{5}{8}$ | 25 | | |
| 67 | $\frac{1}{2}$ | 25 | 170 | 110 |
| 51 | $\frac{1}{2}$ | 25 | 170 | 110 |
| 65 | $\frac{1}{2}$ | 25 | 170 | 110 |
| 60 | $\frac{5}{8}$ | 25 | 170 | 130 |
| 61½ | $\frac{5}{8}$ | 25 | | |
| 64½ | $\frac{5}{8}$ | 25 | 175 | 138 |
| 65 | Shut | 25 | | |
| 25* | $\frac{7}{8}$ | 30 | 160 | 150 |
| 53 | $\frac{7}{8}$ | 25 | 160 | 150 |
| 60 | $\frac{7}{8}$ | 25 | 160 | 150 |
| — | — | — | — | — |
| — | Full | 65 | — | — |
| — | Full | 25 | 175 | 165 |
| 57 | Full | 25 | | |
| 66½ | Full | 25 | 170 | 160 |
| 62 | $\frac{7}{8}$ | 25 | 175 | 140 |
| 67 | $\frac{7}{8}$ | 25 | | |
| 61 | $\frac{7}{8}$ | 25 | 177 | 140 |
| 25 | Full | 35 | | |
| 54⅓ | $\frac{1}{2}$ | 25 | 160 | 115 |
| 64½ | $\frac{1}{2}$ | 25 | | |
| — | — | — | — | — |

86¼ minutes.     ‡ Net time: 46 minutes.

Heaton, was the driver. But of my own experiences, the most
impressive of all, perhaps, was a run in the autumn of 1936
when the 'Flying Scotsman' was running to the 7¼-hour
timing with a call at Newcastle. Throughout from Waverley
to King's Cross we were hauled by the historic engine of the
1925 exchange No 4474 *Victor Wild*, with a heavy load of
475 tons. The running time then allowed was 430 minutes for
the 392·7 miles; our gross running time was 423 minutes
6 seconds inclusive of a permanent way slack that just about
accounted for the odd three minutes, thus showing that an
'A1' could maintain the later 7-hour timing.

The steady trend of development in locomotive engineering
practice that had been so marked a feature of the Gresley
régime was at a very interesting stage in the years 1927 and
1928. Long-lap valves had been tried, and eventually standardized, and next there came a series of experiments leading to
the adoption of higher boiler pressures. These tests were also
carried out on 'Pacific' engines. In July 1927, one of the
original batch of 'A1's, No 4480 *Enterprise*, was put into
traffic fitted with a new boiler having a working pressure of
220 psi. The object was to obtain costs of maintenance and
comparative data as to the life of fireboxes, stays, and tubes,
between boilers carrying 180 psi and 220 psi pressure. The
superheater was enlarged from thirty-two to forty-three
elements, the corresponding increase in heating surface being
from 525 to 706 sq ft, and the higher pressure raised the
nominal tractive effort from the 29,835 lb of the standard
'Pacifics' to 36,465 lb. The heavier boiler and a small re-
distribution of weight elsewhere increased the adhesion from
60 to 66 tons.

*Enterprise* was, of course, fitted with long-lap valves at the
time of her rebuilding, and in traffic she displayed an easy
mastery over any regular task existing on the Southern Area
main line at that time. In some ways she was too powerful, for
even when fully linked up to 15 per cent, it was not possible to
use full regulator without making extravagant gains on schedule time. To investigate further the advantages to be gained
from the use of higher steam pressures another of the 'A1's,

No 2544 *Lemberg*, was fitted with a boiler similar to that of No 4480, but the cylinders were lined up to 18¼-in diameter, thus giving this high-pressure engine a nominal tractive effort equal to that of the standard 180 psi 'Pacifics'.

A series of dynamometer car trials was then conducted, in February 1928, between *Lemberg* and *Solario*, a standard 'A1' fitted with long-lap valves. At that time the expresses between London and the West Riding provided the hardest daily tasks set to the 'Pacifics', and the trials were conducted on the 10.51 AM from Doncaster to King's Cross, and the regular return working, the 4 PM down. The published results of two weeks' running showed no appreciable difference between the two locomotives. The average coal consumption was 3·08 lb per dhp-hour by *Solario* and 3·12 lb by *Lemberg*. The latter engine enjoyed better weather during her week, and on that account her coal consumption per train mile was less than that of her rival – 35·37 against 38·83 lb. Both, however, were excellent figures, considering that the average train-loads were 431 tons from Doncaster to King's Cross, 498 from King's Cross to Peterborough and 339 tons thence to Doncaster.

In ordinary service *Lemberg* earned the reputation of being one of the speediest of all the non-streamlined 'Pacifics'. After the acceleration of 1932 she often worked the 8.40 AM from Doncaster to King's Cross, and with her regular driver Charlie Molson of Doncaster shed, one could always look forward to some sparkling performance on the 63·4 mph run from Grantham to King's Cross. One of the finest of such feats was timed by Mr R. A. H. Weight, on a day when an unusually heavy load for that train was carried, 435 tons gross. A number of delays prevented strict timekeeping, but intermediately there was some grand going including the high maximum, for 1933, of 92½ mph at Essendine. The net time was 97 minutes, a start-to-stop average of 65·3 mph. In the same summer she worked the 'Scarborough Flyer', loaded up to no less than 570 tons gross, non-stop from King's Cross to York, 188·2 miles in 192½ minutes net. In view of these splendid performances it is perhaps significant that the steam port area of this engine was larger, in proportion to the total cylinder volume, than in any other of the Gresley non-streamlined 'Pacifics'; for when the cylinders were lined up to 18¼-in diameter, the original 8-in diameter valves were retained. That feature of her design would certainly help in giving the freedom of exhaust that was so essential for fast and efficient running.

From the data provided from the experimental rebuilding of engines 4480 and 2544 the new so-called 'Super-Pacific' design, class 'A3', was prepared. Engine No 2743 *Felstead*, the first of a batch of ten locomotives, was put into service in August 1928; in these the boiler was identical with that of *Lemberg*, but though the cylinders were increased to 19-in diameter the 8-in diameter piston-valves common to all previous Gresley 'Pacifics' were retained. The nominal tractive effort at 85 per cent boiler pressure was 32,909 lb. Class 'A3' was later increased by conversions of all the remaining class 'A1' engines apart from the two experimental engines, 2544 and 4480, and No 4470, which was rebuilt by Thompson. Soon after the rebuilding of 4480 three others were similarly altered, namely, 2573 *Harvester*, 2578 *Bayardo*, and 2580 *Shotover*. These engines retained their original large cylinders. The last engines built new as class 'A3' were a batch of nine – Nos 2500–8, turned out in 1934–5, which had the modified dome arrangement including a perforated steam collector.

As to the 'A3' performance, the test runs of 2750 *Papyrus* on March 5th, 1935, maximum speed 108 mph, are classics of British locomotive running and are assured of fame equal to that enjoyed by those almost legendary feats of former days, such as the GWR Ocean Mail run of May 9th, 1904, and of the rival Scotch racing trains on the night of August 22nd, 1895. But the subsequent progress in railway speed was such that the record times of *Papyrus* were to become almost a commonplace in the years 1936–9 in the day-to-day running of the streamlined trains. With the 'A4' 'Pacifics' that is understandable, but occasions like those of the week ending March 25th, 1939 leave one rather at a loss for words. Twice in that one week, 'A3's had to take on at short notice the haulage of the up 'Coronation' between Newcastle and King's Cross, and twice in that week the record of *Papyrus* was surpassed, with

AT THE START OF THE GRESLEY ERA – GNR
*Upper:* The 2.10 PM Leeds and Bradford 'Flyer' at Werrington Junction: rebuilt Stirling 2-2-2 engine No 876
*Lower:* Up 'Flying Scotsman' near Potters Bar: non-superheater Atlantic No 278

PRE-GROUPING DAYS ON CONSTITUENTS
*Upper:* Great Central: down Sheffield and Manchester express near
Harrow, hauled by Robinson 4-4-2 No 1084
*Lower:* Great Eastern: Ipswich express passing Brentwood, hauled by
'Claud Hamilton' class 4-4-0 No 1806

PRE-GROUPING DAYS: NORTH EASTERN
*Upper:* Down 'Flying Scotsman' near Lamesley. Class 'V' Atlantic No 1680
*Lower:* Up 'Flying Scotsman' near Birtley. Class 'R1' 4-4-0 No 1244

EAST COAST ATLANTICS
*Upper:* NER 'V' class No 1776 on Newcastle-Liverpool express near Birtley
*Lower:* GNR non-superheater 4-4-2 No 1440 on 2.20 PM 'Scotsman' near Potters Bar

LOCOMOTIVES OF THE GREAT CENTRAL
*Top:* 4-6-0 No 423 *Sir Sam Fay*
*Centre:* Improved 'Director' class 4-4-0 No 506 *Butler-Henderson*
*Bottom:* 2-6-4 mineral tank engine No 272

PRE-GROUPING 4-4-0 DESIGNS
*Top:* Great Eastern, Belpaire 'Claud Hamilton' class No 1831
*Centre:* North British 'Scott' class 4-4-0 No 9424 *Lady Rowena*, in LNER black
*Bottom:* Great Eastern, 'Super Claud' No 8787, one of two engines reserved for Royal train workings between King's Cross and Sandringham

Sir Nigel Gresley: a pencil portrait from *The Engineer*

FAMOUS TANK ENGINE TYPES
*Top:* One of Wilson Worsdell's three-cylinder 4-8-0s for hump shunting at Erimus Yard (1908)
*Centre:* A Gresley 'N2' 0-6-2 for London suburban duties
*Bottom:* Gresley three-cylinder 2-6-2 No 465 class 'V1' for fast suburban service

GREAT NORTHERN 4-4-2S AT WORK
*Upper:* Engine No 1447, with cut-down boiler mountings, leaving York on up express

*Lower:* Two superheater 4-4-2s on up all-Pullman Newmarket race special near Shepreth Branch Junction, Cambridge

FREIGHT AND MIXED-TRAFFIC TYPES
*Upper:* One of the two 'P1' 2-8-2s designed for the Peterborough-London coal traffic
*Lower:* A standard 'K3' 2-6-0 but fitted with Westinghouse brake

*Upper:* The second of the Gresley 'V4' 2-6-2s of 1941
*Lower:* A Great Central 'o4' 2-8-0 rebuilt with Great Northern type boiler (class o4/8)

*Upper:* One of the 'P1' 2-8-2s at work: No 2393 on maximum-load coal train near Sandy

*Lower:* On the GCR line: a down freight passing Guide Bridge, hauled by 'J39' class 0-6-0 No 64712

EST RUNS FROM KING'S CROSS
*Upper:* The pioneer express 2-8-2 No 2001 *Cock o' the North* leaving
with a stopping train on a running-in trip
*Lower:* On the 1923 dynamometer car trials: the Raven 'Pacific' No 2400
ready to leave with the 5.40 PM express

MEDIUM POWER EXPRESS TYPES
*Upper:* The GNR Atlantic No 1419 fitted with booster
*Lower:* The *Claud Hamilton*, as rebuilt with Gresley boiler, superheater and long-travel valves

*Upper:* 'Hunt' class three-cylinder 4-4-0 No 365 *The Morpeth*
*Lower:* 'Sandringham' class 4-6-0 No 2805, originally *Burnham Thorpe* but renamed *Lincolnshire Regiment*

*Upper:* A post-nationalization scene, with a 'B1' 4-6-0 No 61033 *Dibata*, on Manchester express approaching Northolt Junction

*Lower:* One of the Scottish 'Directors', No 62678 *Luckie Mucklebackit*, leaving Edinburgh Waverley

290-ton loads against the 217 tons of the test run. It was a thousand pities that no more detailed records than those of the guard's journal were available, but enough is known to establish them firmly among the finest feats ever achieved by 'A3' 'Pacifics'.

On the first occasion the train arrived punctually and the defect in the booked engine was only discovered when the driver climbed down to give the usual short examination. No 2595 *Trigo* was commandeered on the spot. Although leaving Newcastle 8 minutes late the train was on time by Retford, having covered the 129·7 miles in 120½ minutes. Onwards to London only a single minute was dropped in spite of about five minutes' loss in running through a couple of permanent way slacks. The net time from Newcastle was approximately 225 minutes, an average of 71¾ mph. Two days later, when the circumstances were to a large extent repeated, No 2507 *Singapore* was the engine, with the same crew as before, Driver Nash and Fireman Gilbey of King's Cross. They were 34 minutes late away from Newcastle, but 8½ minutes had been regained by Doncaster. The same relaying slacks as before were experienced, but despite the additional hindrance of a signal check at Bawtry no more time was lost, and King's Cross was reached in 227¼ minutes from Newcastle. Comparison of the journal times on the delayed sections with normal runs suggests that at least 5 minutes were lost by these delays, giving the record net time of 222¼ minutes, an average of 72¼ mph. The time of *Papyrus* with 217 tons was 227½ minutes net.

Another very fast 'A3' performance took place one afternoon when the booked 'A4' for the down 'Coronation' failed at Hitchin. A Great Northern 'Atlantic' took the train to Grantham, where a Doncaster 'A3' No 2744 *Grand Parade* had been got ready to take over. The immediate start was slow, while the driver was clearly taking the measure of the fresh engine, and it took 14 minutes 12 seconds to pass Newark, 14·6 miles. After that, however, time was gradually won back with the full summer load of the 'Coronation', 325 tons gross behind the tender, and the 68·1 miles from Newark

to York were covered in 55 minutes 36 seconds pass to stop.
Restarting, there was some further regaining of time, with the
44·1 miles from York to Darlington covered in 35 minutes
25 seconds, instead of 38 minutes booked. Three successive
permanent way checks prevented any further regaining of
time to Newcastle, where Driver A. J. Taylor of King's Cross
handed over to Driver Stewart of Haymarket.

As from Grantham, the restart was no more than moderate,
but after Alnmouth the fresh driver really began to pile it on.
A maximum of 99 mph was reached at Beal; Berwick, 66·9
miles, was passed in 62 minutes from the start, and then the 1
in 200 gradient from Reston Junction to Grantshouse was
climbed at a sustained 68 mph. Down the Cockburnspath bank
a maximum of 95 mph was attained, and Dunbar, 95·1 miles,
was passed in 87 minutes 21 seconds. Very fast running was
made in conclusion along the Lothian coast with a maximum
speed of 90 mph at Inveresk, and Edinburgh Waverley was
reached in 115 minutes 52 seconds from Newcastle, 124·4
miles, against 120 minutes scheduled. A later chapter of this
book contains details of an even faster run from Newcastle to
Edinburgh, on the post-war 'Talisman'; but this latter run
was made by a Haymarket driver working his regular engine
in contrast to this emergency run, when the first available
'Pacific' had been hurriedly requisitioned at Grantham.

As to heavy load haulage, so far as I know the same engine,
No 2744 *Grand Parade*, still holds the record for the fastest
time ever made from King's Cross to passing Peterborough
with a load of over 500 tons. I was lucky enough to be a
passenger on the 1.20 PM 'Scotsman' on this occasion and
noted the remarkable time of 73 minutes 55 seconds for this
distance of 76·4 miles. With 530 tons behind the tender we
passed Hatfield in 24 minutes 40 seconds, and then put on a
terrific spurt, for those days, averaging 77·8 mph from Hitchin
to Huntingdon. The maximum was 87½ mph. This was at
Whitsun 1932. Then on my very last trip over the East Coast
route before the outbreak of the Second World War, No 2507
*Singapore* was responsible for some further mighty weight-
pulling on the 4.27 PM (Saturdays) non-stop express from

TABLE 19
LNER 4.27 PM YORK–KING'S CROSS
Load: 15 coaches, 504 tons tare, 540 tons full
Engine: 'A3' 4-6-2 No 2507 *Singapore*
Driver: Hunt; Fireman: Cook (King's Cross shed)

| *Distance miles* | | *Sch. min* | *Actual min sec* | | *Speeds mph* |
|---|---|---|---|---|---|
| 0·0 | YORK | 0 | 0 | 00 | |
| 4·2 | Naburn | | 6 | 32 | 57½ |
| 9·7 | Riccall | | 11 | 40 | 72 |
| | | | sigs | | 30 |
| 13·8 | SELBY | 18 | 17 | 38 | 25* |
| 18·4 | Templehirst | | 23 | 30 | 61 |
| 28·0 | *Shaftholme Junction* | | 31 | 53 | 74/75 |
| | | | sigs | | 30 |
| 32·2 | DONCASTER | 38 | 36 | 37 | — |
| 35·0 | *Black Carr Junction* | | 40 | 00 | 61/55½ |
| 42·4 | Scrooby | | 47 | 07 | 73 |
| 49·6 | RETFORD | 54½ | 54 | 23 | 51* |
| 54·5 | *Markham Summit* | | 60 | 24 | 47 |
| 60·8 | Crow Park | | 66 | 00 | 82 |
| 68·1 | NEWARK | 72½ | 72 | 53 | 53/64½ |
| | | | sigs | | 25 |
| 78·5 | Barkston | | 84 | 13 | — |
| 82·7 | GRANTHAM | 88½ | 90 | 48 | 52 |
| 88·1 | *Stoke Box* | | 97 | 39 | 43 |
| 99·6 | Essendine | | 107 | 33 | 86½ |
| 108·7 | *Werrington Junction* | | 114 | 45 | — |
| 111·8 | PETERBOROUGH | 117½ | 119 | 00 | 20* |
| 115·6 | Yaxley | | 124 | 08 | 60 |
| 118·8 | Holme | | 127 | 04 | 72½ |
| 124·7 | Abbots Ripton | | 132 | 28 | 56 |
| 129·3 | HUNTINGDON | 136½ | 136 | 47 | 78 |
| 144·1 | Sandy | | 149 | 02 | 72 |
| 156·3 | HITCHIN | 161½ | 160 | 13 | 56 |
| 159·6 | Stevenage | | 164 | 14 | 46 |
| 170·5 | HATFIELD | 177½ | 175 | 22 | 74½ |
| 175·5 | Potters Bar | | 180 | 16 | 55½ |
| 183·2 | Wood Green | | 187 | 29 | 69 |
| 185·6 | Finsbury Park | | 189 | 58 | — |
| | | | sigs | | |
| 188·2 | KING'S CROSS | 198 | 195 | 21 | |

Net time: 190 minutes.        * Speed restrictions.

York to King's Cross. The log on page 87 gives summarized details of our progress, but to my mind the outstanding feature of the run lay in the steady maintenance of the 74–75 mph on the level road between Selby and Doncaster. This involved an

TABLE 20 LNER 9.27 PM
Engine: class 'A3' 4–6–2
Load: 414 tons tare,
Driver: Douglas; Fireman:

| Distance miles | | Schedule min | Actual | |
|---|---|---|---|---|
| | | | min | sec |
| 0·0 | DUNDEE | 0 | 0 | 00 |
| 0·8 | Esplanade | | 3 | 12 |
| 2·7 | *Tay Bridge South Junction* | 8 | 7 | 44 |
| 8·3 | LEUCHARS JUNCTION | 14 | 13 | 53 |
| 14·6 | Cupar | | 20 | 27 |
| 16·9 | Springfield | | 23 | 00 |
| 20·1 | LADYBANK JUNCTION | 29 | 26 | 28 |
| 21·0 | Kingskettle | | 27 | 22 |
| 24·3 | *Lochmuir Box* | | 31 | 52 |
| — | | | p.w.s. | |
| 28·5 | THORNTON JUNCTION | 41 | 37 | 50 |
| 31·2 | Dysart | | 43 | 35 |
| — | | | p.w.s. | |
| 33·3 | KIRKCALDY | | 46 | 45 |
| 36·5 | Kinghorn | | 51 | 02 |
| 39·1 | BURNTISLAND | 55 | 55 | 10 |
| 41·8 | Aberdour | | 59 | 40 |
| 43·1 | *Dalgetty Box* | | 62 | 05 |
| 46·2 | INVERKEITHING | 65 | 66 | 03 |
| 47·9 | North Queensferry | 70 | 70 | 35 |
| 49·7 | Dalmeny | 73 | 74 | 20 |
| 52·7 | Turnhouse | | 77 | 33 |
| 55·8 | *Saughton Junction* | | 80 | 33 |
| 59·2 | EINDBURGH | 85 | 85 | 43§ |

\* Eased to 55 through station.    † Eased to 53 through station.

output of about 1,600 dhp. Lastly, as indicating some of their work in Scotland, I have tabulated the performance of No 2500 *Windsor Lad*, on the up Aberdonian sleeping-car express – a performance that I was privileged to record from the footplate.

## DUNDEE–EDINBURGH

No 2500 *Windsor Lad*

440 tons full

Hood (Haymarket shed)

| Speeds mph | Regulator | Cut-off per cent | Pressure, psi | |
|---|---|---|---|---|
| | | | Boiler | Steam-Chest |
| — | Full | 65 | 200 | 190 |
| — | Full | 40 | 190 | 175 |
| — | Full | 20 | 200 | 190 |
| 63½* | Shut | 25 | — | — |
| 50 | Full | 20 | 190 | 190 |
| 63½ | Full | 20 | | |
| 49½ | Full | 20 | | |
| 57† | Full | 25 | 190 | 180 |
| 62 | Full | | 200 | 190 |
| 31½ | ½ | 20 | 200 | 120 |
| 57½ | Shut | 20 | | |
| — | | | | |
| 15 | Full | 30 | 200 | 185 |
| 27½ | Full | 20 | | |
| 57 | Shut | 20 | | |
| — | | | | |
| 15 | Full | 25 | 220 | 205 |
| 54½ | Shut | 25 | | |
| 24 | Full | 25 | | |
| 50 | Shut | 25 | | |
| 24‡ | Full | 30 | | |
| 44 | Full | 30 | | |
| 36½ | Full | 30 | | |
| 31½ | ½ | 20 | 205 | 195 |
| 57½ | Shut | 20 | | |
| 25‡ | Full | 40 | | |
| 17½ | Full | 40 | 205 | 195 |
| 41 | Full | 20 | | |
| 69 | Full | 20 | | |
| 57½/62 | Full | 20 | | |

‡ Severe service check.  § Net time: 80½ minutes.

In Chapter Five of this book I have referred at some length to the difficulties of working over the East Coast route north of Edinburgh, and details were tabulated of some runs with North British 'Atlantics' on this same train. It was extremely interesting to observe the actual engine working with a load not far short of the 'Pacific' maximum. The rosters provided for each of the engines in this particular link to make two return trips from Edinburgh to Dundee and back in the 24 hours, 236·8 miles, and *Windsor Lad* was making the last trip of the day. Even with these powerful engines there was little time to spare, and the going was hard on all the banks. A study of the tabulated details shows the extensive use of a full regulator opening, with cut-offs between 30 and 40 per cent on the heaviest banks. Despite such a cut-off as 40 per cent speed fell to 17½ mph on the 1 in 70 climbing up to the Forth Bridge.

It was throughout a fascinating experience on a cold winter's night, with the engine steaming very freely, and riding with that steadiness for which the Gresley 'Pacifics' were famed. Although one could not see much of the road ahead in the darkness the curves could certainly be *felt*, and round them the engine rode with surpassing steadiness. North British men, were, however, not used to rough-riding engines. The Reid 'Atlantics' unlike their Great Northern counterparts were beautifully steady and solid riders. On the faster stretches, as from Leuchars to Ladybank and from the crossing of the Forth Bridge to the outskirts of Edinburgh, *Windsor Lad* was again driven hard. Normally if the regulator was fully open a cut-off of 15 per cent was enough to produce full express speed; but over this severe road it would not have produced a rapid enough acceleration from the point of minimum speed. So I listened, thrilled, to the engine being pounded up to speeds well in excess of 60 mph on full regulator and 20 per cent cut-off.

# CHAPTER EIGHT

# FURTHER THREE-CYLINDER DESIGNS

On January 1st, 1923, the Great Northern Railway, as a separate concern, ceased to exist; but with Gresley appointed as chief mechanical engineer of the newly formed London & North Eastern Railway, a continuance of the traditions of Doncaster was assured, at a time when many famous dynasties of the locomotive world were soon to die out. In the previous chapter a considerable incursion was made into post-grouping history in order to present the whole story of the development of the non-streamlined 'Pacifics'; now, it is necessary to go back to 1923 to review some other events of the first few post-grouping years.

On the Great Northern Railway, three-cylinder propulsion had been given a fairly extended trial, and by the late summer of 1923 Gresley had twelve 'Pacifics' at work, in addition to the '1000' class 'Moguls' (later class 'K3'), and the 2-8-0 mineral engines. The advantages of the three-cylinder type of locomotive were summarized by him, in a paper read before the Institution of Mechanical Engineers in May 1925, as follows:

1. Less coal consumption than with the two-cylinder type of equal power.

2. Increased mileage between general repairs

3. Less tyre wear than with the two-cylinder type.

4. Lighter reciprocating parts can be used, consequently hammer-blow on the rails is reduced, and for equal bridge stresses a greater permissible weight can be allowed on the coupled wheels of the three-cylinder type.

5. More uniform starting effort than with either the two-cylinder type or the four-cylinder with directly opposed cranks.

6. Lower permissible factor of adhesion; thus with a

given weight on the coupled wheels, a higher tractive effort can be obtained without increasing the tendency to slip.

7. An earlier cut-off in full gear.

Gresley was fortunate in being able to subject the two systems of propulsion to a practical test on locomotives that were identical save in the number of cylinders. Trials were carried out in September 1924, with express trains on the Newcastle–Edinburgh road, in which a three-cylinder North Eastern 'Atlantic' (LNER class 'C7') proved superior to the competing two-cylinder engine of class 'C6'; in the following February tests with ex-GNR 2–8–0 locomotives of classes 'O1' and 'O2' gave similar results, this time in heavy coal traffic. The published figures of the latter set of trials sum up concisely the performance of the 'O1' and 'O2' classes, and from this data the following details have been taken, relating to the southbound run from New England yard, Peterborough to Ferme Park.

| Engine No | 3466 | 3479 |
|---|---|---|
| Type | two-cylinder | three-cylinder |
| Load behind tender, tons | 1,310 | 1,315 |
| Average speed mph | 13·2 | 13·6 |
| Boiler pressure (av.) psi | 163½ | 162½ |
| Steam-chest pressure (av.) psi | 107½ | 113½ |
| Superheat temp. (av.) | 500 deg F | 531 deg F |
| Average cut-off per cent | 47 | 47 |
| Water consumed per dhp-hr, lb | 32 | 28·1 |
| Coal consumed per dhp-hr, lb | 5·24 | 4·78 |

It will be seen that in practically identical conditions the three-cylinder engine showed an economy over the two-cylinder of 12 per cent in water consumption and 9 per cent in coal consumption. These results, after those obtained in the trials of the ex-NER 'Atlantics', did much to influence future LNER locomotive policy.

In the middle nineteen-twenties when much interesting passenger engine activity was manifest, little of a corresponding kind was happening in the LNER freight locomotive realm. Having regard to the company's vast mineral traffic, it is remarkable that, with the exception of the two class 'P1' 'Mikado' engines of 1925, not a single new design for the heaviest freight service was turned out after the grouping took place, save for Thompson's rebuilding of the 'O4' with long-lap valves. This may be taken as a compliment to the capacity of the Great Northern and Great Central 'Consolidations', and to the several varieties of North Eastern o–8–o; like the pre-grouping passenger types, these engines were still confined almost exclusively to their original sections. In 1931–2, however, when more locomotives were required for the Great Eastern section, a new series of Great Northern 'O2' three-cylinder 2–8–os were built specially, and ex-ROD 2–8–os of the Great Central type (LNER class 'O4') were to be found in varying numbers over the whole system.

The Gresley 'Mikados' of 1925 were a natural development of the 'Pacific' type for heavy mineral service. They were experimental, not in the locomotive sense but from the operating point of view; it was, indeed, a moot point whether trains of the immense length hauled by Nos 2393 and 2394 were an economical proposition having regard to siding, refuge loop, and yard capacity. Loads of 1,600 tons held no terrors for these capable engines, and special paths had to be arranged in the working timetables for the 100-wagon coal trains that they were rostered to work from Peterborough to Ferme Park. From all accounts, however, the 'Mikados' seem, originally, to have been something of a problem to fire. The boiler was the same as that fitted to the 'A1' 'Pacifics', but, though the cylinders were also the same, the valve gear was modified to give 75 per cent cut-off in full gear, against 65 per cent in the 'A1' engines. The coupled wheels were 5 ft 2 in diameter, and the nominal tractive effort at 85 per cent of the 180 psi boiler pressure 38,500 lb. To assist in the haulage of heavy loads on the long 1 in 200 gradients a booster was fitted to the trailing axle. This auxiliary engine had two cylinders 10-in diameter by 12-in stroke, and provided an additional 9,000 lb of tractive effort when it was in action; it was thus identical in size with that fitted to the 'Atlantic' engine No 4419, though, on account of the higher boiler pressure of the 'Mikados', slightly more powerful. One of the most interesting exploits of No 2394 took place when the design for the express passenger 'Mikados' was in contemplation. As a test she was put on to the 7.45 AM semi-fast train from King's Cross, and attained speeds up to 65 mph on the run to Peterborough.

The first of the 'Mikados', No 2393, was completed in time to take part in the Railway Centenary celebrations at Darlington in 1925. With her was exhibited another remarkable Gresley locomotive, the one and only LNER 'Garratt', which had been completed by Beyer, Peacock & Co Ltd, about the same time. This engine was designed specially for banking duties, and her machinery was the equivalent of two Gresley 'O2' 2–8–0 engines, the wheels, cylinders, and motion being interchangeable. The boiler had all the 'Garratt' characteristics, short length, big diameter, and large tubes; the barrel, though 7-ft diameter, was only 13 ft between the tube plates, and the grate area was no less than 56·4 sq ft. The total heating surface was 3,640 sq ft of which the superheater provided 646 sq ft. The nominal tractive effort of this notable engine was 72,940 lb, the largest of any British type. Although designed for short hauls, she carried 7 tons of coal and 5,000 gallons of water. No 2395 was employed purely as a banking engine, at Wentworth, on the line between Wath marshalling yard and Penistone; the line was used only by mineral trains and avoided Barnsley altogether. The actual method of working the very heavy coal trains was interesting. The maximum load of west-bound trains was 63 wagons, about 1,000 tons loaded, and for this two class 'O4' ex-GCR 2–8–0s were used. The trains were double-headed from Wath to Wombwell, but at the latter point a stop was made, and the assistant engine was transferred from front to rear of the train; thus they continued to Went-worth, where the worst gradient begins. From Wentworth the 'Garratt' assisted in rear up the 1 in 40 gradient, there thus being one 'O4' at the front of the train and one 'O4' and the 'Garratt' in rear. The distance usually assisted was about 2½ miles, and on arrival at West Silkstone Junction, where this goods avoiding line joins the Barnsley–Penistone line, the 'Garratt' came off. She then returned light to Wentworth to assist another train. She managed about eighteen banking trips in the twenty-four hours. After the electrification of this line the 'Garratt' was transferred to Bromsgrove for banking duties on the Lickey incline.

Towards the end of 1924 further multiplication of the '1000' class 'Moguls' began. A batch of fifty locomotives was turned out from Darlington works differing only in certain details, including the boiler mountings, from the original examples, and with typically North Eastern cabs. Hitherto the '1000's or 'K3's as they were classified, had appeared on passenger trains to only a small extent; but they were fast engines, capable of speeds up to 75 mph, and as more became available they were frequently requisitioned for intermediate workings all over the system. After a week's strenuous going on fitted freight trains, their weekend respite often took the form of a trip with a half-day excursion train. It was a striking commentary on their tractive power that in pre-war days with the most famous of all the fast goods trains, the 3.35 PM 'Scotsman', they were rostered to take a maximum of fifty-five wagons on the 111¾ mile non-stop run from Peterborough to York. The booked average speed was 45 mph and the gross load might rise to 650 tons behind the tender.

I had a fine trip on the footplate of No 2450 on this service, details of which are given in the table on page 98.

Sometimes if the arrival from London had been exceptionally early, the train was dispatched about 6.15 PM, and then turned slow road from Essendine to Stoke to let the 'Jubilee' go by, but on my trip we ran in the normal path. This was fortunate, as the 40-minute timing from Westwood to passing Grantham was one of the most strenuous goods train bookings to be found anywhere in the country. There must have been a strong temptation to drop a little time on this section, for it was succeeded by the much easier one of 43 minutes for the 33·1 miles from Grantham to Retford. But Driver Sallins opened No 2450 out to some purpose, made a splendid ascent and kept time.

Full regulator and early cut-off were again the order of the day. Sallins linked up quickly to 20 per cent cut-off and let the engine find her own stride. We topped the fifty line at

Tallington, and it was not until we were well beyond Essendine that an advance in cut-off was made; then it was adjusted by 2 and 3 per cent at a time to a maximum of 28 per cent, and this by no means strenuous working took us over Stoke summit at a minimum speed of 41 mph, which was no better than the booking demands. All the way up boiler pressure was maintained at 175–177 psi and the steam-chest pressure was 170 psi. At Stoke summit Sallins linked up to 15 per cent cut-off; and down the 1 in 200 with no more than 140 psi in the steam-chest, we accelerated rapidly to 65 mph. North of Grantham the engine was eased; with steam-chest pressure down to 110 psi speed gradually dwindled to $48\frac{1}{2}$ mph by the time we passed Newark.

From here it is reasonably hard going right on to York. On full regulator and 20 per cent cut-off we picked up in fine style across the level of the Trent Valley, but then unfortunately, just as we were getting some time in hand to offset the difficulty of the concluding point-to-point times, there came a string of signal checks, culminating in a virtual stop at Retford South. In getting off again No 2450 was linked up to 15 per cent as early as Retford Canal box; we were running at $59\frac{1}{2}$ mph approaching Black Carr Junction and after easing to 46 through Doncaster settled down to a hard spell on full regulator and 20 per cent cut-off along the faintly adverse length to Selby. The top speed here was 56 mph. But only one minute of the six lost at Retford was regained and this was lost again on the tightly-timed last lap, which is 22 minutes from passing Selby to the stop at Severus Junction – a stiff booking considering that a train like the 1.20 PM 'Scotsman' was allowed 17 minutes into York station, a run 2 to $2\frac{1}{2}$ minutes easier. The slightly adverse nature of the road on this section tells heavily on such a train, and in spite of using 22 per cent cut-off instead of the usual 20 on the level, we did not get above $50\frac{1}{2}$ mph. So we were $3\frac{1}{2}$ minutes late on arrival; but our net time was only 147 minutes, a fine average of $45\frac{1}{2}$ mph with such a load.

Equally, the haulage of 400 ton express passenger trains has presented little trouble, and the 'K3's have done excellent work in particular with the London–Leeds expresses over the heavy grades of the West Riding, where maximum speeds up to 79 mph have been recorded with them. Fine running was regularly made on the Sunday excursions from London, as when Mr L. J. Burley timed No 2427, with a fifteen-car train of 500 tons gross, over the 73·9 miles from Peterborough to Finsbury Park in 81 minutes or 78 minutes net. Indeed the 'K3's were second to none among main-line mixed-traffic locomotives, and the only drawback to their universal employment on the system was the heavy loading of 20 tons on each of the coupled axles, which precluded their use over much of the Great Eastern section.

In September 1927, the first of the new intermediate class of express passenger locomotives was turned out from Darlington works, 4–4–0 No 234 *Yorkshire*. Hitherto Gresley had confined the three-cylinder system of propulsion to locomotives intended for the heaviest duties, but this 4–4–0 design marked the beginning of its almost universal adoption on the LNER for new classes. The new 4–4–0s were classed 'D49', but as their names were those of counties served by the LNER they have always been referred to as the 'Shires'. In them the three cylinders drove on to the leading pair of coupled wheels, and the absence of a coupled axle ahead of the driving axle enabled all three cylinders to be set in line, and the three cranks exactly at 120 degrees to each other. In that respect the 'Shires' differed from the 'Pacifics' and the 'K3' 'Moguls'. The valve gear was also simplified by having the rocking levers that operated the valve spindle of the inside-cylinder behind the cylinders, instead of in front. This arrangement eliminated the factor of expansion of the valve spindles which had to be taken into account in the gear fitted to the 'Pacifics' and the 'K3's. The maximum travel of the valves was greater than that of the 'A1' 'Pacifics' – 6 ins against 5¾ ins – and a further important factor towards a free-running engine was the size of the piston-valves in proportion to the cylinders; the valves of the 'Shires' were 8-in diameter as in the 'Pacifics', whereas the 'Shire' cylinders were only 17-in diameter. The coupled wheels were 6 ft 8 in diameter and the weight of the engine in working order was 66 tons, of which 42 tons were available for adhesion.

TABLE 21   LNEI
6.37 PM
Engine: class
Load: 46 wagons and
Driver: Sallins; Fireman

| Distance miles | | Schedule min | Actual min | sec |
|---|---|---|---|---|
| 0·0 | PETERBOROUGH (Westwood Yard) | 0 | 0 | 00 |
| | | | sigs | |
| 0·7 | New England North Box | | 4 | 03 |
| 2·4 | Werrington Junction | | 6 | 40 |
| 7·7 | Tallington | | 13 | 26 |
| 11·5 | ESSENDINE | | 18 | 10 |
| 15·1 | Little Bytham | | 23 | 01 |
| 18·9 | *Milepost* 96 | | 28 | 34 |
| 20·0 | Corby | | 30 | 10 |
| 23·0 | Stoke Box | | 34 | 30 |
| 28·4 | GRANTHAM | 40 | 40 | 33 |
| — | | | easy | |
| 43·0 | NEWARK | 58 | 56 | 50 |
| 50·3 | Crow Park | | 65 | 33 |
| 54·8 | Tuxford | | 71 | 52 |
| | | | sigs | |
| 56·6 | Markham Box | | 75 | 53 |
| | | | sigs sev | |
| 61·5 | RETFORD | 83 | 84 | 40 |
| 66·8 | Ranskill | | 93 | 14 |
| 72·4 | *Milepost* 149½ | | 100 | 28 |
| 76·1 | Black Carr Junction | | 104 | 57 |
| 78·9 | DONCASTER | 104 | 108 | 30 |
| 83·1 | Shaftholme Junction | | 113 | 39 |
| 88·9 | Balne | | 120 | 20 |
| 95·9 | Brayton Junction | | 128 | 35 |
| 97·3 | SELBY | 127 | 130 | 30 |
| 101·4 | Riccall | | 137 | 46 |
| 109·1 | Chaloners Whin Junction | | 147 | 14 |
| 111·8 | YORK (Severus Junction) | 149 | 153 | 25† |

\* Severe service slack.

ETERBOROUGH–YORK
cottish Express Goods
K3' 2–6–0 No 2450
rake van, 610 tons full
russ (New England shed)

| Speeds mph | Regulator | Cut-off per cent | Pressure, psi | |
|---|---|---|---|---|
| | | | Boiler | Steam-Chest |
| — | Full | 65 | 160 | 150 |
| — | Full | 40 | — | — |
| 42½ | Full | 20 | 180 | 175 |
| 51½ | Full | 20 | | |
| 48 | Full | 25 | 180 | 175 |
| 43½ | Full | 28 | 180 | 175 |
| 41 | Full | 28 | | |
| 44 | Full | 28 | 175 | 170 |
| 41 | ½ | 20 | 175 | 120 |
| 65 | ¼ ⅓ | 15 | 175 | 120 |
| 51 | ⅛ | 15 | | |
| 48 | Full | 20 | 175 | 170 |
| 56 | Full | 20 | | |
| 35½ | Full | 20 | 180 | 175 |
| 15 | — | 25 | | |
| — | — | 20 | | |
| — | | — | | |
| 10 | Full | 22 | 160 | 155 |
| 52 | Full | 15 | 175 | 170 |
| 40½ | ¾ ⅖ | 15 | 175 | 150 |
| 59½ | | 15 | 180 | 110 |
| 46 | Full | 20 | 170 | 165 |
| 52 | Full | 20 | 177 | 170 |
| 54 | Full | 20 | 180 | 172 |
| 56 | Shut | 20 | — | — |
| 30* | Full | 32 | — | — |
| 46 | Full | 22 | 175 | 170 |
| 51½ | Full | 22 | | |
| — | | — | | |

Net time: 147 minutes.

The nominal tractive effort of 21,556 lb (at 85 per cent of the working pressure) made the 'Shires' almost equal in power to any of the 'Atlantics' built by the constituent companies of the LNER. The boiler was the same as that used on the 'J39' 0–6–0 goods engines, and alongside those of the Ivatt, Raven, and Reid 'Atlantics' its total heating surface of 1,669 sq ft seemed small; but in conjunction with the customary short cut-off working there never seemed to be any difficulty in providing steam for the most arduous duties. A striking example of their capacity for heavy load haulage was given by a run with the pioneer engine No 234 *Yorkshire* when a load of 480 tons gross was worked over the 44·1 miles from Darlington to York in 48 minutes 41 seconds, a start-to-stop average of 54·2 mph. In the North Eastern area, however, their duties were not usually so heavy; they were put to work mostly on services radiating from Leeds, Hull, and Sheffield, their most important turn being the morning Leeds to Glasgow luncheon-car express from Leeds to Newcastle. In the Scottish area their work was harder. On all routes, at first, they took loads up to the maximum handled by the North British 'Atlantics', and I have seen them pounding away on the Aberdeen road with 380–90 ton gross loads, doing well too. The best performance that I have ever known with a 'Shire' was on the 1.20 PM down 'Scotsman' when No 249 *Aberdeenshire* had to take a 435-ton train from Newcastle to Edinburgh without assistance.

The train was running in two portions on this occasion. How the relief section was loaded I do not know, but the main train brought sixteen vehicles down from London with the then-usual three in front and three on the rear to be detached at Newcastle. Ten coaches would not have been too stiff a job for a 'D49', but on arrival at Newcastle it was found that more accommodation was needed; and so it was decided to send the three front coaches forward to Edinburgh. The task set to No 249 *Aberdeenshire* thus became a formidable one, particularly as the conditional stops at both Dunbar and Drem were to be made.

Under these conditions it was inevitable that time would be lost, but the actual work of the locomotive was magnificent, and allowing for the stops at Alnmouth, Dunbar, and Drem the equivalent non-stop times work out at 75 minutes from Newcastle to Berwick, and 66½ minutes from Berwick to Edinburgh. The going was good enough from Morpeth to Alnmouth with an average of 62·3 mph, from Pegswood to Warkworth, and better still on to Berwick, where we did some really fast running along the coast. But easily the finest feat of the trip, and incidentally one of the finest pieces of 4–4–0 hill-climbing I have ever seen, was the maintenance of a minimum speed of 46½ mph up the 1 in 200 to Grantshouse. This involved an output of about 1,230 dhp, an exceptionally fine figure for a 4–4–0 locomotive. This performance was indeed exceptional in every way for it rarely happened that the 'D49's were set so strenuous a task.

The success attending the moderate advance in steam pressure from the 170–180 psi of the earlier Gresley designs to the 220 psi of the 'A3's resulted in the general adoption of higher pressures for future designs. The first example of this development was to be seen in the 'Sandringham' class of three-cylinder 4–6–0s, LNER class 'B17'. For some time there had been a growing need for a more powerful type of locomotive on the Great Eastern section, though the limitation of both axle-loading and overall length did not appear to offer much chance of an easy solution to the problem. Happily the findings of the Bridge Stress Committee had shown that axle-loading was not the sole criterion of the effect a locomotive has upon the road, and with better balancing and the reduction of hammer-blow due to three-cylinder propulsion, it was found possible to increase the adhesion weight from the 44 tons of the Holden 4–6–0s to 54 tons in the 'Sandringhams'. The engine layout differed from every other Gresley three-cylinder type in that the drive was divided; the outside-cylinders drove on the middle pair of coupled wheels and the inside-cylinder drove on to the leading pair. The principal dimensions were: cylinders, three, 17½-in diameter by 26-in stroke; piston-valves 8-in diameter with a travel in full gear of 5$\frac{21}{32}$ ins; boiler 5 ft 6 ins maximum outside diameter, 14 ft 0 ins between the tube plates, and having tubes of the ample diameter, for their

length, of 2 ins; superheater twenty-four element, affording
344 sq ft of heating surface; total heating surface 2,020 sq ft;
grate area $27\frac{1}{2}$ sq ft; working pressure 200 psi. As usual in
Gresley express locomotives the coupled wheels were 6 ft 8 in
diameter. Although the preparation of the design was beset
with many difficulties, imposed by the nature of the Great
Eastern road, a most successful engine was produced, the
nominal tractive effort of which, 25,380 lb, represented a substantial advance upon the 21,969 lb of the Holden 4–6–0s. The
first batch of 'Sandringhams' was built by the North British
Locomotive Co Ltd, so providing one of the very few instances
of a new Gresley type being built elsewhere than at the railway
company's own works.

At first the 'Sandringhams' did not have much opportunity
for spectacular running. The night Continental expresses had
by that time been decelerated, and other Great Eastern turns,
strenuous enough for the Holden 4–6–0s, did not extend the
'B17's. At the same time as high-speed trials were being carried
out on the Great Northern main line, in preparation for the
striking accelerations of May 1932, No 2800 made one or two
fast trial runs on the Great Eastern section; apart from this,
however, long mileages and the same happy immunity from
casualties as the 'Pacifics' characterized their early work. It was
not until 1936, when the series named after leading association
football teams was turned out from Darlington works, that the
'B17's took their true place in the records of British locomotive
performance. The new batch was sent to Leicester shed, and
the redoubtable enginemen who had made such a reputation
for themselves with the ex-GCR 'Atlantics' took to the 'B17's
immediately, although, of course, they required quite different
driving methods; their exploits on the 6.20 PM down from
Marylebone relieved that train of its one-time difficulties from
the locomotive point of view, and before the war loads of
400 tons went unpiloted. My own experiences on the footplates
of several 'B17's showed their performance to be in the best
Gresley tradition; no driver thought of working with anything
but full regulator, and cut-offs of 15 to 20 per cent produced
the liveliest of running. Easily the most exciting trip I had was

on No 2841 *Gayton Hall*, with the 2.32 AM newspaper express.
The details of this journey are given in the log on page 104,
from which it will be seen that, with the exception of the climb
over the Chilterns, in the amazing start out of Rugby and, of
course, in the initial ascent from Marylebone to Brondesbury,
the engine was worked on 15 per cent cut-off throughout. The
running between Brackley and Rugby is a good example of
what such working produced including such a *minimum* speed
as 68½ mph at Charwelton. Then came that altogether extraordinary start out of Rugby, where the engine was given full
regulator, and where 25 per cent cut-off was maintained to the
top of the Shawell bank. By the LMS viaduct speed had risen
to 51 mph and a maximum of 66 mph was attained in 1¾ miles
from the dead start, on a falling gradient of 1 in 176. After
mounting the Shawell bank at a minimum of 57½ mph, the
driver reverted to 15 per cent, and the run was fitly rounded
off by a maximum of exactly 90 mph near Whetstone. In
descending the final 1 in 176 full regulator was maintained for
two miles from the summit, during which time we accelerated
from 63 to 75 mph; then the regulator was partly closed so that
steam-chest pressure dropped from 175 to 110 psi. With this
latter pressure in combination with 15 per cent cut-off, speed
rose from 75 to 90 mph in five miles of 1 in 176 descent.

My friend Sir James Colyer-Fergusson logged a magnificent
run in the opposite direction on the 8.51 AM express from
Leicester to Marylebone, with a load of no less than 465 tons.
This schedule was one originally designed for operation with
the Great Central 'Atlantics' and 'Director' class 4–4–0s with
loads of around 250 tons; yet here was it being successfully
worked with a load practically double. The driver, Webb of
Leicester, had been a noted runner with 'Atlantics', as I had
personally recorded in past years. He was certainly well served
by his fireman Hayes, on this notable occasion. Minimum
speeds up the long stretches of 1 in 176 ascent, as from Whetstone towards Ashby, and from Braunston, through Catesby
tunnel to Charwelton were 42 and 44 mph respectively, and a
very fine minimum speed of 39 mph up the 1 in 116 ascent into
the Chiltern Hills, to milepost 31½. There was also some fast

TABLE 22 LNER 2.32 AM
Engine: class 'B17' 4-6-0
Load: 271 tons tare,
Driver: Simpson; Fireman:

| Distance miles | | Schedule min | Actual min | Actual sec |
|---|---|---|---|---|
| 0·0 | MARYLEBONE | 0 | 0 | 00 |
| 1·9 | Canfield Place | | 4 | 30 |
| 3·0 | Brondesbury | | 6 | 10 |
| 5·1 | Neasden Junction | | 8 | 32 |
| 9·2 | Harrow | 13 | 12 | 34 |
| 11·4 | Pinner | | 14 | 47 |
| 13·7 | Northwood | | 17 | 00 |
| 16·2 | Watford South Junction | | 19 | 11 |
| 17·2 | RICKMANSWORTH | | 20 | 32 |
| 19·4 | Chorleywood | | 24 | 42 |
| 23·6 | Amersham | | 31 | 50 |
| 28·8 | Great Missenden | | 36 | 51 |
| — | Dutchlands | | — | |
| 33·3 | Wendover | | 40 | 46 |
| 38·0 | AYLESBURY | 44 | 44 | 13 |
| 44·1 | Quainton Road Junction | 52 | 49 | 26 |
| 46·8 | Grendon Junction | | 52 | 17 |
| — | | | — | |
| 54·5 | Finmere | | 59 | 15 |
| 59·3 | BRACKLEY | 67 | 64 | 45 |
| 0·0 | | | 0 | 00 |
| 3·2 | Helmdon | | 5 | 36 |
| 8·1 | Culworth Junction | | 10 | 04 |
| 9·8 | WOODFORD & HINTON | | 11 | 27 |
| 12·2 | Charwelton | | 13 | 32 |
| 19·2 | Braunston | | 19 | 13 |
| 23·9 | RUGBY | 24 | 23 | 46 |
| 0·0 | | | 0 | 00 |
| 3·6 | Shawell Box | | 4 | 47 |
| 6·8 | Lutterworth | | 7 | 58 |
| 15·2 | Whetstone | | 14 | 45 |
| 18·9 | Leicester South Goods Junction | | 17 | 22 |
| 19·9 | LEICESTER | 20 | 19 | 02 |

\* Slight service slack.    † Regulator closed

MARYLEBONE–LEICESTER
No 2841 *Gayton Hall*
00 tons full
Wood (Neasden shed)

| Speeds mph | Regulator | Cut-off per cent | Pressure, psi | |
|---|---|---|---|---|
| | | | Boiler | Steam-Chest |
| — | Full | 65 | | |
| 33 | Full | 25 | 185 | 175 |
| 32 | Full | 15 | | |
| 70½ | Full | 15 | | |
| 53 | Full | 15 | | |
| 66 | Full | 15 | | |
| 59 | Full | 15 | | |
| 75½ | Shut | 15 | | |
| 30 | Full | 30 | | |
| 35 | Full | 30 | 185 | 175 |
| 36 | Full | 15 | | |
| 77½ | Full | 15 | | |
| 63 | Full | 15 | | |
| 84 | Shut | 15 | | |
| — | ⅓ | 15 | 185 | 100 |
| 56* | Full | 15 | | |
| 62 | ⅔ | 15 | 180 | 120 |
| 71 | Full | 15 | 185 | 175 |
| 61½/73 | Full | 15 | | |
| | — | — | | |
| | Full | 65/25 | | |
| 55 | | 15 | 185 | 175 |
| 77 | | 15 | | |
| 72½ | | 15 | | |
| 68½ | ½ | 15 | | |
| 85 | — | 15 | 180 | 125 |
| — | — | — | | |
| | Full | 65/25 | 185 | 175 |
| 66 | Full | 65/25 | | |
| 57½ | Full | 15 | | |
| 90 | ⅜† | 15 | 185 | 110 |
| 81 | ⅜† | 15 | | |
| — | — | — | | |

from full open to ⅔ near Ashby station.

TABLE 23

8.51 AM LEICESTER–MARYLEBONE

Load: 13 coaches, 437 tons tare, 465 tons full

Engine: 3-cylinder 4–6–0 No 2848 *Arsenal*

Driver: Webb; Fireman: Hayes (Leicester shed)

| Distance miles | | Sch. min | Actual min | sec | Speeds mph |
|---|---|---|---|---|---|
| 0·0 | LEICESTER | 0 | 0 | 00 | — |
| 4·7 | Whetstone | | 7 | 45 | 50 |
| 9·2 | Ashby | | 13 | 55 | 42 (min) |
| 13·1 | Lutterworth | | 18 | 59 | |
| 19·9 | RUGBY | | 25 | 12 | 73½/63 |
| 24·6 | Braunston | | 29 | 23 | 70 |
| 31·6 | Charwelton | | 32 | 42 | 44 |
| 34·0 | WOODFORD | 37 | 39 | 53 | — |
| 37·0 | Culworth | | 42 | 40 | 69/60 |
| 40·6 | Helmdon | | 45 | 58 | — |
| 43·8 | Brackley | | 48 | 46 | 79 |
| 48·6 | Finmere | | 52 | 37 | 69 |
| 54·3 | Calvert | | 57 | 03 | 80½/72 |
| 56·3 | *Grendon Junction* | 56 | 58 | 45 | 63* |
| 59·0 | Quainton Road | 59 | 61 | 14 | 71 |
| 65·2 | AYLESBURY | 65 | 66 | 37 | 69 |
| 69·8 | Wendover | | 71 | 54 | — |
| 71·9 | *Milepost* 31½ | | 75 | 05 | 39 |
| 74·3 | Great Missenden | 76 | 77 | 37 | 71 |
| 79·5 | Amersham | | 82 | 33 | 55 |
| 81·5 | Chalfont | 83 | 84 | 26 | 80 (max) |
| 85·9 | Rickmansworth | 87½ | 88 | 11 | slack |
| — | | | p.w.s. | | |
| 93·9 | HARROW | 97 | 98 | 47 | — |
| 98·0 | *Neasden Junction* | 101½ | 103 | 12 | 68 |
| 100·1 | Brondesbury | | 105 | 21 | 49 |
| 103·1 | MARYLEBONE | 109 | 110 | 06 | |

Net time: 109 minutes.          * Speed restriction.

downhill running from Woodford, with maximum speeds of 80
mph or a little under on the 1 in 176 descents. In view of feats like
this and that of *Gayton Hall* on the newspaper train it is sad to
recall that much of this line is now closed and the track lifted.

The 'Sandringham' class engines have not always had the
best of reputations for good riding; but I must admit that in
my own experience they were usually good, and on one trip

exceptionally so. This latter was in British Railways days, when engines were not always kept in the best of condition. I had an engine pass to ride the up 'Fenman' from Cambridge to Liverpool Street one morning, and was delighted to find the engine was a 'Sandringham' and not the expected 'B1'. *Lambton Castle*, then numbered 61623, proved a veritable ghost engine skating along with scarcely a sound from her exhaust, and the smoothest and quietest action one could imagine on a reciprocating steam locomotive.

The 'Sandringhams' shared with the 'King Arthurs' of the Southern the distinction of being able to take full regulator at once from a standing start. On several engines of both classes I have seen drivers open up, and put the regulator hard against the stop, and the locomotive get away without a trace of slipping. With a load of only 'nine', such vigorous methods were not needed on 'The Fenman'; but the initial opening at Cambridge was wide enough for all that, giving 175 psi steam-chest pressure, against 210 in the boiler. From Trumpington Box, just over a mile out, the regulator was absolutely full open, and thus it remained until we were over Elsenham summit. As can be seen from the accompanying log we covered the 20·1 miles from Cambridge to this point in 23 minutes 36 seconds.

The climb is nowhere severe, as the worst pitches are $2\frac{1}{2}$ miles at 1 in 163–135–153 from Great Chesterford to the north end of Audley End tunnel, and the $4\frac{3}{4}$ miles at 1 in 182–245–176–322 from Newport to Elsenham. For most of the distance the engine was working in 20 per cent cut-off, with what might be termed an 'academic' increase to 21 per cent for the steepest pitch immediately after Great Chesterford. Here the minimum speed was 46 mph, and after touching 63 mph in the Newport dip Elsenham summit was cleared at a minimum speed of $50\frac{1}{2}$ mph.

The usual slack to 30 mph through Bishops Stortford was preceded by a short permanent way slowing; and then we got away once more for an enjoyable spin down the Lea Valley. Sixty miles per hour was reached at the twenty-eighth milepost $2\frac{1}{2}$ miles south of Bishops Stortford, and at this point cut-off was shortened to 15 per cent, and the regulator eased back to give about 150 psi steam-chest pressure. For 20 miles of gradual descent the average speed was 71·7 mph, and on passing Tottenham, 49·7 miles from the start, the actual time was 52 minutes 18 seconds or about 50¾ minutes net.

TABLE 24

### EASTERN REGION: 'THE FENMAN'
### CAMBRIDGE–LIVERPOOL STREET

Load: 9 cars, 299 tons tare, 320 tons full
Engine: class 'B17' 4–6–0 No 61623 *Lambton Castle*

| Distance miles | | Time min sec | | Speeds mph |
|---|---|---|---|---|
| 0·0 | CAMBRIDGE | 0 | 00 | — |
| 3·3 | Shelford | 5 | 28 | 48 |
| 6·7 | Whittlesford | 9 | 09 | 56 |
| 10·0 | Great Chesterford | 12 | 33 | 58½ |
| 12·5 | Milepost 43¼ | 15 | 23 | 46 |
| 14·0 | Audley End | 17 | 12 | 49 |
| 15·8 | Newport | 19 | 07 | 63 |
| 20·1 | Elsenham | 23 | 36 | 50½ |
| 22·3 | Stansted | 24 | 44 | 72 |
| | | | p.w.s. | — |
| 25·3 | BISHOPS STORTFORD | 30 | 13 | — |
| 31·2 | Harlow | 36 | 56 | 70 |
| 38·6 | Broxbourne | 42 | 58 | 74 |
| 42·9 | Waltham Cross | 46 | 31 | 71 |
| 49·7 | TOTTENHAM | 52 | 18 | — |
| 50·8 | *Coppermill Junction* | 53 | 28 | slack |
| | | | p.w.s. | — |
| 52·7 | Hackney Downs | 58 | 18 | |
| 54·6 | Bethnal Green | 62 | 48 | |
| | | | sigs | |
| 55·7 | LIVERPOOL STREET | 66 | 48 | |

The last stages of the run, with the heavy slack at Coppermill Junction, cautious running over the crowded and winding stretch from Hackney Downs to Bethnal Green, and two slight checks into the bargain, were inevitably slow, and the six miles from Tottenham into Liverpool Street took 14½ minutes. But the net time of 63 minutes with its start-to-stop average speed of 53 mph bespoke good work, especially in relation to the ease with which it was done.

# CHAPTER NINE

# EXPERIMENTS AND REBUILDINGS

While the broad principles of Gresley's standard practice were being developed, and duly embodied in new express passenger types, the quest for increased efficiency was being pursued in several other ways. To investigate the possibility of improving boiler performance, feed-water heaters of various types were tried; extended tests were made with poppet-valves; and earlier experiments with boosters were followed by two particularly interesting applications. For a time, also, it seemed that Gresley was feeling his way towards some policy of boiler standardization, since boilers of his own design were fitted to certain ex-GCR and ex-NER locomotives. The tests of feed-heating and poppet-valves were made in a very practical way; their application to certain locomotive classes of moderate or indifferent performance improved the engines that were equipped from the operational point of view, and at the same time gave valuable running experience with the devices in question before any inclusion of them in first-class express passenger locomotives.

Before grouping, there was a Great Eastern 4-4-0 of the 'Claud Hamilton' class, No 1791, fitted with the Weir feed-water heater and pump, though this apparatus was removed in 1924. Isolated applications were also made of the Dabeg heater on a class 'O2' 2-8-0 and of the Worthington apparatus on an ex-Great Eastern 4-6-0, No 8509, and on an ex-North British 'Atlantic', No 9903 *Cock o' the North*. But the only type that was tried extensively was the ACFI. This was already in regular use on the Continent, and the observed performance of some 2,000 locomotives that were so fitted justified the manufacturer's claim that economies of 10 to 12 per cent in coal, and 15 per cent in water, were realized with the added advantage of 10 per cent reduction in feed density when using hard water. These increases in efficiency were, of course, over similar locomotives on which the feed water was not heated at all. The LNER, however, was already using a form of feed-water heater in the Davies & Metcalfe exhaust steam injector which, while not giving so high an efficiency, was a great deal simpler. The tests were therefore to find out whether the higher service efficiency of the ACFI apparatus was enough to justify the higher initial cost.

Two of the ex-NER three-cylinder 'Atlantics' Nos 728 and 2206 (class 'C7') were equipped, but Gresley's most extensive trials of the ACFI system were made on ex-GER 4-6-0 express engines of what were LNER class 'B12'. Whatever its effect in improving performance, the two cylindrical chambers saddling the boiler and the profusion of connecting pipes sadly impaired the handsome appearance of these engines, and was partly responsible for their being nicknamed 'hikers', though this is sometimes claimed to be of Scottish origin. The drafting to the Great Eastern system of some thirty 'Sandringhams' released a number of the 'B12's, and these were sent to Scotland for service on the GNS section. Here, limitations of axle-loading had hitherto precluded the transference of more powerful types from other sections, and apart from the assistance of a few rebuilt Holmes 4-4-0s from the North British, the whole of the work in the far north-east was still being done by the little Manson and Pickersgill 4-4-0s. The Scottish enginemen found that on the 'B12's coal had to be shifted quite a long way in comparison, from the shovelling plate to the fire door; this distance, requiring a step or two on the fireman's part, is credited in Scotland with having given rise to the 'hiker' nickname.

The results obtained were evidently encouraging, for Gresley carried the trials a stage further by equipping two of the 'Pacifics'. From experience gained with the 'B12's a number of modifications to the standard apparatus were suggested to the manufacturers, with the results that the two 'Pacifics' were equipped with a considerably improved type of feed-water heater that was fitted inside the smokebox. This reduced the loss of heat due to radiation, to which the standard equipment, fixed in exposed position on the boiler, was susceptible; the

appearance of the engines was also much improved, as compared with the 'B12's. These 'Pacific' tests were of further
value as giving results at two differing boiler pressures, one
engine, No 2576 *The White Knight*, being an 'A1' with 180 psi
pressure, and the other, No 2580 *Shotover*, an 'A3' with 220
psi. This modified form of ACFI heater was also fitted to the
first of the 2–8–2 express engines in 1934. Although no figures
have been published it would seem that any improvement
realized in thermal efficiency, over engines fitted with the
standard arrangement of injectors, was outweighed by the
extra first cost and maintenance charges of the ACFI heater
and its steam-driven pump; for it was not applied to any new
engines after 1934. As in engine No 10000, and all Gresley's
experimental work, once trials were embarked upon they were
not lightly abandoned.

Concurrently, another series of tests was in progress on
poppet-valves, which on theoretical grounds could be arranged
to provide a steam distribution nearer to the ideal than piston-
valves of the conventional type. The full valve opening, for
example, was available no matter how early the cut-off, and
more complete expansion of the steam was made possible by
having the release position independent of the cut-off. The
ex-GER 4–6–0s again featured in the first use of poppet-valves
on the LNER, No 8516 being equipped in 1927 with the Lentz
oscillating-cam gear. As a result of this application, which gave
valuable running experience, and a marked improvement in
coal consumption, a batch of ten new 'B12's having the Lentz
OC valve gear was ordered from Beyer, Peacock & Co Ltd.
These engines, Nos 8571–80, were put into service in 1928, and
although in external appearance they conformed generally to
the original Holden design, the Gresley touch was apparent in
the cutting away of the coupling-rod splashers. In the following
year two of the ex-GCR four-cylinder 4–6–0s of the 'Lord
Faringdon' class were fitted with the Caprotti valve gear, and
this brought about a substantial improvement in the work of a
class with a distinctly shaky reputation.

So far, it will be appreciated that the trial of poppet- versus
piston-valves had not been made on equal terms, since the GC

4-6-os, and the ex-GER 'B12's could hardly be called modern engines. When turning out his own 'D49' class of three-cylinder 4-4-os Gresley equipped six of them with poppet-valves driven by oscillating cams, the motion being provided by the usual arrangement of the Walschaerts gear. Direct comparison with the piston-valve engines was thus possible, and in 1929 the trials were carried further when two more 'D49's, No 336 *Buckinghamshire* and No 352 *Leicestershire*, were fitted with poppet-valves operated by rotating cams. The driving mechanism for this gear was simple, consisting of a longitudinal shaft driven by a bevel gear off the driving axle, and it was probably on account of this simplicity that the RC gear received the most extended trial of all. As applied to 'D49' engines Nos 336 and 352 this gear provided only five positions of cut-off, ranging from 15 to 75 per cent in full gear, and it was not possible to work the engine with the gear between any two of these positions. In contrast to the Caprotti gear, which also employs rotating cams and which provides for infinitely fine adjustment anywhere between 3 per cent and full gear, the RC arrangement makes an engine somewhat inflexible in service. Yet the limitation so imposed in normal working cannot have been unduly severe, for in 1932, when further 4-4-0 locomotives were required for intermediate service in the North Eastern area, a new series of 'D49's was turned out, all having the RC poppet-valve gear. These engines were named after famous hunts, and their nameplates were distinguished by the figure of a fox above the lettering. The two experimental engines, Nos 336 and 352, were, at the time, renamed *The Quorn* and *The Meynell* respectively.

On at least one occasion, however, the inflexibility of the RC poppet-valve arrangement resulted in the failure of a locomotive to carry out a task of a special kind. About the time that the 'Hunts' were built one of the ex-NER three-cylinder 'Atlantics', No 732, was rebuilt with a front end identical with that of the 4-4-os and one day in 1936 this engine was requisitioned for the up 'Silver Jubilee' when the booked engine ran hot and had to come off, at York. The driver found that one cut-off position was not sufficient to do the job, and the next, if used continuously, would 'just about have killed the fire-man', to quote his own words. In this connexion it may be recalled that in the only application of RC poppet-valve gear made on the GWR the two-cylinder 4–6–0 No 2935 *Caynham Court* had a mechanism giving nine, instead of five cut-off positions, ranging from 10 to 85 per cent. The one-time 'uniflow' three-cylinder 4–4–2 No 2212 was also rebuilt with RC poppet-valve gear.

Next to be recorded are the further experiments made with boosters. Great Northern 'Atlantic' No 4419, the first LNER engine to have a booster, was fitted with one similar to those in fairly common use in America. This apparatus had a gear ratio of 2·57 to 1, and in extensive trials it was found that 15 mph was about the maximum speed at which the booster could be used; above that the demands on the locomotive boiler were too great owing to the high rotational speed of the auxiliary engine. That Gresley had in mind a method of operation differing considerably from that of contemporary American practice is clear from the specification he laid down for the booster equipment of some further 'Atlantic' engines. An increased pull of 2 tons was to be provided on starting, and the booster had to be capable of cutting-in smoothly at 30 mph so that this speed could be sustained up a 1 in 96 gradient with a train-load of 400 tons. This envisaged the continued use of the ex-NER three-cylinder 'Atlantics' of the LNER class 'C7' as reserve engines for the Anglo-Scottish expresses north of York, the booster to be brought into use on the Cockburnspath bank south of Dunbar, and, of course, in starting.

To do this the gear ratio of the auxiliary engine was, after considerable experiment and research, fixed at 1 to 1, on a machine having two cylinders 10½-in diameter by 14-in stroke. In 1931 two 'C7' 'Atlantics' Nos 727 and 2171 were equipped, a novel feature being that the booster engine was carried on a four-wheel bogie; the locomotive and tender were articulated, with the rear end of the engine and the front end of the tender carried on this bogie. In rebuilding these two locomotives Gresley fitted enlarged boilers having 200 psi pressure, against the previous 170, and with grate area increased from 27 to

30 sq ft. Despite the reduction in the booster gear ratio the rebuilt 'C7's had, with the booster in action, a higher nominal tractive effort than the 'C1' engine No 4419, owing to the greater cylinder volume and higher working pressure. On test one of the rebuilt 'C7's started a load of 746 tons, exerting a drawbar pull of 12¼ tons whereas with the booster cut out the drawbar pull in starting a load of 486 tons was 9 tons. Both these tests were made on level track.

A further development came in January 1932. For some time traffic conditions in the hump marshalling yard at Wath had been growing more arduous. There Robinson's ex-Great Central three-cylinder 0–8–4 tanks were at work; and the maximum load they could restart without assistance on the 1 in 107 gradient leading to the hump was 45 loaded 10-ton coal wagons. To handle increased loads in all weathers No 6171 of this class was rebuilt with a superheater-equipped boiler, and a reversible booster was fitted to the trailing bogie; all previous applications on the LNER for use in main-line traffic had been of uni-directional boosters, though on an engine used for hump work it was obviously necessary that the auxiliary should be effective when working with chimney or bunker first. Another interesting feature of this rebuilding was that the bogie wheels were coupled, providing the auxiliary engine with valuable extra adhesion weight. With the booster in operation, the nominal tractive effort of the locomotive was increased by 35 per cent, and its practical effect was to enable sixty-two-wagon trains, about 1,000 tons loaded, to be operated successfully over the hump. Two new engines of the same type, Nos 2798 and 2799, were built at Gorton later in the same year; they were identical with No 6171 except that the side tanks were cut away at the front end to improve the driver's outlook.

Another interesting tank locomotive conversion, in 1931, was that of the ex-NER class 'D' 4–4–4s, the first of which were built at Darlington in 1913. To assist in the handling of the heavy Tees-side traffic these engines were altered to 4–6–2s, which change, while not adding to the nominal tractive effort, substantially increased the adhesion weight from 40 to

$52\frac{1}{4}$ tons. Even before the conversion of the 4–4–4s there had been 4–6–2 tanks at work in this area. A batch of class 'A5' engines was built specially by R. & W. Hawthorn Leslie & Co Ltd, showing once again Gresley's partiality towards Great Central designs; but in them the characteristically handsome Robinson outline was marred by the use of a 'Shire' type built-up chimney, and a dome no higher than that of a 'Pacific'.

Lastly, in connexion with Gresley's modifications certain changes in boilers require mention. In 1929 two of the ex-GCR 2–8–0s of class 'O4', Nos 6287 and 6371, were turned out with Great Northern type boilers, as used on the 'O2' engines. To accommodate these, the frames had to be lengthened at the trailing end, and in some further conversions a modified form of 'O2' boiler, with shorter barrel, was fitted. These later rebuilds retained their Great Central cabs, whereas Nos 6287 and 6371 acquired a curious-looking single-windowed affair. The re-buildings with modified 'O2' boilers proved successful, and after 1939 a considerable number of the class was so altered; these conversions were classed 'O4/7'. A similar process was applied in 1929 to one of the Raven express passenger 'Pacific' engines, No 2404 *City of Ripon*. This was not done in the interests of standardization, for the North Eastern chassis was too long to allow of an 'A1' boiler being used. The new boiler was fitted to obtain better evaporation, by the use of a wide firebox and a barrel coned at the rear end. The advantages gained, however, were evidently not sufficiently marked to justify the continued existence of the 'A2's and No 2404 was scrapped at the same time as the four other engines of the class, in 1936–7.

The greatest experiment of Gresley's whole career, and not the least notable from the fact that it was unsuccessful, was the four-cylinder compound 4–6–4 built at Darlington, No 10000. The first appearance of this unique locomotive was at the close of 1929, little more than a year after the 'A3's had come out, and this may have given rise to ideas that the two designs were in some way connected; that the trial of 450 psi pressure in No 10000 was a sequel to the success of the previous moderate increase, from the 180 psi of the 'A1's to the 220 psi of the

'A3's. Actually, however, the conception of a high-pressure locomotive design dates back almost to pre-grouping days, and was unaffected by any current events on the LNER. In a paper read before the Institution of Mechanical Engineers on January 23rd, 1931, Gresley tells that he was so impressed by the striking increases in efficiency obtained in land and marine boilers by the use of high steam pressure that he began to formulate a design of locomotive which it was hoped would realize the same advantages. By September 1924 his own ideas were sufficiently advanced for him to approach Mr Harold Yarrow, of Glasgow, with a view to the latter's firm building a high-pressure boiler of the water-tube type suitable for a loco-motive. It is striking evidence of the amount of painstaking work put into the design of engine No 10000 that nearly three years were spent in preparing the design of the boiler alone; and that although the order for the boiler was placed with Yarrow early in 1928 it was not completed until October 1929. The engine ran its trial trip on December 12th, 1929.

The working pressure was 450 psi, and to obtain the greatest possible range of expansion the engine was arranged as a com-pound having two high-pressure cylinders 12-in diameter and two low-pressure 20-in diameter, all four cylinders having 26-in stroke. On trial it was found that a more equal dis-tribution of the work between the high- and low-pressure cylinders was obtained by reducing the diameter of the high-pressure cylinders to 10 ins. Although using only two sets of valve gear, Gresley introduced an arrangement making it possible to vary the cut-off in the high-pressure cylinders independently of that in the low-pressure; the advantages of having this provision will be manifest to anyone who has studied the working of the De Glehn compounds in France. The details of this gear were fully described by Gresley in the paper previously referred to. The paper itself, and the sub-sequent discussion, covers no less than 106 pages, and is a document of absorbing interest. The aerodynamic screening at the front end attracted a lot of attention at the time, and its unconventional appearance prepared us for *Cock o' the North* four years later.

In his paper Gresley was able to report that No 10000 'has worked trains of over 500 tons weight for long distances at express speeds with consistent success and reliability, and although it has not been possible so far to carry out any extensive trials, there is every indication that it will prove more economical in fuel consumption than express engines of the latest normal types'. During the summer of 1930 she was working in the ordinary Gateshead 'Pacific' link, including the long-mileage double-manned turn, beginning with the 11.17 AM from Newcastle to Edinburgh; this latter included the 43 minute Darlington–York run of the evening Glasgow–Leeds dining-car express. Mr R. A. H. Weight timed her from Darlington to York, 44·1 miles, at exactly 60 mph from start to stop with a load of 440 tons. On July 31st, 1930, she worked the 'Flying Scotsman' non-stop from Edinburgh to King's Cross, returning on the corresponding train next day; I witnessed her arrival on the up journey, dead on time. In general performance, however, the early promise of success was not realized, and No 10000 proved a troublesome engine to maintain; but although posterity will remember her best in her rebuilt form as a giant in the noble regiment of blue streamliners, the boldness of the original conception, and the superb engineering put into her construction, must not be lightly dismissed.

# CHAPTER TEN

# THE GIANT 2-8-2s

In striking contrast to the trend of locomotive practice else-where Gresley did not develop a policy of rigid standardization of types. On the main lines, of course, his 'Pacifics', his 'K3' 'Moguls', and other types were already in widespread use, but where special conditions of road and traffic existed, he pre-ferred to build special engines for the job rather than use the largest standard type permissible, and double-head when re-quired. Since the introduction of third-class sleeping-cars a serious operating problem had existed on the East Coast main line north of Edinburgh, where the heavy gradients compelled the limitation of 'Pacific' loads to maximum tonnages of 440 tons southbound and 480 tons northbound. The problem of designing a locomotive that would haul loads of 550 tons over that difficult road was not merely one of producing a machine big enough. The curves are as exacting as the gradients, and in any proposed design almost as much attention had to be given to its likely behaviour as a vehicle as to its haulage ability. The Gresley 'Pacifics' had an excellent reputation for good riding, though the same could not be said for the 'Moguls' or the 'Sandringham' class 4-6-0s.

Gresley was intensely aware of all that was then going on in France. He kept closely in touch with André Chapelon of the Paris–Orleans, and Jean Lancrenon of the Nord, and the per-formance of the latest 'Pacifics' on those two railways interested him very keenly. He was particularly impressed with the free running of these engines, and with the minimal back pressure when working extremely hard. The large direct ports and pas-sages and the internal streamlining seemed to him the key to the very high power output of those French 'Pacifics' in re-lation to their nominal tractive effort. On the LNER the outcome of much careful study was the celebrated No 2001 *Cock o' the North*. This new locomotive was turned out of Doncaster

works in May 1934, to a mighty fanfare of trumpets. It was a
time of intense effort by all the British railways to regain some
of their lost traffic, when no chance of advertisement was to be
lost. In the great size, unorthodox lines, and challenging name
of No 2001 the publicists found a plethora of material, and the
engine duly featured in radio programmes and numerous
highly coloured newspaper stories. The name was lifted from
another Scottish engine, the North British 'Atlantic' No 9903,
which thereupon received the name of the pioneer of her class,
*Aberdonian*, the latter having just been scrapped.

   *Cock o' the North* was the most powerful passenger engine in
Britain at the time of construction, and it remained so until the
'P2' class, of which No 2001 was the pioneer, was rebuilt by
Edward Thompson as 'Pacifics'. Although the design broadly
followed established Gresley practice, the French influence was
to be seen in that the internal steam passages were streamlined
to a greater extent than in previous LNER locomotives, and the
freedom of the exhaust was increased by use of the Kylchap
arrangement of double chimney and blastpipe. Equipment included the ACFI feed-water heater and poppet-valves operated by rotary cam gear, originally capable of infinitely variable
adjustment of cut-off. The leading dimensions were: cylinders
(3) 21-in diameter by 26-in stroke; coupled wheels 6 ft 2 in
diameter; total heating surface 3,490 sq ft; grate area 50 sq ft;
boiler pressure 220 psi; total weight of engine and tender in
working order $165\frac{1}{2}$ tons; tractive effort at 85 per cent working
pressure 43,462 lb. In view of the soft exhaust which it was
expected would result from the low back-pressure aimed at,
the smokebox was provided with an arrangement of aerodynamic screening to lift the exhaust steam and smoke clear of
the cab; *Cock o' the North* was not unlike No 10000 in this
respect though the latter engine had not the wedge-fronted cab
that was later proved so efficacious as a smoke lifter on the
later 2–8–2s of class 'P2' and the streamlined 'Pacifics'.

   The early days of the 'A1' 'Pacifics' were soon vividly recalled by a high-output test from King's Cross to Grantham
and back, with a 650-ton load. In the course of this trip a remarkable climb from Peterborough to Stoke summit was made

with an average speed of 60·3 mph throughout from Tallington to the summit box; during this fine exhibition a drawbar horse-power of no less than 2,090 was recorded. Another feature of this engine's working was demonstrated during this test. When the reverser was put into mid-gear the valves were lifted from their seats, and the engine then coasted with the utmost free-dom. I had an example of this myself very shortly afterwards. Service trials were conducted between Doncaster and King's Cross, mostly on the up Yorkshire express then due at 1.55 PM and returning on the 4 PM down. On these trials *Cock o' the North* proved such a flyer as to astonish even those intimately connected with the design. Maximum speeds up to 85 mph were attained with ease, a speed almost unheard of then with eight-coupled wheels. To the attainment of such speeds the poppet-valves, with their exceptionally free exhaust, con-tributed largely, combining very effectively with the Kylchap double blastpipes and chimney. During this period M. Lanc-renon paid a visit to England, and for his benefit No 2001 with the dynamometer car was put on to the 1.20 PM 'Scotsman', and worked that train to York. I understood at the time that the Frenchman was highly delighted with the performance.

During the period of the ordinary test running with No 2001 between Doncaster and King's Cross I was able to travel down to Peterborough one afternoon, and although the year 1934 was well before the days when I was privileged to ride in the dynamometer car I culled some interesting information from one of the testing staff. The log is tabulated herewith. We took a very heavy train of 585 tons out of King's Cross and began rather inauspiciously. Immediately upon entering Gas Works tunnel the engine went into a violent slip, so violent indeed that those on the footplate thought the roof of the tunnel had been damaged, and that water from the Regents Canal was pouring down. But mastery was soon gained, and although the run was not a spectacular one from the viewpoint of times and speeds the actual engine performance was very fine. We had a very good example of the engine's freedom in coasting when steam was shut off at Connington, and the next five level miles were covered, without steam, at an average speed of 60 mph.

*Cock o' the North* went to Scotland in time to assist in the working of the August holiday traffic of 1934. At that time through locomotive working was in force between Edinburgh and Aberdeen, and a run on the up 'Aberdonian', timed by Mr W. A. Willox, showed the capabilities of the great engine to the full. With a load of 550 tons the 40·6 miles from Aberdeen to Montrose were covered in exactly 50 minutes start to stop, an average of 48·7 mph over that severe road that gave an arrival 8 minutes early at Montrose. The first sojourn in Scotland of No 2001 was short, however, for in December 1934 she was shipped across to France for trials at the Vitry testing plant of the OCEM. This step was in some ways to be expected, for not only was Gresley at pains to acknowledge his indebtedness to French practice for certain features of the design, but he was also one of the staunchest advocates of a similar testing station in this country. He certainly publicized the fact that no suitable testing plant existed in Great Britain, and that for an engine to be scientifically tested it had to be sent to France. At that time, of course, the Swindon plant was in its original condition and could certainly not have absorbed the maximum output of an engine like *Cock o' the North*.

In the autumn of 1934 the second 2-8-2 express engine No 2002 *Earl Marischal* was turned out from Doncaster works. It differed from *Cock o' the North* in several important respects. Instead of RC poppet-valves No 2002 had 9-in diameter piston-valves, with Walschaerts gear and the usual Gresley derived motion for the inside-cylinder; and in place of the ACFI feed-water heater No 2002 was fitted with a Davies & Metcalfe exhaust injector. Like No 2001 the second engine ran for some time between King's Cross and Doncaster and considerable trouble was experienced with smoke obscuring the driver's outlook. The aerodynamic screening at the front end, which had proved quite successful with the sharp exhaust from the poppet-valves of *Cock o' the North*, was not so effective with the very soft blast of *Earl Marischal*, which also had a double chimney and the Kylchap exhaust arrangement. A solution to the difficulty was found by adding side-plates, somewhat similar to those used on contemporary express locomotives of the Southern Railway. But the plates fitted to *Earl Marischal* proved to be a temporary measure only, because the front end was subsequently altered to correspond with that of the 'A4' 'Pacifics', to be described in the next chapter.

TABLE 25
LNER 4 PM KING'S CROSS–PETERBOROUGH
Load: 548 tons tare, 585 tons full
Engine: 2–8–2 No 2001 *Cock o' the North*

| Distance miles | | Actual min   sec | Speeds mph |
|---|---|---|---|
| 0·0 | KING'S CROSS | 0    00 | — |
| 2·6 | Finsbury Park | 6    55 | 38 |
| 5·0 | Wood Green | 10    13 | 53½ |
| 9·2 | New Barnet | 15    37 | 44 |
| 12·7 | Potters Bar | 20    26 | 44 |
| 17·7 | HATFIELD | 25    55 | 67 |
| 23·5 | *Woolmer Green* | 31    51 | 50½ |
| 28·6 | Stevenage | 37    16 | 62/55 |
| — | | sigs | 50 |
| 31·9 | HITCHIN | 40    42 | — |
| 35·7 | Three Counties | 44    31 | 66/62 |
| 41·1 | Biggleswade | 49    27 | 71½ |
| 44·1 | Sandy | 52    05 | 64½ |
| 47·5 | Tempsford | 55    05 | 69 |
| 51·7 | St Neots | 58    52 | 64½ |
| 56·0 | Offord | 62    38 | 69 |
| 58·9 | HUNTINGDON | 65    15 | 66 |
| 62·0 | *Milepost* 62 | 68    22 | 54 |
| 67·4 | *Connington* | 73    22 | 73 |
| 72·6 | Yaxley | 78    48 | — |
| — | | p.w.s. | |
| 75·0 | *Fletton Junction* | 82    58 | |
| 76·3 | PETERBOROUGH | 85    50 | |

Before this there had been other experiments with smoke-deflecting devices on the LNER, and although they are not directly connected with the 'P2' engines they can conveniently be described at this point. The serious accident to the 'Royal Scot' at Leighton Buzzard LMSR in March 1931 drew attention to the trouble experienced on certain modern types of locomotive with smoke beating down, and although the standard Gresley 'Pacifics' of the 'A1' and 'A3' classes did not generally suffer in this way, some experimental modifications were made to the 'A3's No 2747 *Coronach* and No 2751 *Humorist* which had the upper part of the smokebox cut away on a slope, after the style of the streamlined 'A4' 'Pacifics'. On these 'A3's the original circular shell was retained to form a funnel, with the idea of inducing a strong upward current of air just behind the chimney. *Humorist* had a modified version of the same device in which the smokebox shell was cut away and a trough, to produce the requisite air current, was made by fitting two inclined deflector plates to the smokebox top; this queer *ensemble* was completed by a perfectly plain stovepipe chimney.

The normal smokebox was restored some years afterwards when *Humorist* was fitted with Kylchap double blastpipe and an elongated version of the standard 'Pacific' chimney; but the soft blast resulting from this exhaust arrangement compelled a return in 1938 to the small deflector plates, though this time with a normal round-topped smokebox. The absence of any lip on the elongated stove-pipe chimney was presumably to eliminate any projection that might cause eddies and so interfere with the lifting of the exhaust steam. From the footplate the effectiveness of the large deflector plates on *Earl Marischal* was obvious; the exhaust from the chimney was lifted by the inner screening, but at the same time given a lateral deflection, and the large plates produced an upward air current that counteracted the latter effect.

When No 2002 was handed over to the running department in Scotland in the early summer of 1935, she was a superb locomotive. On the 'A1' and 'A3' 'Pacifics' there was usually a drop of about 10 psi in the pressure between the boiler and the steamchests when the regulator was fully open; but on *Earl Marischal* there was no drop at all – a striking tribute to the design of the steam passages. The riding, as I was able to observe on some footplate journeys, was easy and buoyant; indeed it was more like that of a carriage than of a locomotive. As to the performance, there was the same sensitivity to small changes in cut-off as was characteristic of the 'Pacifics'. In this respect *Earl Marischal* showed up to considerable advantage over the poppet-valve engine *Cock o' the North*, as the latter

TABLE 26  L[
Engine: 2–
Load: 479 tons [
Driver: Arbuthnot; Firen

| Distance miles | | Time min sec | | Speeds mph |
|---|---|---|---|---|
| 0·0 | ABERDEEN | 0 | 00 | — |
| 0·6 | *Ferryhill Junction* | 2 | 19 | — |
| 1·1 | *Milepost 240* | 3 | 28 | 30 |
| 3·1 | *Milepost 238* | 6 | 55 | 37½ |
| 4·8 | Cove Bay | 9 | 40 | 35½ |
| 6·1 | *Milepost 235* | 11 | 48 | 38 |
| 7·1 | *Milepost 234* | 13 | 18 | 41½ |
| 8·2 | Portlethen | 14 | 33 | — |
| 10·4 | Newtonhill | 16 | 55 | 61 |
| 11·6 | Muchalls | 18 | 05 | 61 |
| 13·6 | *Milepost 227½* | 20 | 14 | 52 |
| 16·2 | STONEHAVEN | 23 | 24 | 63† |
| 0·9 | *Milepost 224* | 2 | 46 | 28 |
| 1·9 | *Milepost 223* | 4 | 57 | 28½ |
| 2·6 | Dunnottar | 6 | 16 | 32½ |
| 2·9 | *Milepost 222* | 6 | 50 | 38 |
| 3·9 | *Milepost 221* | 8 | 23 | 39 |
| 4·7 | *Milepost 220¼* | 9 | 39 | 36 |
| 5·5 | Carmont | 10 | 43 | 47½ |
| 7·2 | Drumlithie | 12 | 50 | — |
| 11·2 | Fordoun | 16 | 43 | 64½ |
| 14·5 | Laurencekirk | 19 | 59 | 60 |
| — | *Milepost 209¼* | — | — | 57½ |
| 17·7 | Marykirk | 23 | 11 | 64 |
| 19·8 | Craigo | 25 | 11 | 67 |
| 21·9 | *Kinnaber Junction* | 27 | 50 | 15 |
| 24·5 | MONTROSE | 32 | 05 | — |
| 0·7 | *Milepost 30* | 2 | 03 | 26 |
| 1·7 | *Milepost 29* | 4 | 21 | 26½ |
| 2·1 | Usan | 5 | 15 | — |
| 2·7 | *Milepost 28* | 6 | 31 | 30½ |
| 3·7 | *Milepost 27* | 8 | 26 | 32 |
| 4·9 | Lunan Bay | 10 | 14 | — |
| 7·5 | Inverkeilor | 12 | 56 | 63½ |
| 10·7 | Letham Grange | 16 | 20 | 54½ |
| — | | — | — | 62 |
| 13·1 | *St Vigeans Junction* | 19 | 00 | 20 |
| 13·7 | ARBROATH | 20 | 43 | — |

* 65 per cent for short distance from sta[

| Regulator opening | Cut-off per cent | Pressure, psi | |
|---|---|---|---|
| | | Boiler | Steam-Chest |
| Full | 65 | 190 | 190 |
| Full | 38 | — | — |
| Full | 25 | 220 | 220 |
| Full | 25 | — | — |
| Full | 25 | 220 | 220 |
| Full | 25 | — | — |
| Full | 20 | 215 | 215 |
| 1/2 | 18 | 215 | 170 |
| 3/8 | 18 | 215 | 160 |
| 3/4 | 22 | 215 | 190 |
| 1/16 | 18 | 215 | 70 |
| — | — | — | — |
| Full | 32* | 195 | 195 |
| Full | 32 | — | — |
| Full | 25 | 220 | 220 |
| Full | 25 | — | — |
| Full | 25 | — | — |
| Full | 25 | 215 | 215 |
| 5/8 | 25 | 220 | 200 |
| 1/2 | 18 | 220 | 80 |
| 3/8 | 22 | 190 | 150 |
| 5/8 | 25 | 215 | 200 |
| 1/4 | 18 | — | 80 |
| — | — | — | — |
| 5/8 | 20 | 190 | 180 |
| — | — | — | — |
| — | — | — | — |
| Full | 32* | 215 | 215 |
| Full | 32 | — | — |
| Full | 27 | — | — |
| Full | 27 | 200 | 200 |
| Full | 27 | — | — |
| 1/2 | 18 | 210 | 80 |
| 1/2 | 22 | 200 | 175 |
| 3/4 | 18 | — | — |
| 1/4 | 18 | 200 | 80 |
| 1/16 | 18 | — | — |
| — | — | — | — |

Maximum before stop.

TABLE 27   L:
Load: 493 tons t
Engine: 2-
Driver: Shedden; Firema

| Distance miles | | Schedule min | Actual | |
|---|---|---|---|---|
| | | | min | sec |
| 0·0 | DUNDEE | 0 | 0 | 00 |
| 0·8 | Esplanade | — | 3 | 02 |
| — | Top of 1 in 114 | — | — | |
| 2·7 | *Tay Bridge South Junction* | 8 | 7 | 38 |
| 4·6 | St Fort | — | 10 | 32 |
| 8·3 | LEUCHARS JUNCTION* | 14 | 14 | 22 |
| 11·6 | Dairsie | — | 18 | 06 |
| 14·6 | Cupar* | — | 21 | 10 |
| 16·9 | Springfield | — | 23 | 47 |
| 20·1 | LADYBANK JUNCTION* | 29 | 27 | 25 |
| 21·0 | Kingskettle | — | 28 | 21 |
| 23·1 | Falkland Road | — | 31 | 02 |
| 24·3 | *Lochmuir* | — | 33 | 37 |
| 25·9 | Markinch Junction | — | 36 | 02 |
| — | *Pitfall** | | p.w.s. | |
| 28·5 | THORNTON JUNCTION | 41 | 40 | 42 |
| 29·6 | *Randolph Siding* | — | 42 | 40 |
| 31·2 | Dysart | — | 45 | 05 |
| 31·9 | Sinclairtown | — | 45 | 48 |
| 33·3 | KIRKCALDY | — | 47 | 07 |
| 34·4 | *Invertiel Junction* | — | 48 | 10 |
| 36·5 | Kinghorn* | — | 50 | 27 |
| 39·1 | BURNTISLAND* | 55 | 54 | 37 |
| 41·8 | Aberdour | — | 58 | 59 |
| 43·1 | *Dalgetty Box* | — | 61 | 29 |
| 46·2 | Inverkeithing | 65 | 65 | 37 |
| 47·9 | North Queensferry | — | 69 | 52 |
| 49·7 | Dalmeny | 73 | 73 | 24 |
| 52·7 | Turnhouse | — | 76 | 40 |
| 55·8 | *Saughton Junction* | — | 79 | 40 |
| 58·0 | Haymarket | 82 | 81 | 47 |
| 59·2 | EDINBURGH (Waverley) | 85 | 84 | 57 |

* Service sla

30 tons full
No 2001, *Cock o' the North*
Hardisty (Haymarket shed)

| Speeds mph | Regulator opening | Cut-off per cent | Pressure, psi | |
|---|---|---|---|---|
| | | | Boiler | Steam-Chest |
| — | 3/5 | 65 | 190 | 180 |
| 19½ | 3/4 | 25 | 200 | 200 |
| — | 3/4 | 18 | — | — |
| 33 | 1/2 | 18 | 200 | 200 |
| 61 | 3/5 | 18 | 195 | 180 |
| 55 | Shut | — | — | Nil |
| 49 | 3/5 | 18 | 200 | 190 |
| 56 | 3/5 | 18 | — | — |
| 60 | Shut | — | — | Nil |
| 55 | 3/5 | 18 | 195 | 180 |
| 47½ | 3/5 | 18 | — | — |
| 57 | Shut | — | — | Nil |
| 51 | 3/5 | 18 | 190 | 180 |
| 60 | 3/5 | 18 | — | — |
| 33 | 3/4 | 18 | 195 | 190 |
| 25½ | Shut | — | — | Nil |
| 52 | Shut | — | — | Nil |
| 19 | Shut | — | — | Nil |
| — | 3/4 | 25 | 210 | 205 |
| 33 | 3/4 | 18 | — | — |
| 55 | Shut | — | — | Nil |
| 61 | Shut | — | — | Nil |
| 65 | Shut | — | — | Nil |
| 58½ | Shut | — | — | Nil |
| 25 | Shut | — | — | Nil |
| 46 | Shut | — | — | Nil |
| 25 | 3/4 | 35 | 205 | 200 |
| 45 | 3/4 | 18 | — | — |
| 33 | 3/4 | 25 | 201 | 207 |
| 31 | Shut | 18 | — | Nil |
| 24 | 3/4 | 25 | — | — |
| 19 | 3/4 | 35 | 210 | 205 |
| 42 | 3/4 | 18 | — | — |
| 68 | 3/4 | 18 | — | — |
| 59 | 3/4 | 18 | — | — |
| 64 | 3/4 | 18 | 160 | 150 |
| — | Shut | — | — | Nil |
| — | — | — | — | — |

was running in 1935; at that time the RC valve arrangements had been changed, and as with the RC poppet-valve gear fitted to the 'Hunt' class 4-4-os the 2-8-2 then had a fixed cut-off corresponding to each cam, and no intermediate positions could be used. Footplate observations on *Cock o' the North* showed that the driver worked at three positions, 18, 25, and 35 per cent, changes of 7 and 10 per cent compared with the adjustments of 2 or 3 per cent at a time that produced such excellent results on *Earl Marischal*. It seemed a pity that the gear originally fitted to No 2001, which was capable of finer adjustment of cut-off, was not retained on *Cock o' the North*; for as things were in 1935 the poppet-valve engine was certainly not operating on equal terms with its piston-valve rival. In these circumstances the subsequent conversion of No 2001 to piston-valves was practically inevitable.

During the summer of 1935, with two 'P2' engines available, the diagrams were arranged so that No 2001 made two return trips from Edinburgh to Dundee, and that No 2002 made corresponding trips from Dundee to Aberdeen. There were then six express trains in each direction between Edinburgh and Aberdeen, and from that time onwards two in each direction could be worked by 'P2's. It worked out that all the heaviest trains except one were 2-8-2 hauled, the exception being the down 'Aberdonian', leaving Edinburgh at 4.15 AM. The up 'Aberdonian' leaving Aberdeen at 7.35 PM was 'P2' hauled throughout, with 2001 relieving 2002 at Dundee. The work of both these engines was very fine, as I had opportunity to observe from the footplate. Loads up to 600 tons were tackled with complete success, and with such performance in view authorization was given for the construction of four more, in 1936, to provide enough 'P2's to handle the entire service north of Edinburgh, except, of course, for extras and excursions. These four engines were built new with streamlined front ends exactly corresponding to the 'A4' 'Pacific' engines of 1935. The four new engines were:

| 2003 | *Lord President* | 2005 | *Thane of Fife* |
| 2004 | *Mons Meg* | 2006 | *Wolf of Badenoch* |

Engine No 2005 took her name from a North British 'Atlantic', No 9871, scrapped about that time, but the other three names were new.

My footplate runs with Nos 2001 and 2002 in 1935 gave extremely good results, and very full details are set out in the tables on pages 124-7 of a run with the 10.20 AM up from Aberdeen, and with No 2001 on the up 'Aberdonian' at night. Each engine was double-manned in its day's work, and I had the good fortune to travel with both crews regularly allocated to No 2002. There was a considerable difference between them. The driver on the early train worked in the orthodox Gresley manner, with full regulator for all the hard work, and cut-off adjusted to suit. The man on the late turn, using no more than a partly opened regulator and longer cut-offs, definitely burned more coal, and the performance lacked something of the snap and exhilaration that No 2002 provided when she was handled in the textbook manner. The run tabulated with No 2002 was that on the morning train, when a really magnificent performance was put up. I was travelling elsewhere in the following summers, and saw nothing of the work of the later 'P2's. They did equally good work.

When the war came, and the loads grew still heavier, the 'P2's were worth their weight in gold, though with gradually diminishing standards of maintenance they fell a prey to the troubles inherent in the Gresley conjugated valve gear. They were, of course, no worse than any other Gresley three-cylinder type; but when Edward Thompson was on the war-path, as told in Chapter Eleven, this small class of only six locomotives provided a perfect 'guinea-pig' for his trials of the new cylinder, valve, and wheel arrangements. By removing the leading pair of coupled wheels he could rebuild the engines so easily. It was nevertheless a great pity that these magnificent engines were so treated, for in subsequent years there was never anything to touch them on the Aberdeen road.

# CHAPTER ELEVEN

## THE STREAMLINE AGE

The year 1935 was memorable in Gresley's career. It began with the brilliant performances of 'A3' 'Pacific' No 2750 *Papyrus*, on the King's Cross–Newcastle test runs in March; and mid-summer saw the 2–8–2 express engines handling the heaviest loads with comparative ease on the Edinburgh–Aberdeen route. Yet few, if any, of the most ardent LNER enthusiasts were prepared for the events of late September 1935. The idea of a high-speed service between London and Newcastle was prompted by the striking success of the high-speed diesel-electric railcars introduced in 1933 on the Union Pacific and Burlington Railroads in the USA, and on the German State Railways. Gresley was quick to realize the importance of these innovations, and personal experience of the running of the 'Flying Hamburger' so impressed him that the question of purchasing a similar train for experimental purposes on the LNER was seriously considered.

In preparing, in the most detailed manner, a design for service in England the makers of the German railcar were not able to promise a higher average speed than 63 mph between London and Newcastle, against the 77·4 mph of the 'Flying Hamburger' between Berlin and Hamburg; the difference was due to the heavier gradients and speed restrictions of the LNER main line. Furthermore the passenger accommodation was cramped and hardly likely to attract passengers used to the spacious comfort of standard East Coast rolling stock. In his presidential address to the Institution of Mechanical Engineers in 1936 Gresley records how, at this stage in the investigation, Sir Ralph Wedgwood, then chief general manager of the LNER, suggested that with an ordinary 'Pacific' engine faster overall speeds could be maintained with a train of much greater weight, capacity, and comfort. The *Papyrus* trial proved this contention to be correct, and that it might even have been possible to work a four-hour service between King's Cross and Newcastle by 'A3' engines, with a load of 200–220 tons.

At that time, however, the principle of streamlining, to reduce air resistance at high speed, was being applied to locomotives, and it seemed probable that some saving in power might be effected by modifying the form of the standard 'Pacifics' at the front end. Experiments were conducted at the National Physical Laboratory to determine a form that would both reduce air resistance and lift the exhaust steam effectively at high speed. The investigation, which was made with scale models, gave the following results:

HORSEPOWER SAVED BY STREAMLINING

| Speed | | 60 | 70 | 80 | 90 |
|---|---|---|---|---|---|
| Horsepower required to overcome head-on air resistance | { 'A3' 4–6–2 | 97·21 | 154·26 | 230·51 | 328·49 |
| | Streamlined } 4–6–2 | 56·39 | 89·41 | 133·61 | 190·40 |
| Horsepower saved by streamlining | | 40·82 | 64·85 | 96·90 | 138·09 |

These results indicated a probable saving in power output of about 10 per cent in the working of the new service, a forecast that was confirmed in practice. The now familiar wedge-shaped form also proved most successful in smoke deflection; in this design an important feature was the slight depression immediately behind the chimney, without which it was found that, in a side wind, the eddy currents on the leeward side of the engine caused quite serious obscuring of the driver's outlook.

Furthermore, the publicity value of streamlining was an important point in attracting business to a new train service on which extra fares were to be charged for the privilege of higher speed. 'Streamline' was at that time a popular catchword, and its apparent sales value was reflected in the singular promiscuity with which it was applied, to toothbrushes, for example, domestic kettles, and even signal-boxes! Into such a world emerged Gresley's new 'Pacific' No 2509 *Silver Link*. This apparition upset all one's well-established notions of what a locomotive, or at any rate a British locomotive, should look like; she provided a feast for the sensation-mongers and a butt for the cynics who averred that the streamlining was merely a rather feeble pandering to popular taste. Among connoisseurs of the graceful in locomotive lines, many were genuinely appalled at this new development; and although the majority of railway enthusiasts have since become reconciled their first reaction is still a vivid memory. In brief, the engine created a profound sensation.

The timing of the 'Silver Jubilee' required speeds of 70 to 75 mph to be sustained up 1 in 200 banks, with a gross load of 235 tons behind the tender; on the level the schedule demanded sustained speed of 85 to 90 mph. The locomotives would be working their hardest at 75 mph and over, in striking contrast to normal conditions on the heavy East Coast trains; and to provide for this some important changes from the 'A3's were made in the design. The exhaust was made freer, by use of 9-in diameter piston-valves, against the previous 8 ins, and the pressure-drop between boiler and steam-chest was virtually eliminated by streamlined passages, as well as by the increased fluidity of the steam itself, due to the higher boiler pressure of 250 psi and a higher degree of superheat. The softer blast resulting from the freer exhaust would have created less draught in the firebox had the 'A3' boiler been retained, with, possibly, an adverse effect upon the steaming; so in the 'A4's the boiler barrel was shortened from 19 ft to 18 ft, and the consequent reduction in tube heating surface was compensated for by the use of a combustion chamber. The cylinders of the 'A4's were slightly smaller, 18½-in diameter against 19 ins.

In the haulage of the 'Silver Jubilee' the 'A4's leapt into immediate fame. The trial run of September 27th, 1935, was only part of *Silver Link*'s amazing début; then, although only three weeks out of the shops, she twice attained 112½ mph, and sustained an average of 100 mph for 43 miles on end. A significant feature of the run was the average of 108·7 mph over the 10·6 miles from Biggleswade to St Neots, a stretch that has as much adverse as favourable grading. Three days after this brilliant display she went into regular working on the 'Silver Jubilee', and duly performed the double journey, 536½ miles daily, for the first fortnight of the service. That this arduous duty was accomplished without any mechanical troubles was indeed a great tribute to design and workmanship. The Jubilee year, which had witnessed such a succession of triumphs for his locomotives, was fittingly crowned by the honour of knighthood conferred on Gresley himself, in recognition of his work – *The Times* happily expressing it – 'as engineer and speeder-up to the LNER'.

Four streamlined 'Pacifics' were built for the 'Silver Jubilee' service, and three were stationed at King's Cross. The fourth, No 2511 *Silver King*, was spare engine and allocated to Gateshead shed; there she stood pilot for the up 'Jubilee', afterwards usually operating the long double-manned Newcastle–Edinburgh–York–Newcastle turn beginning with the 11.10 AM non-stop express to Edinburgh. Although from the inception of the service it was clear that the 'A4' 'Pacifics' were masters of their work, it was nearly a year later that the first technical details of their running were published. With the dynamometer car added to the train, increasing the tare load to 254 tons, trial runs were made between Newcastle and King's Cross and Newcastle and Edinburgh. On the first run, on August 27th, 1936, No 2512 *Silver Fox* fractionally improved upon the maximum speed record of the previous September by attaining 113 mph in the descent of the Stoke bank. On the northbound trip on the same day No 2509 *Silver Link* made some outstanding running up the same incline; the 15·3 miles from Tallington to Stoke summit were covered at an average speed of 82·7 mph with the locomotive working in 18 per cent cut-off and a wide-open regulator. Both runs were made in ordinary service, and the speed of 113 mph attained by *Silver Fox* has remained the British record by a considerable margin, for a train carrying fare-paying passengers. The work of No 2511 *Silver King* between Newcastle and Edinburgh included a most exceptional ascent of the Cockburnspath bank, in which 68 mph was sustained up the 1 in 96 gradient. This required a

| Distance miles | | Schedule min | Actual min | sec |
|---|---|---|---|---|
| 0·0 | GRANTHAM | 0 | 0 | 00 |
| 2·3 | *Milepost* 107¾ | — | 4 | 24 |
| 4·2 | Barkston | — | 6 | 31 |
| 6·0 | Hougham | — | 8 | 05 |
| 9·9 | Claypole | — | 11 | 08 |
| 14·6 | NEWARK | 15 | 14 | 47 |
| | | | | eased ove |
| 17·4 | *Bathley Lane* | — | 17 | 01 |
| 20·9 | Carlton | — | 19 | 46 |
| 21·9 | Crow Park | — | 20 | 35 |
| 26·4 | Tuxford | — | 24 | 39 |
| 28·2 | *Markham* | — | 26 | 22 |
| 30·0 | Gamston | — | 28 | 00 |
| 32·0 | *Grove Road* | — | | — |
| 33·1 | RETFORD | 32½ | 30 | 44 |
| 34·1 | *Canal* | — | | — |
| 36·2 | Sutton | — | 34 | 17 |
| 38·4 | Ranskill | — | 36 | 18 |
| 40·3 | Scrooby | — | 37 | 52 |
| 42·2 | Bawtry | — | 39 | 27 |
| 44·0 | *Milepost* 149½ | — | 41 | 04 |
| 45·8 | Rossington | — | 42 | 37 |
| 47·7 | *Black Carr Junction* | — | 44 | 07 |
| 50·5 / 0·0 } | DONCASTER | { 50 / 0 | 48 / 0 | 47 / 00 |
| 2·1 | Arksey | — | 4 | 28 |
| 4·2 | *Shaftholme Junction* | — | 6 | 46 |
| 7·0 | Moss | — | 9 | 22 |
| 10·0 | Balne | — | 11 | 53 |
| 11·3 | Heck | — | 12 | 56 |
| 13·8 | *Templehirst* | — | 15 | 01 |
| 17·0 | *Brayton Junction* | — | 17 | 36 |
| | | | | sigs |
| 18·4 | SELBY | 20 | 20 | 10 |
| 19·1 | *Barlby Junction* | — | 21 | 26 |
| 25·1 | Escrick | — | 27 | 53 |
| 28·0 | Naburn | — | 30 | 25 |
| 30·2 | *Chaloners Whin Junction* | — | 32 | 26 |
| | | | | sigs |
| 32·2 | YORK | 37 | 36 | 43 |

* Service slack.   † Advanced to 20 per cent

io 4498 *Sir Nigel Gresley*
re, 510 tons full
earce (King's Cross shed)

| Speeds mph | Cut-off per cent | Pressure, psi | |
|---|---|---|---|
| | | Boiler | Steam-Chest |
| — | 65 | 215 | 215 |
| — | 15 | 225 | 225 |
| 62 | — | — | — |
| 72 | 15 | 220 | 185 |
| 82/74 | — | — | — |
| 79 | — | shut off steam | |
| 72 | 15 | 215 | 215 |
| 77½ | 15 | — | — |
| — | 20† | — | — |
| 62 | 25 | — | — |
| 64 | 15 | 225 | 225 |
| — | 15 | 225 | 225 |
| 82 | — | shut off steam | |
| 47* | 25 | 220 | 220 |
| — | 15 | 220 | 220 |
| 64 | 15 | — | — |
| 66½ | 15 | — | — |
| 75 | 15 | 210 | 210 |
| 69 | 20 | 210 | 210 |
| 67 | 15 | — | — |
| 77½ | 15 | — | — |
| — | — | — | — |
| — | — | — | — |
| — | 60 | 235 | 235 |
| — | 18 | 235 | 235 |
| 62½ | 15 | — | — |
| 69½ | — | — | — |
| 75 | — | 230 | 230 |
| 71½ | — | — | — |
| 74½ | — | 235 | 235 |
| 79 | — | — | — |
| 20 | — | — | — |
| — | 35 | 235 | 235 |
| — | 15 | — | — |
| 66 | — | 230 | 230 |
| 70½ | — | — | — |
| — | — | — | — |
| — | — | — | — |
| — | — | — | — |

troughs

2 miles beyond Crow Park station.

drawbar hp output of 1,460 whereas Gresley, in his presidential address to the Institution of Mechanical Engineers, stated that the average dhp required to work the 'Silver Jubilee' between King's Cross and Newcastle was no more than 620; in the Cockburnspath ascent, however, the pull of gravity on the locomotive and tender had to be overcome.

Until January 1937 there were only four engines of the 'A4' class, but in that month No 4482 *Golden Eagle* was turned out, the first of a new series, built for the 'Coronation' express and general use on the fastest ordinary trains. Encouraged by the success of the 'Silver Jubilee', the LNER provided even more lavish passenger accommodation on the six-hour London–Edinburgh flyer, bring the tare weight up to 312 tons, against the previous 220 tons; this entailed even harder work, though it was coal consumption rather than actual locomotive capacity that tended to govern performance on that train. It seems a little strange that on this hardest of all East Coast turns the engines worked through from London to Edinburgh. With a normal consumption of about 3 lb of coal per dhp-hour, roughly $7\frac{1}{2}$ tons was burnt on that journey, and it did not need much in the way of cross winds or other adverse conditions to increase consumption to something very near the total capacity of the tenders – 9 tons; indeed, on one occasion the up 'Coronation' ran out of coal by Hitchin. Changing engines at Newcastle would have made all the difference. It was on the up 'Coronation' that I recorded one of the most astonishing pieces of high-speed running that has ever been made with a British passenger train, under ordinary, as against test conditions. That most famous of NE area drivers, Walker, of Gateshead, was making his first trip on the train, and owing to over-emphasizing some of the slacks we passed Grantham just over a minute late. With the engine working – so Walker told me afterwards – in 15 per cent cut-off Stoke summit was breasted at $64\frac{1}{2}$ mph; no change was subsequently made, and the engine accelerated to 106 mph, before Essendine. What made this descent so very exceptional, however, was the way in which the speed was sustained afterwards; for the average speed from Essendine to Helpston Box was no less than 104·8 mph. About half this distance of 6·7 miles is downhill at 1 in 264 and 1 in 440, but between Tallington and Helpston, where we continued running at 105–106 mph, the gradient changes between 1 in 528 and dead level. The engine was 4491 *Commonwealth of Australia* and the gross load 325 tons.

TABLE 29
LNER KING'S CROSS–YORK
'The Coronation'
Load: 312 tons tare, 325 tons full
Engine: class 'A4' 4–6–2 No 4490 *Empire of India*

| Distance miles | | Sch. min | Actual min sec | | Speeds mph |
|---|---|---|---|---|---|
| 0·0 | KING'S CROSS | 0 | 0 | 00 | — |
| 2·6 | Finsbury Park | | 5 | 23 | — |
| 5·0 | Wood Green | | 8 | 06 | 65 |
| 12·7 | Potters Bar | | 15 | 59 | 55 |
| 17·7 | Hatfield | 18½ | 20 | 06 | 86½ |
| 23·5 | *Woolmer Green* | | 24 | 28 | 70½ |
| 31·9 | HITCHIN | 29½ | 31 | 18 | 94/88 |
| 41·1 | Biggleswade | | 37 | 23 | 92 |
| 51·7 | St Neots | | 45 | 02 | 74 |
| 56·0 | Offord | | 48 | 29 | 77/72 |
| 58·9 | HUNTINGDON | 48½ | 50 | 43 | 77½ |
| 62·0 | *Milepost 62* | | 53 | 14 | 73½ |
| 67·4 | *Connington* | | 57 | 08 | 95 |
| 76·4 | PETERBOROUGH | 63½ | 64 | 21 | 15* |
| 84·8 | Tallington | | 72 | 29 | 86 |
| 88·6 | Essendine | | 75 | 11 | 90 |
| 97·1 | Corby | | 81 | 25 | 76/80½ |
| 100·1 | *Stoke Box* | | 83 | 48 | 74 |
| 105·5 | GRANTHAM | 87½ | 87 | 52 | 82/74* |
| 120·1 | NEWARK | 99½ | 98 | 12 | 90/62* |
| 131·9 | Tuxford | | 107 | 29 | 75 |
| 138·6 | RETFORD | 114½ | 112 | 35 | 84/62 |
| 145·8 | Scrooby | | 118 | 32 | 82 |
| 149·5 | *Milepost 149½* | | 121 | 44 | 67 |
| 156·0 | DONCASTER | 128½ | 127 | 43 | 77/59* |
| 160·2 | *Shaftholme Junction* | | 131 | 14 | 76½ |
| 173·0 | *Brayton Junction* | | 140 | 24 | 88 |
| — | | | sigs | | 25 |
| 174·4 | SELBY | 144 | 142 | 43 | — |
| 184·0 | Naburn | | 151 | 42 | 82 |
| 188·2 | YORK | 157 | 157 | 07 | |

* Speed restrictions.

As an example of the work of the 'A4's in ordinary East Coast service I have tabulated very full details of a footplate journey on No 4498 *Sir Nigel Gresley* on the 5.45 PM from King's Cross, as between Grantham and York. On this occasion a maximum of 79 mph was attained on level track with the engine working in 15 per cent cut-off. This performance, involving an output of 1,760 dhp, was an impressive exposition of the capabilities of these engines (see pages 134–5).

Four engines of the class were when new fitted with double chimneys and the Kylchap exhaust arrangements, and several of the finest performances recorded in pre-war days with Gresley 'Pacifics' were made by members of this quartet. No 4468 *Mallard* on July 3rd, 1938, secured for Britain the world's record speed with steam by attaining 126 mph, on a test run down Stoke bank. No 4901 *Capercaillie*, working a colossal wartime load of 665 tons tare and 730 tons gross, averaged 75·9 mph over the 25 miles from Otterington to Poppleton Junction; this achievement over an almost level road must have involved a continuous output of about 2,100 dhp. On a footplate journey with No 4902 *Seagull* on the 1.20 PM down 'Scotsman', we were running past Hitchin in 16 per cent cut-off with the regulator partly closed and yet were accelerating at such a rate as to increase the speed from 84 to 95 mph in three miles; indeed, with the controls unchanged it is possible that we might have gone over the hundred at Arlesey, 480-ton load notwithstanding, had not the driver almost closed his regulator just below Cadwell in order to keep to the 90-mph limit.

The down 'Coronation', booked to cover the 188·2 miles from King's Cross to York in 157 minutes start to stop, was the fastest train in the British Commonwealth, and to show the kind of running that was needed to keep time I have tabulated a run with engine No 4490 *Empire of India*. So far as the reverse direction of running is concerned I have tabulated the section from Stoke tunnel to Peterborough, when engine No 4491 attained a maximum speed of 106 mph (see opposite).

So far as heavy load pulling was concerned an outstanding run was made on June 30th, 1938, at the inauguration of the new air-conditioned stock for the 'Flying Scotsman'. I was favoured with an invitation for this memorable run, made as far as Stevenage in six-wheeled ECJS coaches of 1888, hauled by the Stirling eight-footer No 1. Then at Stevenage we changed into the new train, headed by the 'A4' No 4498 *Sir*

TABLE 30
LNER THE UP 'CORONATION'
GRANTHAM–PETERBOROUGH
Load: 312 tons tare, 325 tons full
Engine: 4–6–2 No 4491 *Commonwealth of Australia*

| Distance miles* | | Sch. min | Actual min sec | | Speeds mph |
|---|---|---|---|---|---|
| 162·8 | GRANTHAM | 150½ | 151 | 53† | 69 |
| 168·2 | *Stoke Box* | | 156 | 48 | 64½ |
| 171·2 | Corby | | 159 | 14 | 85 |
| 176·1 | Little Bytham | | 162 | 25 | 98 |
| — | | | | | 106 |
| 179·7 | Essendine | | 164 | 30 | 104 |
| 183·5 | Tallington | | 166 | 40 | 106 |
| — | | | | | 104 |
| 186·4 | *Helpston* | | 168 | 20 | 106 |
| 188·8 | *Werrington Junction* | | 169 | 47 | |
| 191·9 | PETERBOROUGH | 174 | 172 | 45† | |

* From start at Newcastle. † Passing times in each case.

Average speeds:
Corby–Werrington 17·6 miles: 100·1 mph
Little Bytham–Helpston 10·3 miles: 104·5 mph

*Nigel Gresley.* The accompanying log gives details of the magnificent run that followed. The part I found so impressive was the very high speed maintained with this 500-ton load after we had got down to virtually level track after Biggleswade.

The introduction of the new air-conditioned stock on the 'Flying Scotsman' in 1938, and the establishment of a *minimum* tare load, with 14 coaches, of 503 tons, led certain observers to comment that such a tonnage would be beyond the capacity of the 'A4' engines as an all-weather figure during the winter months. This did not prove to be the case, and during the winter of 1938–9 which included a good deal of severe weather the 'Flying Scotsman' had a fine record of punctuality. The 'classic of classics' in the way of heavy-load haulage by the 'A4' engines in pre-war years occurred one morning in September 1938 when the down 'Scotsman' had three extra coaches added

TABLE 31
LNER STEVENAGE–GRANTHAM
Demonstration run: June 30th, 1938
Load: 14 coaches (air conditioned), 503 tons tare, 510 tons full
Engine: 4–6–2 No 4498 *Sir Nigel Gresley*

| Distance miles | | Actual min sec | | Speeds mph |
|---|---|---|---|---|
| 0·0 | Stevenage | 0 | 00 | — |
| 3·3 | HITCHIN | 5 | 21 | 62½ |
| 7·1 | Three Counties | 8 | 24 | 83½ |
| 10·0 | *Langford Bridge* | 10 | 34 | 79½ |
| 12·5 | Biggleswade | 12 | 20 | 90 |
| 15·5 | Sandy | 14 | 22 | 86 |
| 18·9 | Tempsford | 16 | 43 | 88 |
| 23·1 | St Neots | 19 | 45 | 80½ |
| 27·4 | Offord | 23 | 07 | 71½* |
| 30·3 | HUNTINGDON | 25 | 37 | 69 |
| 33·4 | *Milepost* 62 | 28 | 28 | 62½ |
| 38·8 | *Connington* | 32 | 45 | 90 |
| 44·0 | Yaxley | 36 | 28 | 75 |
| 47·8 | PETERBOROUGH | 40 | 38 | 15* |
| 50·9 | *Werrington Junction* | 45 | 25 | 60 |
| 56·2 | Tallington | 50 | 35 | 64½ |
| 60·0 | Essendine | 54 | 15 | 60 |
| 63·6 | Little Bytham | 57 | 51 | 60 |
| 68·5 | Corby | 63 | 08 | 53/57 |
| 71·5 | *Stoke Box* | 66 | 28 | 53 |
| 73·4 | Great Ponton | 68 | 23 | 68½ |
| 76·9 | GRANTHAM | 72 | 23 | |

* Speed restrictions.
Average speed: Three Counties–Yaxley 36·9 miles:
78·8 mph

to the standard fourteen-coach air-conditioned formation, making a somewhat staggering tare load of 593 tons. The engine, No 4490 *Empire of India*, was in its original condition, with single blastpipe, and it was manned by a Gateshead crew, Driver Dalrymple and Fireman Armstrong. In assessing the merit of what transpired it must be remembered that the air-conditioned stock required extra electrical energy to be generated for the forced draught ventilation, and this was reckoned as equal to the haulage of another coach, as compared with the former Scottish express stock.

The log of this remarkable performance is tabulated overleaf. It was not surprising that a little time was dropped on the heavy initial gradients out of King's Cross. These had to be tackled before the engine had warmed up. Later, the long and equally steep ascent to Stoke summit was cleared at 48 mph, yet in the early stages a speed of 39 to 40 mph was the sustained minimum up the 1 in 200 to Potters Bar. But it was soon evident that no half-hearted attempt was being made to keep time. This huge train was worked up to 91 mph at Arlesey, and with such remarkable minimum speeds as 72 mph at St Neots and 59 mph at milepost 62, the fast schedule allowance to Peterborough was maintained. 'Even time' from the start was achieved soon after Abbots Ripton. The passage through Peterborough was followed by magnificent hill-climbing, with the 20·6 miles from Werrington Junction to the summit box covered in 20 minutes 54 seconds. So Grantham was reached a minute early, after a late start of 2 minutes from King's Cross.

The second stage of the 'Flying Scotsman's' journey was then timed very sharply, with only 83 minutes allowed for the 82·7 miles from Grantham to York. A notable feature of the run was the scrupulous care with which the driver observed the various speed restrictions, such as the 60 mph over Newark troughs, 55 mph through Retford, and 60 at Doncaster. Had he run harder at any of these locations it would have made things easier afterwards. Once again 'even time' was achieved from the start, this time by Doncaster. The slight slack through this centre was followed by some superb running on the dead level that follows, rising to 72 mph after Templehirst. The only signal check of the entire journey came in the approach to Selby, and cost about a minute in running. The concluding point-to-point allowance, on this stage, was very sharp – only 16 minutes for the 13·8 miles into York. This section was commenced slowly, and followed by slight rising gradients, and

TABLE 32
## KING'S CROSS–NEWCASTLE
'The Flying Scotsman'
Load: 17 coaches, 593 tons tare, 635 tons full
Engine: class 'A4' 4–6–2 No 4490 *Empire of India*

| Distance miles | | Sch. min | Actual min sec | | Speeds mph |
|---|---|---|---|---|---|
| 0·0 | KING'S CROSS | 0 | 0 | 00 | — |
| 2·6 | Finsbury Park | | 7 | 33 | — |
| 5·0 | Wood Green | | 10 | 58 | 50 |
| 9·2 | New Barnet | | 16 | 55 | 40 |
| 12·7 | Potters Bar | | 22 | 17 | 39 |
| 17·7 | HATFIELD | 24 | 27 | 22 | 76 |
| 23·5 | *Woolmer Green* | | 32 | 17 | 65 |
| 28·6 | Stevenage | | 36 | 36 | 72 |
| 31·9 | HITCHIN | 38 | 39 | 07 | 85 |
| 37·0 | Arlesey | | 42 | 33 | 91 |
| 41·1 | Biggleswade | | 45 | 30 | 82 |
| 44·1 | Sandy | | 47 | 46 | 74 |
| 47·5 | Tempsford | | 50 | 28 | 77 |
| 51·7 | St Neots | | 53 | 55 | 72 |
| 56·0 | Offord | | 57 | 13 | 80/67* |
| 58·9 | HUNTINGDON | 59 | 59 | 48 | 70 |
| 63·5 | Abbots Ripton | | 64 | 05 | 59 |
| 69·4 | Holme | | 68 | 30 | 85 |
| 76·4 | PETERBOROUGH | 76 | 75 | 23 | 27* |
| 79·5 | *Werrington Junction* | | 80 | 09 | 58 |
| 84·8 | Tallington | | 85 | 18 | 66 |
| 88·6 | Essendine | | 88 | 50 | 62 |
| 92·2 | Little Bytham | | 92 | 17 | 60 |
| 97·1 | Corby | | 97 | 35 | 53 |
| 100·1 | *Stoke Box* | | 101 | 03 | 48 |
| 102·1 | Great Ponton | | 103 | 03 | 71 |
| 105·5 | GRANTHAM | 110 | 107 | 55 | — |
| 4·2 | Barkston | | 7 | 55 | 68 |
| 9·9 | Claypole | | 12 | 35 | 79 |
| 14·6 | NEWARK | 15 | 16 | 19 | 60* |
| 21·9 | Crow Park | | 23 | 25 | 70 |
| 28·2 | *Markham Box* | | 29 | 27 | 57 |
| 33·1 | RETFORD | 33 | 34 | 00 | 55* |
| 38·4 | Ranskill | | 39 | 13 | 69 |
| 44·0 | *Milepost 149½* | | 44 | 14 | 58½ |
| 45·8 | Rossington | | 45 | 58 | 74 |
| 50·5 | DONCASTER | 49 | 50 | 18 | 60* |
| 54·7 | *Shaftholme Junction* | 53 | 54 | 18 | 67 |
| 60·5 | Balne | | 59 | 21 | 70 |
| 64·3 | Templehirst | | 62 | 41 | 72 |

TABLE 32 (*continued*)

| Distance miles | | Sch. min | Actual min sec | Speeds mph |
|---|---|---|---|---|
| — | | | sigs | 20 |
| 68·9 | SELBY | 67 | 67 45 | — |
| 73·0 | Riccall | | 73 20 | 61 |
| 78·5 | Naburn | | 78 35 | 66 |
| 80·7 | *Chaloners Whin Junction* | | 80 40 | 57* |
| 82·7 | YORK | 83 | 84 55 | |
| 5·5 | Beningbrough | | 8 40 | 59 |
| 11·2 | Alne | 14 | 14 08 | 65 |
| 16·1 | Pilmoor | | 18 48 | 63 |
| 22·2 | THIRSK | 25 | 24 30 | 66 |
| 30·0 | NORTHALLERTON | 32½ | 31 43 | 63 |
| 33·7 | Danby Wiske | | 35 13 | 66 |
| 38·9 | *Eryholme* | 41 | 39 58 | 64 |
| 41·5 | Croft Spa | | 42 16 | 69 |
| 44·1 | DARLINGTON | 46 | 44 40 | 54* |
| 49·5 | Aycliffe | | 50 46 | 52 |
| 54·2 | Bradbury | | 56 11 | 51 |
| 57·0 | Ferryhill | 60½ | 58 56 | 66 |
| 61·9 | Croxdale | | 63 35 | — |
| 66·1 | DURHAM | 72 | 69 06 | 30* |
| 71·9 | Chester le Street | | 75 38 | 69 |
| 74·7 | Birtley | 81 | 78 00 | 73 |
| 77·6 | Low Fell | | 80 28 | — |
| 80·1 | NEWCASTLE | 90 | 86 00 | |

* Speed restrictions.

ended by the need for restraint over Chaloners Whin Junction and in the approach to York. There it was not surprising that a minute was dropped.

In the working of the King's Cross–Newcastle double-home turns it was generally considered that the stretch from York to Darlington was the one most critical to the performance of the engine. By York there had been ample time for the fire to get dirty, and the steaming to deteriorate; but on this splendid occasion Driver Dalrymple was able to begin gaining time at once, in recovery of a late start of five minutes from York. Despite the gradually rising character of the line the attainment of 'even time' from the start a third time was only narrowly missed: 44·1 miles to Darlington in 44 minutes 40 seconds. Eventually four out of the five minutes arrears were recovered and Newcastle was reached only a single minute late. This was certainly a wonderful performance that deserves the closest study in all its details.

In the autumn of 1937 yet another special express train service, the 'East Anglian', was introduced. The booked speed, however, cannot have been much to Gresley's liking, for the timings of 80 minutes for the 68·9 miles between Liverpool Street and Ipswich, and 51 minutes for the 46·2 miles on to Norwich, were no faster than some already in force – with trains, moreover, of considerably greater weight than the luxurious six-coach set, taring 219 tons, built specially for the 'East Anglian' service. A much faster schedule was at one time contemplated, but unfortunately it was found impossible, because of the density of traffic, to arrange suitable high-speed paths without providing extra track facilities. So far as locomotive power alone was concerned it should have been easily possible with 'Sandringham' class engines to do London–Ipswich in 65 minutes, and Ipswich–Norwich in 45 minutes. Nevertheless, two of the class were specially allocated to the service and streamlined after the style of the 'A4' 'Pacifics'. These two engines, originally No 2859 *Norwich City* and 2870 *Manchester City*, were renamed *East Anglian* and *City of London* respectively; the latter took the title previously borne by the ex-GCR two-cylinder 4–6–o No 5427, of the 'Sir Sam Fay' class. These two engines were painted in the standard apple-green livery, and the coaches were of the usual varnished teak.

# CHAPTER TWELVE

# PERFORMANCE OF PRE-GROUPING ENGINES 1927-39

In the late nineteen-thirties the LNER remained a line of immense locomotive variety. I have written earlier of Sir Nigel Gresley's policy of retaining pre-grouping engines in regular service, and the complete absence of any moves to flood the lines with Doncaster principles and Doncaster designs. To what extent this was a studied policy of Sir Nigel himself, and how much it was dictated by the overall financial situation of the company, it is not now possible to say. The plain fact is that the LNER did not pay a dividend on its ordinary shares for many years. We do know also that Gresley was a close personal friend of the chief general manager, Sir Ralph Wedgwood, and there is no doubt that their minds were in complete accord over locomotive building policies. The pre-grouping engines were maintained in excellent condition and continued to do good work, though when the company was engulfed in all the manifold difficulties of war conditions the average age of the LNER locomotive stock began to tell heavily against it. There were some who sought to lay the blame for this, after his death, upon Sir Nigel Gresley and his policies. Purely upon engineering grounds there is some justification for this; but to reach such a conclusion is to ignore completely the financial state of the company in the 1930s.

Whatever the reasons, however, the result was to make the LNER the most fascinating of all the grouped railways to the connoisseur of locomotives. In East Anglia the rebuilt 'B12' 4-6-0s and 'D16' 4-4-0s were doing remarkable work; in the West Riding and in North Eastern England it did not need much contriving to get runs with early Robinson 4-6-0s, North Eastern 'Atlantics', and engines like the Worsdell 'R1' class 4-4-0s (then class 'D21'). In Scotland the North British 'Atlantics' were disappearing, but 'Scotts', 'Glens', and the

Scottish version of the Great Central 'Director' class were ubiquitous. As for the large-boilered Great Northern 'Atlantics' they were doing some of the finest work of their entire careers. In this chapter therefore I have brought together a collection of running experiences with a miscellaneous collection of pre-grouping locomotives. Of these only the Great Eastern 'B12' and 'D16' classes were to any degree modified from their pre-grouping condition.

TABLE 33
WAKEFIELD–DONCASTER
5.30 PM ex Leeds

| Engine No Engine Class Load tons E/F | 6099 'B4' 313/340 | | | 6102 'B4' 343/365 | | |
|---|---|---|---|---|---|---|
| Distance miles | min | sec | mph | min | sec | mph |
| 0·0  WAKEFIELD | 0 | 00 | | 0 | 00 | |
| 1·7  Sandal | 3 | 10 | 51 | 3 | 00 | 48 |
| 4·0  Hare Park | 6 | 05 | 46 | 6 | 00 | 44½ |
| 5·5  Nostell | 8 | 05 | 44½ | 8 | 10 | 41 |
| 8·0  Hemsworth | 11 | 05 | 60 | 11 | 10 | 61 |
| 11·2  South Elmsall | 14 | 05 | 71½ | 14 | 00 | 74 |
| 13·3  Hampole | 15 | 55 | 72 | 15 | 55 | 69 |
| 15·9  Carcroft | 18 | 00 | — | 18 | 10 | 66 |
| — | sigs | | | sigs | | |
| 19·6  Marshgate Jcn | 22 | 00 | sig | 22 | 55 | sig |
| | 28 | 15 | stops | 24 | 40 | stop |
| 19·9  DONCASTER | 34 | 05 | | 28 | 00 | |

Schedule: 24 minutes.     Net time: 22½ minutes in each case.

To open the ball there are two runs on the 5.30 PM express from Leeds to King's Cross, which in the late 1920s was usually worked as far as Doncaster by a Great Central 4–6–0 of the 'Immingham' class, LNER class 'B4'. These engines when superheated had a boiler standard with the celebrated 'O4' 2–8–0s. The train was usually piloted to Wakefield by a small GNR 4–4–0, and the two runs are therefore tabulated as between Wakefield and Doncaster. The line falls steeply from the start to the crossing of the long viaduct by Sandal, and then comes a stiff climb of four miles, nearly all at 1 in 150 to a summit point half a mile south of Nostell. After that there is an almost continuous descent to Hampole, where the line is flattening out to dead level approaching Doncaster. On the first run, with engine No 6099 and a 340-ton load, we touched 51 mph over Sandal viaduct, and then cleared the Nostell bank at a minimum speed of 44½ mph. On the comparison run, with a somewhat heavier train, engine No 6102 got off the mark very smartly from Wakefield, but then fell away to 41 mph at Nostell summit.

The remarkable thing about these two runs, made at an interval of two years apart, is the very close correspondence of the running times. This correspondence was continued on the fast descent to Doncaster. At that time I was taking my passing times at stations to the nearest five seconds. Had I been working to the nearest second, as I did in later years, the coincidence of the times might have been closer still. Both engines ran freely down the bank, with maximum speeds of 72 and 74 mph, though both were badly delayed in the approach to Doncaster. Both runs were made at times of heavy traffic, when there was some congestion due to remarshalling of certain trains.

Turning now to the Great Eastern, the introduction of the new 'East Anglian' express in 1927, with two of the 'Sandringham' class engines streamlined like the 'A4' 'Pacifics' to haul it, caused considerable interest, not so much in the running of the train itself, which was an easy task with a load of no more than 230 tons, but in the comparisons it afforded with past and current running on the Great Eastern lines. At that time the '1500' class 4–6–0s in their original condition (LNER class 'B12') were still doing remarkably fine work, while the 'Claud Hamilton' 4–4–0s altered only by the addition of superheaters, were admirably maintaining the wonderful reputation they earned on their first introduction some thirty years earlier. The rebuilds of both types, 'B12/3' and 'D16/3' were outstanding engines. As in more recent times some of the fastest running was made between Ipswich and Norwich, and the following runs are taken from a large collection made by Mr K. Braine Hartnell.

This line is an ideal racing ground. There are some sharp rises and falls, but except for the 2 miles of 1 in 131 constituting Haughley bank, and against down trains, the majority of the gradients can be rushed. There is a very gradual rise out of Ipswich as far as Stowmarket; then comes Haughley bank, and then a series of sweeping ups and downs that can be taken at top speed. There are tabulated first three runs on trains making an intermediate stop at Stowmarket. The first of these, with a 'Claud Hamilton' rebuilt as 'D16/3', was a brilliant affair, and included some very fast running typical of these

TABLE 34

IPSWICH–NORWICH

| Engine No | 8808 | | 8870 | | 8556 | |
|---|---|---|---|---|---|---|
| Engine type | 4-4-0 | | 4-4-0 | | 4-6-0 | |
| Engine class | 'D16/3'* | | 'D15' | | 'B12/3' | |
| Load tons E/F | 260/280 | | 293/310 | | 431/460 | |
| Distance miles | | | | | | |
| | min | sec | min | sec | min | sec |
| 0·0　IPSWICH | 0 | 00 | 0 | 00 | 0 | 00 |
| 4·9　Claydon | 7 | 25 | 7 | 45 | 7 | 40 |
| 11·9　STOWMARKET | 15 | 10 | 15 | 20 | 15 | 00 |
| 2·3　Haughley | 4 | 30 | 4 | 35 | 5 | 00 |
| 6·0　Finningham | 9 | 20 | 9 | 37 | 10 | 30 |
| 14·4　DISS | 16 | 23 | 17 | 02 | 17 | 50 |
| 19·9　Tivetshall | 21 | 08 | 22 | 00 | 22 | 55 |
| 26·1　Flordon | 26 | 01 | 27 | 14 | 27 | 58 |
| 29·1　Swainsthorpe | 28 | 20 | 29 | 46 | 30 | 30 |
| 31·4　Milepost 112 | 30 | 05 | 31 | 35 | 32 | 20 |
| 34·4　NORWICH | 34 | 37 | 36 | 00 | 37 | 10 |
| Speeds | mph | | mph | | mph | |
| Before Stowmarket | 63 | | 63 | | 61 | |
| Haughley bank | 40 | | 39 | | 33 | |
| Diss | 83 | | 82 | | 81 | |
| Tivetshall | 65 | | 61 | | 56 | |
| Flordon | 84 | | 79 | | 82 | |
| Swainsthorpe | 75 | | 66 | | 66 | |
| Milepost 112 | 82 | | 78 | | 79 | |

* With piston valves.

Great Eastern engines fitted with Gresley boilers, and long-travel valves. It will be seen from the table that three independent maximum speeds of over 80 mph were attained.

The next run was with an original 'Claud' modified only by superheating, and was another grand effort, with a 310-ton train. The opening run to Stowmarket was little slower than that of the fully rebuilt engine, and then over the racing stretches this old engine, still with its original valve gear, produced successive maximum speeds of 82, 79 and 78 mph. Then, to conclude the table, there is the remarkable performance of the rebuilt 'B12/3' 4-6-0 No 8556, with a load of no less than 460 tons. To Stowmarket this heavily-loaded engine made the fastest time of all. On Haughley bank somewhat naturally the uphill speeds were below those of the 4-4-0s, with an attained maximum before the summit of 33 mph against 40 and 39 mph on the two preceding trips. But once past Finningham the driver got No 8556 going in tremendous style, and his three successive maximum speeds of 81, 82, and 79 mph were up to the finest standards of the route, regardless of the load.

Then there are two quite outstanding runs on trains booked non-stop from Ipswich to Norwich, both tabulated. In studying the first of these, made by an unrebuilt 'Claud Hamilton' 4-4-0, it is amusing to recall that the luxury East Anglian express, with a 230-ton load, hauled by a streamlined 'Sandringham' 4-6-0 was allowed 51 minutes from Ipswich to Norwich. As will be seen from the table the 4-4-0 No 8864 was doing 65 mph through Stowmarket, fell only to 52 mph on Haughley bank, and then produced speeds of 86, 83 and 78 mph at the maximum points of the subsequent racing stretch. Such speeds were virtually unheard of in the old days of the Great Eastern Railway! But so far as maximum speeds were concerned this was a mere nothing to the exploits of the 'B12/3' engine No 8535, in charge of a driver who was anxious to make up as much as possible of a late start. On this run speed was worked up to 72 mph at Stowmarket, and Haughley bank was cleared at 58 mph. A truly record-breaking flight then developed, but just as speed reached a full 90 mph

TABLE 35
IPSWICH–NORWICH

| Engine No | 8864 | 8535 |
|---|---|---|
| Engine type | 4–4–0 | 4–6–0 |
| Engine class | 'D15' | 'B12/3' |
| Load tons E/F | 231/245 | 280/305 |

| Distance miles | | min sec | min sec |
|---|---|---|---|
| 0·0 | IPSWICH | 0  00 | 0  00 |
| 4·9 | Claydon | 6  50 | 7  05 |
| 11·9 | STOWMARKET | 13  30 | 13  35 |
| 14·2 | Haughley | 15  50 | 15  38 |
| 17·9 | Finningham | 19  45 | 19  12 |
| — | | — | mishap |
| 26·3 | Diss | 26  30 | 25  59 |
| — | | — | 29  19 |
| 31·8 | Tivetshall | 31  00 | 37  09 |
| 38·0 | Flordon | 35  55 | 42  26 |
| 41·0 | Swainsthorpe | 38  22 | 44  49 |
| 43·3 | *Milepost* 112 | 40  12 | 46  35 |
| | | sig stop | sigs |
| 46·3 | NORWICH | 51  45 | 52  29 |
| Net time *min* | | 44¾ | 43½ |

| Speeds | mph | mph |
|---|---|---|
| Stowmarket | 65 | 72 |
| Haughley bank | 52 | 58 |
| Before Diss | 86 | 90 |
| Tivetshall | 65 | 55 |
| Flordon | 83 | 84 |
| Swainsthorpe | 70 | 72 |
| Milepost 112 | 78 | 81 |

approaching Diss a carriage door flew open, and the train
came to a sudden stop. After a halt of 3¼ minutes the driver
was not long in working his engine back into the same hurricane
stride, and despite this stop and adverse signals at the finish
the total time from Ipswich to Norwich was only 52½ minutes.
These five runs certainly show the Great Eastern line at its
very finest in the 1930s.

A number of the unrebuilt 'B12' 4–6–0s were transferred to
Scotland to work on the GNSR line, but I had no opportunity of

travelling behind them on those duties. Their tractive power was certainly welcome on a route where relatively small 4–4–0s had previously been the only source of main-line engine power for passenger and goods alike. A typical run of early grouping days was one I enjoyed on the 3.30 PM from Inverness to Aberdeen, in 1928. This train took the former Highland route from Elgin, and it was at Keith that the GNSR engine came on. This proved to be one of the batch built in James Johnson's time, No 6907 of LNER class 'D41', and she gave us the pleasant little run tabulated herewith. I have not got the intermediate schedule times, but we were running punctually throughout.

The line is level, and slightly falling from Keith to Cairnie Junction, and near this latter point there begins a 15-mile

TABLE 36
KEITH–ABERDEEN
Load: 201 tons tare, 215 tons full
Engine: Johnson 4–4–0 No 6907

| Distance miles | | Actual min   sec | | Speeds mph |
|---|---|---|---|---|
| 0·0 | KEITH | 0 | 00 | |
| 4·3 | Grange | 7 | 00 | 53 |
| 5·1 | Cairnie Junction | 7 | 48 | 58½ |
| 8·0 | Rothiemay | 10 | 55 | 46½ |
| 12·5 | HUNTLY | 17 | 00 | |
| 5·0 | Gartly | 9 | 15 | 46 |
| 8·0 | Kennethmont | 13 | 45 | 35½ |
| 9·7 | Wardhouse | 16 | 00 | 53 |
| 13·2 | Insch | 19 | 35 | 63½/46 |
| 16·2 | Oyne | 23 | 05 | 60 |
| 19·4 | Pitcaple | 26 | 30 | 53/56 |
| 20·4 | INVERAMSAY | 28 | 00 | |
| 3·5 | INVERURIE | 5 | 50 | 51 (max) |
| 3·5 | Kintore | 6 | 10 | 52½ |
| 6·3 | Kinaldie | 9 | 15 | 56 |
| 8·6 | Pitmedden | 10 | 40 | 58½ |
| 10·6 | DYCE | 14 | 15 | |
| 2·0 | Bucksburn | 4 | 15 | |
| 3·7 | Woodside | 6 | 00 | 53 |
| 4·9 | Kittybrewster | 7 | 50 | |
| 5·9 | ABERDEEN (SCHOOLHILL) | 9 | 40 | |

climb to Kennethmont summit. The actual gradients change almost incessantly, but as far as Gartly the average inclination is about 1 in 200. There is a sharp 1½ miles at 1 in 100 after Gartly, but the final 1½ miles to the summit are on easy grades. Engine No 6907, hauling 215 tons, touched 58½ mph at Cairnie, and had fallen to 46½ mph before shutting off steam for the stop at Huntly. Restarting, speeds varied between 40 and 46 mph on the broken rise to Gartly, and fell to 35½ mph on the 1 in 100 pitch. After that it is downhill almost all the way to Aberdeen, but no more than moderate speeds were needed to keep time. From Inverurie to Dyce the line is little more than dead level; but the pronounced fall recommences after Dyce, and the final approach to Aberdeen is down a gradient of 1 in 72. My logging on this journey ended with the stop at the Schoolhill ticket platform.

Having arrived back in North British territory we can pass on to some of the excellent work done by various classes of 4-4-0. The 'Scott' class has already featured in Chapter Five, as assistant engines to the 'Atlantics' on the East Coast workings. Elsewhere, although the Scottish variants of the Great Central 'Director' class, LNER class 'D11/2' had taken over most of the harder duties, between Edinburgh and Glasgow the 'Scotts' were still being extensively used, and in 1936 I clocked an excellent run with one of them on the Glasgow connexion off the 1.20 PM ex-King's Cross. This run is tabulated, and *Claverhouse* certainly made some brisk running. On the gradual rise at 1 in 960 that extends from Haymarket West Junction to Philpstoun we accelerated well to 65 mph. There was some smart running between stops and then the engine ran at 60 to 65 mph on the dead level from Falkirk until approaching the permanent way slack at Waterside Junction. The total running time for this journey of 47·3 miles was 68¼ minutes and the total overall time was exactly 71 minutes.

I had no detailed timings with the 'Director' class 4-4-0s over this route, but in my travelling diaries there are notes of several punctual runs on the 6 PM from Glasgow to Edinburgh, which then made four stops within an overall time of 75 minutes. One of the most interesting runs I had with a 'Director'

in Scotland was in 1927 on the 10.7 AM express from Edinburgh
to Perth via the Forth Bridge. This is a difficult road, and one
did not ordinarily look for any sustained fast running. The
merit of the work of No 6387 *Lucy Ashton*, as tabulated herewith, lay in the hill-climbing. From Inverkeithing, for ex-

TABLE 37
### EDINBURGH (WAVERLEY)–GLASGOW
Load: 232 tons tare, 245 tons full
Engine: class 'D30' 4–4–0 No 9415 *Claverhouse*

| Distance miles | | Actual min sec | Speeds mph |
|---|---|---|---|
| 0·0 | WAVERLEY | 0 00 | |
| 1·2 | Haymarket | 3 10 | |
| 3·5 | *Saughton Junction* | 6 07 | 53½ |
| 8·2 | Ratho | 11 19 | 64½ |
| — | | p.w.s. | 42 |
| 14·5 | Philpstoun | 18 48 | 62 |
| 17·6 | LINLITHGOW | 22 47 | |
| 2·2 | Manuel | 4 03 | 53 |
| — | | p.w.s. | |
| 4·7 | POLMONT | 8 08 | |
| 3·2 | FALKIRK HIGH | 6 13 | |
| 6·2 | Castlecary | 8 23 | 61½ |
| 10·3 | Croy | 12 23 | 60 |
| — | *Waterside Junction* | — | 64½ |
| — | | p.w.s. | 30 |
| 15·5 | Lenzie | 18 55 | 52 |
| 20·2 | Cowlairs | 25 06 | |
| 21·8 | QUEEN STREET | 31 08 | |

ample, up to Dunfermline the gradient is 1 in 89, and the
minimum sustained speed was 29 mph. On restarting, up a
continuous 1 in 74–72, speed was quickly worked up to
27 mph, and increased to 29 mph on the 1 in 100 between
Halbeath and Cowdenbeath. Sharp switchback gradients follow on to Kinross, and then an excellent flying run was taken
at the climb to Glenfarg. It is certainly quite short from this
side, but the last 1½ miles at 1 in 100 were taken at a minimum
speed of 39 mph.

A fortnight later I travelled by the 8.10 PM express from

Perth; but a load of 326 tons tare was considered too great for
a 'Director' class to handle unassisted up the very severe climb
from Bridge of Earn to Glenfarg, 6 miles continuously at 1 in
75, and so engine No 6390 *Hobbie Elliott* had the assistance of
a rebuilt Holmes 4–4–0 of LNER class 'D31', No 9214. Between

TABLE 38

EDINBURGH–PERTH

Load: 273 tons tare, 295 tons full

Engine: class 'D11/2' 4–4–0 No 6387 *Lucy Ashton*

| Distance miles | | Actual min sec | | Speeds mph |
|---|---|---|---|---|
| 0·0 | EDINBURGH (WAVERLEY) | 0 | 00 | |
| 1·2 | Haymarket | 3 | 40 | |
| 5·3 | Turnhouse | 8 | 10 | 54 |
| 8·3 | Dalmeny | 11 | 50 | 43 |
| 10·0 | *Forth Bridge North* | 14 | 45 | 60 after |
| 12·0 | INVERKEITHING | 17 | 25 | slack |
| 13·5 | Rosyth | 20 | 35 | 34/29 |
| 15·7 | DUNFERMLINE | 25 | 30 | |
| 2·2 | Halbeath | 7 | 20 | 26½ |
| 5·6 | Cowdenbeath | 13 | 55 | 29 |
| 7·8 | Kelty | 16 | 50 | 53 |
| | | p.w.s. | | 40 |
| 10·0 | Blairadam | 20 | 35 | 28½/45 |
| 13·7 | KINROSS JUNCTION | 25 | 55 | |
| 3·6 | Mawcarse Junction | 6 | 20 | 48½ |
| 7·1 | Glenfarg | 11 | 00 | 39 |
| | | slack | | 70½ (max) |
| 13·7 | Bridge of Earn | 18 | 25 | |
| 15·2 | *Hilton Junction* | 20 | 05 | |
| 17·2 | PERTH | 24 | 00 | |

the two of them they made light of the train. Glenfarg was
taken at a minimum speed of 27 mph, but perhaps the best
piece of hill-climbing was that up the 1 in 70 from Inverkeithing to the Forth Bridge. Passing the junctions at 25 mph
they accelerated smartly up the bank, and entered upon the
bridge at 33 mph.

On the Aberdeen road, until the introduction of the 2–8–2
engines in 1934–5, 4–4–0s continued to play a major part in
the express workings. Because of underline bridge restrictions

there were limitations to the combinations of engines that could be used on double-headed trains. 'Pacifics' were not allowed to be piloted and nothing larger than the superheated 'Scotts' could be used in combination with 'Atlantics'. One could not run two three-cylinder 4-4-os of the 'Shire' class together, but a 'Shire' and a 'Director' was a frequent combination, and one could always look for a very lively run on the up 'Aberdonian', if Haymarket shed had not got an 'Atlantic' available, and put on two 'Directors' instead. One can indeed look wistfully back to the great variety of locomotives then to be seen passing through stations like Inverkeithing and Dundee, in these days of dull diesel haulage; but from the viewpoint of the man with the stop-watch the West Highland line in the early 1930s provided some of the most rewarding experiences.

There, the 'Glen' class 4-4-0 engines were allowed a maximum tare load of 180 tons. The introduction of 'K2' class 2-6-0 engines enabled loads of 220 tons to be taken without pilot assistance, but whereas train workings north of Fort William were handled mostly by the latter engines, in the early 1930s traffic south of that point was more equally shared between the two classes. There is first tabulated a run on a popular excursion from Glasgow, which always carried a heavy load. The two 'Glen' class engines employed, with 170 tons apiece, were each loaded nearly to the maximum. From Upper Helensburgh almost to Arrochar the run was made in thick driving mist, and the rails in consequence were slippery, yet on the 1 in 59 ascent from the start at Garelochead a speed of 23 mph was attained, and increased to 37½ on the continuation of the climb to Glen Douglas, in this case rising at 1 in 80. No advantage could be taken of the easy grading between Arrochar and Ardlui, where the line winds along the hillside above Loch Lomond, and then comes 7½ miles of hard climbing. The 1 in 65 grade is relieved by several short level or easier strips, but even so, to run the 7 miles between posts 28 and 35 at an average speed of 28·9 mph was an excellent feat. Crianlarich was reached 3 minutes early.

From here, after a brief favourable strip in crossing to the opposite side of Strathfillan, climbing is continuous and almost

entirely at 1 in 60 to the summit 1,024 ft above sea level, at
milepost 43. Between posts 37 and 43 an average speed of
27 mph was maintained, the absolute minimum being 26 mph.
After a cautious descent to Bridge of Orchy, including the

TABLE 39

### HELENSBURGH–FORT WILLIAM

Load: 46 axles, 341 tons tare, 365 tons full

Engines No 9035 *Glen Gloy* and No 9221 *Glen Orchy*

(both class 'D34')

| Distance miles | | Actual min sec | | Speeds mph |
|---|---|---|---|---|
| 0·0 | Upper Helensburgh | 0 | 00 | — |
| 6·9 | Garelochhead | 12 | 05 | — |
| 1·3 | Whistlefield | 5 | 05 | 23 |
| 6·2 | *Glen Douglas* | 14 | 58 | 37½ |
| 10·6 | Arrochar | 21 | 51 | |
| 8·0 | Ardlui | 12 | 30 | — |
| 8·4 | *Post 28* | 13 | 24 | 35 |
| 15·4 | *Post 35* | 27 | 55 | 26 |
| 16·7 | Crianlarich | 30 | 35 | — |
| 0·7 | *Post 37* | 1 | 48 | — |
| 5·0 | Tyndrum | 11 | 17 | 26 |
| 6·7 | *Post 43* | 15 | 05 | 28¼ |
| 12·5 | Bridge of Orchy | 23 | 06 | — |
| 15·7 | *Post 52* | 26 | 55 | 42½ |
| 21·2 | Gortan | 38 | 53 | 27 |
| 28·1 | Rannoch | 48 | 00 | |
| 1·6 | *Post 66* | 4 | 52 | 21 |
| 7·3 | *Corrour* | 14 | 17 | 46 |
| 8·5 | Fersit | 14 | 12 | — |
| 1·2 | Tulloch | 3 | 25 | |
| 5·7 | Roy Bridge | 9 | 57 | |
| 3·0 | Spean Bridge | 6 | 00 | |
| 8·5 | *Mallaig Junction* | 11 | 35 | 59 |
| 9·5 | Fort William | 14 | 05 | |

negotiation of the famous horseshoe curve, the climbing is continuous again to Gortan crossing-place, but at rather easier
grades. After the slack for tablet exchange at Bridge of Orchy,
speed rose, up 1 in 240, to 42½ mph at post 52, while on the
subsequent length at 1 in 66 a minimum of 27 mph was

registered. Beyond Gortan, the 7 miles of undulation across the Moor of Rannoch to Rannoch station were run smartly in a time of 9 minutes 7 seconds to the stop. The restart from Rannoch is made up 1½ miles at 1 in 53. At the top of this grade speed had risen to 21 mph. The remainder of the climbing, to the summit of the route at Corrour crossing, is broken by several short downhill strips, and the five miles from post 66 to post 71 were covered in 8 minutes 7 seconds, speed rising at one point to 46 mph. On the occasion of this run, day-excursion traffic was so heavy as to necessitate the running of a relief train; as the latter had not cleared Tulloch, our train was held up for 3 minutes at Corrour, but despite this delay the arrival at Fort William was exactly to time. The whole distance from Corrour is steeply downhill, but owing to severe curvature, no fast running is possible until after Spean Bridge, and even here did not rise above 59 mph. Thus the overall time for the 97¾ miles from Upper Helensburgh to Fort William was 195 minutes as booked, while the running time of 175 minutes gave an average speed of 33½ mph.

In the next table details are given of two southbound runs, both with 'Glen' class engines hauling the maximum rostered load. In this direction, on starting from Fort William, the engines are faced with 28 miles of continuous climbing, during which the line rises practically from sea level to an altitude of 1,347 ft at Corrour. The grade therefore averages 1 in 110. On the 5.12 PM train engine No 9494 passed Corrour, 28·2 miles in 59 minutes 25 seconds inclusive of two stops, at Spean Bridge and Tulloch, totalling 3 minutes 10 seconds. Engine No 9035 achieved the even finer feat of reaching Corrour in 57 minutes 56 seconds. The average speed from start to stop, in the latter case inclusive of the same two stops, was 29 mph throughout. For 4–4–0 locomotives of such moderate dimensions these were first-class efforts, but even so were very little faster than the timetable demanded. Continuing across Rannoch Moor, No 9494 completed the 7·3 miles to the Rannoch stop in 10 minutes 20 seconds not exceeding 54 mph, but No 9035 made some brisk running, and by covering the same distance start to stop in 9 minutes 43 seconds reached Rannoch

in a time only 33 seconds more than that of No 9494, Corrour
stop included. Speed was maintained at 62½ mph for some
distance, though suitably reduced, of course, for the concluding two miles, which are sharply curved.

TABLE 40
FORT WILLIAM–GLASGOW

| Engine No 4–4–0 No Engine name Load tons tare/full Driver | 9494 *Glen Loy* 182/190 D. Ross (Eastfield) | | 9035 *Glen Gloy* 180/190 W. Carr (Fort William) | |
|---|---|---|---|---|
| Distance miles | Time min sec | Speed mph | Time min sec | Speed mph |
| 0·0 Fort William | 0 00 | — | 0 00 | — |
| 3·4 *Post 96½* | 7 15 | 23½ | 7 14 | 27¼ |
| 8·4 *Post 91½* | 15 07 | 47½ | 14 29 | 53 |
| 9·5 Spean Bridge | 16 30 | — | 15 37 | — |
| 1·4 *Post 89* | 3 35 | 40 | 3 49 | 39½ |
| 4·4 *Post 86* | 9 10 | 26 | 9 06 | 26 |
| 6·4 *Post 84* | 12 45 | 39 | 12 45 | 37½ |
| 8·4 *Post 82* | 16 37 | 26½ | 17 13 | 22 |
| 8·7 Tulloch | 17 20 | — | 17 48 | — |
| 3·0 *Post 78¾* | 7 30 | 37½ | 7 35 | 41½ |
| 6·7 *Post 75* | 15 17 | 25 | 15 11 | 22½ |
| 8·7 *Post 73* | 19 40 | 32½ | 19 55 | 32 |
| 10·0 *Corrour* | { pass | 25¼ | 22 41 | 27 |
| | { 22 25 | 54 | 23 35 | — |
| 17·3 Rannoch | 32 45 | — | 33 18 | 62½ |
| 6·9 *Gortan* | 10 15 | 53 | 10 35 | — |
| 8·7 Bridge of Orchy | 12 00 | 60 | 21 33 | 58½ |
| 12·5 *Post 45* | 19 25 | 31½ | 28 15 | 37 |
| 14·5 *Post 43* | 24 00 | 25 | 32 48 | 23 |
| 16·2 Tyndrun | 26 25 | 52 | 35 15 | — |
| 21·2 Crianlarich | 33 30 | | 42 25 | |
| 16·7 Arrochar | 30 55 | | 28 57 | — |
| 4·4 *Glen Douglas* | 11 05 | 23 | 11 46 | 20½ |
| 10·6 Garelochhead | 20 45 | 56 | 22 28 | |
| 19·6 Craigendoran | 37 25 | | 15 10 | |
| | | | 2 signal stops | |
| 22·5 GLASGOW (Queen Street) | 64 55 | | 37 42 | |

The difficulties of the remainder of the run are confined to the short length at 1 in 55 from the horseshoe curve to post 43, and the restart from Arrochar. This latter is a particularly difficult bank, as it is a constant succession of reverse curves, in addition to the heavy grade. Here on both runs, the speed fell to lower minima than on any other part of the journey. Little need be said about the remaining sections, except to mention the very steady speed maintained on the winding descents, without a constant irritating succession of brake applications. Quite apart from the comfort of travelling it bespeaks skilful driving. The two trains were respectively 1¼ and 1 minute early at Rannoch, and 3½ and 4½ minutes early at Crianlarich. Beyond this point, the King's Cross 'sleeper', no conditional stops being called, had an easy task. The afternoon train did well to reach Glasgow on time after several delays beyond Craigendoran.

These runs were logged in 1932 and 1934, and although there was officially a speed restriction of 40 mph throughout from Craigendoran to Fort William it was honoured more in the breach than in the letter. I rode on the footplate of 'Glen' class engines on several occasions and they were extremely free runners. The speed limit had to be enforced much more rigorously when heavier engines were introduced, and I have described elsewhere in this book, in some detail, a run with the pioneer 'K4' 'Mogul' the log of which came under the closest scrutiny at headquarters before I was permitted to publish the results.

And so I come finally to the Great Northern, and really it is difficult to find adequate superlatives to describe the work of the large-boilered 'Atlantics' in the years 1930-9. After the long trial of Great Central engines on the Pullman trains was ended the 'C1' class had these celebrated trains to themselves. They did wonderfully consistent work, though their use precluded the strengthening of the train-formation at times of heavy traffic beyond eight Pullmans. The normal load of the 'Queen of Scots' express was seven. One took almost for granted the fact that an 'Atlantic' would put up a good show, but the feats that put these engines on a pedestal, even among the ranks of the immortals of the locomotive world, were the three occasions when the failure of 'Pacifics' on the 1.20 PM 'Scotsman' led to the requisitioning of 'Atlantics' at a moment's notice from Grantham shed, and the making of runs onwards to York that were verily in heroic vein.

I must, however, take the ordinary run of 'Atlantic' performance before the exceptional. I had ten runs altogether on the Pullman trains, two in the down direction and eight in the up. In the earlier years of my travelling I hoped sometime to catch a Great Central engine on the up 'Queen of Scots'; but on the days I travelled I always had a 'C1' 'Atlantic'. The results make my record of these engines all the more remarkable. Never once, on these fast schedules, was there any time to book against the engine, even including some journeys made in stormy winter weather; and the net gains on schedule on seven of the up runs were 8½, 2, 15, 5, 13¾, 5, and 17 minutes. The last mentioned gave a net time of 176 minutes for the 185·8 miles from Leeds Central to King's Cross, and is one of the classics of my personal collection of logs. The eighth run was made on a snowy winter's night on the Harrogate Sunday Pullman, when we had no less a celebrity at the head of the train than the pioneer engine, No 251 – or 3251 as she then was. We got a bad road as far as Grantham, but then did splendidly up to London, covering the 105½ miles from Grantham to King's Cross in 104¼ minutes pass to stop, with an eight-car train of 325 tons gross behind the tender.

The normal up Pullman runs gave the following overall results:

TABLE 41

| Engine No | Load tons full | Sch. time min | Actual min | sec | Net time min | Max speed mph |
|-----------|----------------|---------------|------------|-----|--------------|---------------|
| 3280 | 295 | 205 | 209 | 55 | 186½ | 84 |
| 3284 | 325 | 195 | 191 | 15 | 181¼ | 88 |
| 4436 | 285 | 193 | 193 | 00 | 188 | 85 |
| 4444 | 300 | 195 | 195 | 25 | 190 | 82 |
| 4444 | 335 | 205 | 194 | 45 | 190 | 85½ |
| 4450 | 335 | 205 | 203 | 45 | 203 | 85 |
| 4456 | 290 | 193 | 189 | 35 | 176 | 93 |

TABLE 42
## 'QUEEN OF SCOTS' EXPRESS
### LEEDS–KING'S CROSS
Load: 7 cars, 277 tons tare, 290 tons full
Engine: GN 4–4–2 No 4456
Driver: W. Worboys; Fireman: C. Fisher (King's Cross shed)

| Distance miles | | Sch. min | Actual min | sec | Speeds mph |
|---|---|---|---|---|---|
| 0·0 | LEEDS | 0 | 0 | 00 | — |
| 0·5 | Holbeck | — | 2 | 08 | — |
| 2·5 | Beeston | — | 6 | 12 | 43 |
| 5·6 | Ardsley | | 10 | 52 | 39 |
| 7·5 | Lofthouse | | 13 | 12 | 59 |
| 9·9 | WAKEFIELD | 18 | 15 | 52 | 40* |
| 11·6 | Sandal | | 17 | 53 | 59 |
| 13·9 | Hare Park | | 20 | 23 | — |
| 15·4 | Nostell | | 22 | 10 | 50 |
| 17·9 | Hemsworth | | 24 | 50 | — |
| 21·1 | South Elmsall | | 27 | 37 | 75 |
| 23·3 | Hampole | | 29 | 22 | 76½ |
| 25·8 | Carcroft | | 31 | 26 | — |
| | | | sigs | | |
| 29·8 | DONCASTER | 39 | 36 | 05 | — |
| 32·6 | *Black Carr Junction* | | 39 | 48 | 59 |
| 34·5 | Rossington | | 41 | 48 | 56 |
| 36·3 | *Milepost 149½* | | 43 | 48 | 52½ |
| 38·1 | Bawtry | | 45 | 42 | — |
| 40·0 | Scrooby | | 47 | 33 | 65 |
| 41·9 | Ranskill | | 49 | 15 | — |
| 44·1 | Sutton | | 51 | 15 | 67½ |
| 47·2 | RETFORD | 56 | 54 | 00 | 73 |
| 50·3 | *Gamston* | | 56 | 49 | 64½ |
| 52·1 | *Markham* | | 58 | 33 | 60 |
| 53·9 | Tuxford | | 60 | 09 | 74 |
| 59·4 | Carlton | | 64 | 20 | 82 |
| 65·7 | NEWARK | 73 | 69 | 30 | 64 |
| 70·4 | Claypole | | 73 | 52 | 68 |
| 74·3 | Hougham | | 77 | 27 | 64½ |
| 76·1 | Barkston | | 79 | 10 | 62 |
| 78·0 | *Milepost 107¾ (Peascliffe)* | | 81 | 06 | 58 |
| 80·3 | GRANTHAM | 88 | 83 | 24 | 64 |
| 83·8 | Great Ponton | | 86 | 52 | 58 |
| 85·7 | *Stoke* | | 88 | 55 | 55 |
| 88·7 | Corby | | 91 | 38 | 77½ |
| 93·6 | Little Bytham | | 95 | 10 | 90 |
| 97·2 | Essendine | | 97 | 32 | 93/90 |
| 101·0 | Tallington | | 100 | 03 | 92 |

TABLE 42 (*continued*)

| Distance miles | | Sch. min | Actual min sec | Speeds mph |
|---|---|---|---|---|
| 103·9 | Helpston | | 102  01 | 88 |
| | | | p.w.s. | 35 |
| 106·3 | *Werrington Junction* | | 104  19 | — |
| 109·4 | PETERBOROUGH | { pass | 109  40 | — |
| | | 117 | 114  25 | |
| 110·8 | *Fletton Junction* | | 117  59 | |
| 113·2 | Yaxley | | 121  00 | 54 |
| 116·4 | Holme | | 124  07 | 67 |
| 118·4 | *Connington* | | 125  53 | 68½ |
| 122·3 | Abbots Ripton | | 129  44 | 57 |
| 126·9 | HUNTINGDON | 135 | 133  58 | 77½ |
| 129·8 | Offord | | 136  12 | 79 |
| 134·1 | St Neots | | 139  40 | 71 |
| 138·4 | Tempsford | | 143  11 | 76½ |
| 141·7 | Sandy | | 145  58 | 70 |
| 144·7 | Biggleswade | | 148  30 | 70½ |
| 147·2 | *Langford Bridge* | | 150  47 | 65 |
| 150·1 | Three Counties | | 153  24 | 69 |
| 153·9 | HITCHIN | 160 | 156  56 | 62½ |
| 157·2 | Stevenage | | 160  29 | 53½ |
| 159·1 | *Langley Junction* | | 162  31 | 64½ |
| 160·8 | Knebworth | | 164  08 | 60 |
| 162·3 | *Woolmer Green* | | 165  36 | — |
| 163·5 | Welwyn Garden City | | 168  20 | — |
| 168·1 | HATFIELD | 174 | 170  23 | 82 |
| 173·1 | Potters Bar | | 174  40 | 69 |
| 176·6 | New Barnet | | 177  40 | 74 |
| 180·8 | Wood Green | | 181  09 | 70 |
| 183·2 | FINSBURY PARK | | 183  25 | — |
| | | | sigs | |
| 185·8 | KING'S CROSS | 193 | 189  35 | — |

\* Service slack.

The run of 4456 was something of a phenomenon, even for the middle 1930s. In the first place she was not the booked engine for the job. At King's Cross and Copley Hill sheds 'Atlantics' in the very prime of condition were set aside for the working of the Pullman trains, but on this occasion a slight defect on the London engine made a substitute necessary. Copley Hill had nothing suitable, so Doncaster sent 4456, the first engine available. She arrived at Leeds looking grubby; there was no time to clean her up to Pullman standards, while to crown all the water troughs at Werrington were under repair and we should have to stop for water at Peterborough. The engines of all Pullman trains had to be thrashed good and hard on the climb to Ardsley. The King's Cross driver duly set about her in the traditional style, and to our delight she responded magnificently. With 50 per cent cut-off and full regulator she gave us a thrilling 39 mph sustained up the 1 in 100 to Ardsley; her beat was true, her steaming perfect and from this early stage one forgot completely that she was a hurriedly provided spare engine. What a ride she gave us! With her rolling and swaying, and much sharp 'tail-wag', we had a high old time on the footplate; her 'tail-wag' was transmitted to the tender. No coal pusher was needed on this engine! After each spell of fast running the footplate was ankle deep in Rossington 'hards'.

What an engine! The harder she was flogged the faster she went, and the freer she steamed. The work between Newark and Grantham was an almost exact counterpart of those heavy load runs tabulated on page 70, as the drawbar horsepower averaged 850, showing a pull of 5,050 lb, or 29 per cent of the nominal tractive effort; this was really better, since the horse-power effort was made at higher speed, while on the Hunting-don–Hitchin stretch, done at an average of 70·7 mph against a rising gradient of 1 in 610, the horsepower was 820, and the drawbar pull 4,370 lb. Here the engine was matching Church-ward's famous target of a drawbar pull of 2 tons at 70 mph – 1·95 to be exact – but with an engine having a cylinder capacity of only 80 per cent of that of the 'Stars' and with 170 lb pressure instead of 225! On the footplate, of course, the supreme thrill of a journey that was packed with incident was the topping of Stoke summit, when we stormed up from Newark doing our 850 dhp, and the driver left the regulator and cut-off un-touched for the descent to Werrington. It was as much the anticipation of what was going to happen as what actually did happen, and I was not disappointed! Earlier that day going down to Leeds on No 4423 I had clocked my very first 90 any-where, and on this return trip No 4456 gave me an *average* of 90·5 mph for over 10 miles, and a maximum of 93. This is, so far as I know, the fastest ever recorded with one of the 'Atlantics'. With the controls untouched from the positions used on the climb from Newark to Stoke the rate at which steam was being used was increased by nearly 50 per cent and yet the boiler pressure was held unvaryingly at 165 to 170 psi. The full log of this magnificent run is tabulated herewith.

Next I come to the 'emergency' runs between Grantham and York. On two out of the three occasions it was extremely fortunate that an experienced recorder was travelling on the train, and this makes credible the fact that a very similar performance was achieved on a *third* occasion. Curiously enough they were separated by roughly two years. The first of these three runs took place in 1934 when Driver Samwells of King's Cross had to give up his regular 'A3' 'Pacific', No 2744 *Grand Parade*, at Grantham, and got in exchange the 'Atlantic' No 4415. The second run took place in 1936, when Driver Walker of Gateshead had to give up another 'A3' No 2595 *Trigo*, while the third occasion was in February 1938, when Driver Peachey of King's Cross did equally well with the 'Atlantic' No 3285. The three runs may be summarized thus:

TABLE 43
GRANTHAM–YORK: 82·7 miles

| Engine No | Driver | Load, tons full | Actual time min   sec | Net time min |
|-----------|--------|-----------------|-----------------------|--------------|
| 4415 | Samwells | 545 | 86   56 | 86¾ |
| 4404 | Walker | 585 | 87   40 | 86½ |
| 3285 | Peachey | 540 | 89   00 | 86 |

The first two runs are tabulated in full detail. The first was logged by my friend A. F. Webber, and the second by Mr Cecil J. Allen. Both were remarkable pieces of locomotive performance, and the second all the more so because it was made by a North Eastern driver and fireman who had never been on one of those engines before. The result emphasizes the outstanding quality of the design and the simplicity of the controls and firing. Both engines were being worked practically at the limit of the boiler, with the regulator wide if not necessarily full open, and probably a cut-off of at least 40 per cent. There would be no difficulty with that excellent front-end design in passing such volumes of steam freely through the cylinders. The fact that a strange driver and fireman could step on one of these engines, drive away, and make such a

TABLE 44
GRANTHAM–YORK

| Run No<br>Engine No<br>No of coaches<br>Load tons tare<br>Load tons full | | 1<br>4415<br>16<br>506<br>545 | | 2<br>4404<br>17<br>546<br>586 | |
|---|---|---|---|---|---|
| *Distance*<br>*miles* | *Sch.*<br>*min* | *Actual*<br>*min   sec* | *Speeds*<br>*mph* | *Actual*<br>*min   sec* | *Speeds*<br>*mph* |
| 0·0 | GRANTHAM | 0 | 0   00 | | 0   00 | |
| 4·2 | Barkston | | 8   22 | 61 | 8   17 | — |
| 6·0 | Hougham | | 10   05 | 71 | 10   03 | — |
| 9·9 | Claypole | | 13   22 | 74 | 13   23 | 74 |
| 14·6 | NEWARK | 15 | 17   13 | 68/73 | 17   23 | |
| 21·9 | Crow Park | | 23   18 | — | 24   19 | 64 |
| 25·8 | *Dukeries Junction* | | 27   01 | 57½ | 28   30 | 48 |
| 28·2 | *Markham Box* | | 29   41 | 53 | 31   31 | 48½ |
| 33·1 | RETFORD | 35 | 34   16 | 72½ | 36   15 | 77½ |
| 36·2 | Sutton | | 36   56 | 69 | 38   49 | 72½ |
| 38·4 | Ranskill | | 38   52 | 71½ | 40   37 | 74 |
| 40·3 | Scrooby | | 40   26 | 72 | 42   08 | 75 |
| 42·2 | Bawtry | | 42   04 | — | 43   43 | — |
| 44·0 | *Milepost 149½* | | 43   44 | 67 | 45   22 | 61 |
| 47·7 | *Black Carr Jcn* | | 46   56 | 70½ | 48   38 | 72½ |
| 50·5 | DONCASTER | 53 | 49   34 | 59½ | 51   19 | 55 |
| 54·7 | *Shaftholme Jcn* | | — | — | 55   36 | 62½ |
| 57·5 | Moss | | 56   34 | 64 | 58   15 | 64 |
| 60·5 | Balne | | 59   23 | — | 61   02 | 65 |
| 61·8 | Heck | | 60   36 | — | 62   17 | 60 |
| 64·3 | Templehirst | | 63   03 | 65 | 64   42 | 66 |
| 67·5 | *Brayton Junction* | | 66   04 | — | 67   41 | — |
| 68·9 | SELBY | 73 | 67   35 | 24 | 69   17 | 30 |
| 73·0 | Riccall | | 75   08 | 50 | 75   18 | 55 |
| 78·5 | Naburn | | 81   11 | 58 | 80   56 | 60 |
| 80·7 | *Chaloners Whin Jcn* | | 83   33 | — | 83   09 | — |
| | | | — | — | sigs | |
| 82·7 | YORK | 90 | 86   56 | — | 87   40 | — |

phenomenal run on the spur of the moment is a resounding tribute to the design.

This is not to belittle the work of the King's Cross men who both did so well in similar circumstances. They and their respective firemen would be familiar with the engines, because all the King's Cross men then working on the London–Newcastle double-home turns had graduated through the Pullman link. A study of the table containing the logs shows that Driver Samwells did considerably the faster work in the earlier stages, including the remarkable minimum speeds of 53 mph at Markham summit and no less than 67 mph at Pipers Wood (milepost $149\frac{1}{2}$). After that there was some very level pegging onwards to Selby, with Driver Walker taking the honours by reason of his heavier load; then Walker drew clean ahead by a rather faster passage through Selby. In any account of LNER steam these two runs must rank with the greatest of the streamlined 'A4' performances.

# CHAPTER THIRTEEN

# 'V2's AND THE EARLY
# WAR YEARS

At about the same time as the 'P2' engine No 2003 *Lord President* was turned out, there appeared the first of the 2–6–2 express engines, No 4771 *Green Arrow*. As was the case with nearly all Gresley's most successful designs, very few of these locomotives were built until thorough service trials had been carried out. Of the 'Green Arrows', class 'V2', only five were built in 1936. These were stationed at widely separated depots, and foreshadowed the eventual use of the new class as express passenger and mixed-traffic engines over the entire East Coast route. No 4771 was stationed at King's Cross, 4772 and 4773 at York, 4774 at Peterborough, and 4775 at Dundee. Although they were designated mixed-traffic engines, the use of 6 ft 2 in coupled wheels in combination with an efficient modern front end made them eminently suitable for any express passenger duty, except perhaps the streamlined trains. The design was derived to a large extent from that of the 'A3' 'Pacifics' although some interesting variations are shown by table 45, on page 168.

A study of these dimensions reveals once again Gresley's then well-established practice of working out each new design entirely on its merits, without any particular concern for the possible incorporation of existing standard parts. By making the cylinders of the 'V2's $\frac{1}{2}$ in larger in diameter, the front end could have been made interchangeable with that of the 'A3's; but in that case the cylinder volume would have been disproportionately large in relation to the evaporative heating surface, which, with a boiler barrel shorter by 2 ft, was less than that of the 'A3's by 305 sq ft. So an entirely new front-end design was prepared, in which the cylinders, steam-chests, smokebox saddle, and outside steam-pipes were incorporated in a single steel casting. The boiler was of the same diameter as that of the 'A3' class; the shortening took place in the parallel portion at the front end. As in the 'P2's and in the final batch of 'A3's the boiler was fitted with a steam collector instead of a dome, and through this collector passed all steam entering the regulator. This device proved very effective in counteracting any tendency to prime, and, to minimize any wire-drawing effects at the point of entry to the collector, the cross-sectional area of the slotted holes cut in the top of the boiler barrel-plate was double that of the full regulator opening.

TABLE 45

## COMPARATIVE DIMENSIONS OF 'V2' AND 'A3' CLASS LOCOMOTIVES

|  |  | 'V2' class 2–6–2 | | 'A3' class 4–6–2 | |
|---|---|---|---|---|---|
| Cylinders (3) | *in* | 18½ by 26 | | 19 by 26 | |
| Coupled-wheels, diameter | *ft in* | 6 | 2 | 6 | 8 |
| Total wheelbase (engine) | *ft in* | 33 | 8 | 35 | 9 |
| Total length over buffers (engine and tender) | *ft in* | 66 | 5 | 70 | 5 |
| Length of boiler barrel | *ft* | 17 | | 19 | |
| Total evaporative heating surface | *sq ft* | 2431 | | 2736·6 | |
| Grate area | *sq ft* | 41¼ | | 41¼ | |
| Boiler pressure | *psi* | 220 | | 220 | |
| Adhesion weight | *tons cwt* | 65 | 12 | 66 | 3 |
| Weight of engine in working order | *tons cwt* | 93 | 2 | 96 | 5 |
| Weight of engine and tender in working order | *tons cwt* | 144 | 2 | 154 | 3 |
| Nominal tractive effort at 85 per cent working pressure | *lb* | 33,730 | | 32,909 | |

It will be seen that, although the 2–6–2 wheel arrangement was used, the total engine wheelbase was only 25 in less than that of the 'Pacifics'. This was partly accounted for by the spacing of the coupled wheels; in the 'A3's the driving axle was 7 ft 3 ins from both the trailing and leading coupled axles, whereas in the 'V2's the trailing coupled axle was 8 ft 3 ins from the driving axle. In comparison with the original 'A3's their appearance suffered somewhat from the height of the running-plate which left the coupled wheels completely exposed, and from the shape and position of the steam collector; a touch of distinction was provided, however, by the wedge-shaped front of the cab, so designed to induce air currents for deflecting any exhaust steam which tended to beat down. Taken all round, the ‘Green Arrows’ embodied, in a single outstanding design, every feature that Gresley, in his long career, had found to give efficient and reliable service. The only possible omission was the Kylchap double blastpipe and chimney, although at the time *Green Arrow* was built, that device was still only in experimental use on the LNER.

In regular express passenger service before the war their work was practically indistinguishable from that of the ‘Pacifics’. At first they were chiefly to be seen on relief portions of regular trains, but their running in these circumstances was such that as more became available, they were regularly drafted to top-link duties; the ‘Yorkshire Pullman’ with its 60 mph timing between Doncaster and King's Cross was a case in point. With loads of about 400 tons, their speeds down the Stoke bank were just as fast as those of the ‘Pacifics’ on the Leeds ‘Breakfast Flyer’. There was a run by No 4817, on which a maximum of 93 mph was attained near Essendine, and the 17·6 miles from Corby to Werrington Junction were run at an average speed of 86·2 mph. The load behind the tender on this occasion was 380 tons gross. Speeds of 90 mph were not uncommon with ‘V2’s on the Great Central section also. With the exception of the special test runs with engines Nos 4472 and 2750 before the introduction of the ‘Silver Jubilee’ service, speeds of 90–92 mph also seemed to be about the maximum regularly attained by the ‘A1’ and ‘A3’ ‘Pacifics’, and thus it would appear that air resistance, rather than piston speed, was the limiting factor, where other considerations, such as front-end design, were equally favourable. A piston speed equivalent to that of No 4817 at Essendine would be equal, with a ‘Pacific’, to 101 mph.

It was significant of the versatility of the ‘V2’s that their work on first-class express passenger traffic came so much into the limelight. In connexion with express goods traffic, I was fortunate in having an opportunity of observing the work, between

King's Cross and Peterborough, of *Green Arrow* herself, on the famous 3.35 PM down Scottish goods. The running made on that occasion had a special significance in later years, for the similarity of the load to those of wartime East Coast expresses helped to show how easily the 'V2's could make the moderate speeds then demanded. I should add, however, that on my 1937 trip *Green Arrow* was in the 'pink' of condition. From Sandy to Peterborough we had a load of 47 vehicles, all four-wheelers; the actual gross load was estimated at 610 tons, but, having due consideration for the higher frictional resistance of goods wagons, this would have been equal to about 700 tons of bogie passenger stock. With this load *Green Arrow* ran at 62 mph on the level on 18 per cent cut-off with the regulator only partly open, and with 160 psi in the steam-chest as against a boiler pressure of 220 psi.

The acceleration out of Sandy also was most impressive. The engine was started on 65 per cent cut-off with the regulator opened to give 140 psi in the steam-chest. After about 200 yds the regulator was opened to the full, linking up began, and, exactly a mile out, the cut-off was down to 18 per cent. This adjustment was maintained as far as Tempsford, 3·4 miles out, where the regulator was partly closed; by that time the speed was 53 mph. In the earlier stages of the journey, with a lighter load of 42 vehicles, 550 tons behind the tender, the hill-climbing had also been very good; details of the working again show complete mastery over the load. The start from King's Cross goods station was made on 65 per cent cut-off, and a partly opened regulator, but, as soon as the train was on the move, and indeed, before we entered Copenhagen tunnel, the cut-off was shortened to 40 per cent and the regulator opened to the full. As we gathered speed the cut-off was reduced by steps of 2 or 3 per cent until it was down to 25 per cent on passing Holloway summit; yet notwithstanding this comparatively easy steaming, we averaged 18 mph up the 1 in 107 gradient between Belle Isle and Holloway North Down box. Belle Isle, of course, was passed at no more than walking pace, as we had started from the goods terminus. Full details of the running are given in table 46, page 172.

This performance makes an interesting comparison with that of an 'A1' 'Pacific' with a 520-ton load. The latter engine, on the 1.20 PM 'Scotsman', passed Belle Isle in full cry, with wide-open regulator and 47 per cent cut-off; by Holloway summit her driver had linked up to 28 per cent, yet even with this flying start his average over the same section was only $21\frac{1}{2}$ mph. The steam-chest pressures recorded on *Green Arrow* were indeed a tribute to the design of the steam passages, for with full regulator there was never a drop of more than 5 psi between the boiler and the steam-chest. In explanation of our apparently wholesale disregard of schedule time north of Hitchin, allowance is made for side-tracking, if necessary, to clear the way for the 'Yorkshire Pullman'. In addition to being delayed somewhat on the slow line between Woolmer Green and Hitchin South, we were held longer than usual owing to the 4 PM down Yorkshire express being divided. On this account we were only just on time at Sandy. From there onwards, however, Driver Hart certainly showed off the paces of his engine, and incidentally showed the 'Yorkshire Pullman' a very clean pair of heels.

On the Edinburgh–Aberdeen route the 'V2's were rostered to take the same loads as the 'A1' and 'A3' 'Pacifics'. The maximum tonnages are of interest when compared with those laid down for other classes over this route, as shown in the table on page 174. Limits were also laid down for the 'D49' class when piloted. Two 'D49's were allowed to work in double-harness north, but not south of Dundee; the maximum tonnage for such a pair was 600 northbound and 550 southbound. The same limits applied south of Dundee for a 'D49' piloted by a 'B12' ex-GER 4–6–0. After all the North British 'Atlantics' of class 'C11' had been scrapped, nothing larger than a 'D49' was allowed to be piloted. Due to their shorter wheelbase and a general handiness the 'V2's became very popular on that route, and they worked passenger, express fish and other fast freight trains turn and turn about with the 'Pacifics'. These duties were typical of their widespread use over the LNER system.

On the Great Central section, the Leicester top-link engine-

TABLE 46   LNER 3.35 PM
Engine: class 'V2' 2–6–2
Load: to Sandy 42 vehicles, 550 tons gross;
Driver: Hart; Fireman:

| Distance miles | | Schedule min | Actual | |
|---|---|---|---|---|
| | | | min | sec |
| 0·0 | KING'S CROSS (Goods) | 0 | 0 | 00 |
| | | | sigs | |
| 2·0 | Finsbury Park | | 6 | 43 |
| | | | sigs | |
| 4·4 | Wood Green | | 11 | 06 |
| 8·6 | New Barnet | | 18 | 48 |
| 12·1 | Potters Bar | | 24 | 12 |
| 17·1 | HATFIELD | 30 | 30 | 18 |
| 22·9 | *Woolmer Green* | | 37 | 04 |
| 30·6 | *Hitchin South* | 53½ | 58 | 50 |
| 0·7 | HITCHIN | 4 | 3 | 00 |
| 4·5 | Three Counties | | 9 | 46 |
| 9·9 | Biggleswade | | 15 | 40 |
| 12·9 | SANDY | 35 | 19 | 35 |
| 3·4 | Tempsford | | 6 | 18 |
| 7·6 | St Neots | 18½ | 11 | 12 |
| 11·9 | Offord | | 15 | 56 |
| 14·8 | HUNTINGDON | 30 | 18 | 56 |
| 17·9 | *Milepost* 62 | | 22 | 54 |
| 19·4 | Abbots Ripton | | 24 | 39 |
| 25·3 | Holme | | 30 | 34 |
| 28·5 | Yaxley | | 33 | 53 |
| 32·3 | PETERBOROUGH | | 38 | 40 |
| | | | sigs | |
| 33·0 | *Westwood Junction* | 54 | 42 | 00 |

\* Crossover slack to slow line.

men, as might be expected, made some very fast runs with
'V2's on the pre-war 6.20 PM down express from Marylebone
and have worked them up to 90 mph as readily as the Great
Northern men seemed to do. But perhaps the most outstanding
performance in high-speed passenger service took place when
No 4789 was drafted at very short notice to work the streamlined 'West Riding Limited' on its 68½ mph start-to-stop
booking from King's Cross to Leeds. A number of delays were

KING'S CROSS (GOODS)–PETERBOROUGH
No 4771 *Green Arrow*
to Peterborough 47 vehicles, 610 tons gross
Cook (King's Cross shed)

| *Speeds mph* | *Regulator* | *Cut-off per cent* | *Pressure, psi* | |
|---|---|---|---|---|
| | | | *Boiler* | *Steam-Chest* |
| | Full | 65 | 175 | 170 |
| | | 18 | — | — |
| 45½ | | 18 | 195 | 190 |
| 35¼ | | 18 | | |
| 32 | ½ | 18 | 190 | 120 |
| 63 | Full | 18 | 195 | 185 |
| 20* | — | 18 | | |
| | 3/5 | 18† | 200 | 140 |
| 57/53 | 2/5 | 18 | 195 | 100 |
| 62 | 2/5 | 18 | 195 | 100 |
| 53 | Full | 18 | 200 | 195 |
| 48¾ | ½ | 18 | 200 | 130 |
| 59 | 7/8 | 18 | | |
| — | | 18 | 200 | 185 |
| 46 | | 18 | | |
| — | ¼ | 18 | 200 | 75 |
| 66 | 3/8 | 18 | 185 | 160 |
| — | | 18 | 185 | 160 |
| — | | 18 | 185 | 160 |

† Linked up to 18 per cent near Cadwell Box.

experienced *en route*, but the net time was estimated at 167 minutes for the 185·7 miles, within four minutes of booked time and involving an average speed from start to stop of 66·7 mph. The load was the usual one of 278 tons tare, 290 tons gross. Shortly before the outbreak of war a similar case occurred in the North Eastern area where another 'V2', No 4782, worked the down 'Coronation' forward to York. Under wartime traffic conditions the 'V2's were interchangeable with the 'Pacifics' on all the heaviest duties, and through Gresley's 'big engine' policy the LNER, with over 130 'V2's in service by the middle of the war, was fortunate in having nearly 250 locomotives capable of handling the entire range of main-line duties, on routes where engines of such weight could be operated.

TABLE 47

MAXIMUM TONNAGES ALLOWED OVER EDINBURGH–ABERDEEN ROUTE

|  | 'D49' Class 4–4–0 | 'C11' Class 4–4–2 | 'A1' and 'A3' Class 4–6–2 | 'V2' Class 2–6–2 | 'P2' Class 2–8–2 |
|---|---|---|---|---|---|
| Aberdeen to Dundee | 310 | 340 | 420 | 420 | 530 |
| Dundee to Edinburgh | 340 | 370 | 450 | 450 | 550 |
| Edinburgh to Dundee | 340 | 370 | 480 | 480 | 550 |
| Dundee to Aberdeen | 340 | 370 | 480 | 480 | 530 |

With the locomotives for the East Anglian service mentioned in Chapter Eleven we come to the end of Gresley's express passenger designs; but before concluding the story with the two remarkable mixed-traffic classes 'K4' and 'V4' mention must be made of the rebuilding of three locomotives, all isolated examples, yet each one significant of the general trend in LNER practice towards the end of Gresley's chieftainship. First, in 1936, one of the celebrated ex-NER 4–4–0s of class 'R' (LNER class 'D20') was fitted with long-travel valves. This reconstruction was considerably less extensive than that previously carried out on the 'Claud Hamiltons', for on engine No 2020 the original boiler, and – more surprising – the original chimney and dome, were retained. The alteration to the motion was as follows:

|  | Original NER class 'R' | LNER 'D20' rebuilt |
|---|---|---|
| Piston-valves | 8¾-in dia | 10-in dia |
| Lap | 1⅛ ins | 1⅝ ins |
| Travel in full gear | 4³⁄₃₂ ins | 6 ins |

The outward appearance of No 2020 was changed somewhat by the seemingly inevitable raising of the running-plate, and as the upward curve took place in front of the leading splasher the effect was not pleasing. No 2020 was the only engine of the class to be altered, but the new arrangement of the motion should have enhanced the excellent reputation of the 'D20's for high-speed running with moderate loads. I have, however, not seen any detailed logs of her running.

After this came the rebuilding of an ex-NER class 'S3' three-cylinder mixed-traffic 4–6–0. Engines of that class, later LNER class 'B16', had three sets of Stephenson link motion, but in 1938 No 2364 was fitted with new cylinders, Walschaerts gear for the outside-cylinders, and the Gresley derived motion for the inside-cylinder. Piston-valves, 9-in diameter, which had a travel of 6 ins at the maximum cut-off of 68 per cent, were used. This rebuilding was carried out at Darlington works, and as with the 'D20' the original North Eastern boiler, chimney, and dome were retained. No 2364 in her modified form, classified 'B16/2', proved a great success and many more engines of the 'B16' class were similarly converted.

The last rebuilding to be mentioned was that of the four-cylinder Ivatt 'Atlantic' No 3279, briefly referred to in Chapter Six. In 1938 this engine was reconstructed as a two-cylinder machine with 20-in by 26-in cylinders and outside Walschaerts gear. The cylinders and valves were similar to those of the 'K2' 'Moguls', but although the 2–6–0s and the rebuilt 4–4–2 No 3279 had 10-in diameter piston-valves, the 'Atlantic' had long laps and a valve-travel in full gear of 6 ins against the $5\frac{9}{32}$ ins of the 'Moguls'. It would have been interesting to see whether No 3279 with her modern front end could have equalled or eclipsed the maximum efforts of the standard '251' class engines. She was stationed at New England, and there is no recorded instance of her having to take over at a moment's notice the haulage of a 550-ton East Coast express, as the Grantham 'C1's did on certain memorable occasions. Nevertheless this rebuilding, by Gresley himself, was actually a curtain raiser to the production of the 'B1' 4–6–0, by Thompson, and indeed all his standard two-cylinder types. He also used the 20-in by 26-in cylinders of the 'K2' 'Moguls', with long-lap valves.

Mention of the 'K2' 'Moguls' brings me to the West Highland line, and to the special 2–6–0s designed by Gresley to deal with the severe operating conditions obtaining there. Hitherto, the maximum load permitted without a pilot had been 220 tons, and winter and summer alike a good deal of double-heading was necessary. In preparing a new locomotive design for this road Gresley was handicapped not only by limitations on axle-loading but also by the curvature; but by the use of coupled wheels of only 5 ft 2 in diameter an engine of high tractive effort was produced. This was classed 'K4', and the leading dimensions make an interesting comparison, shown on page 178, with those of previous 'Moguls' for the GNR and LNER.

The cylinders of the new class were the same as those of the 'K3's but the heaviest demands for steam would be intermittent, and in any case at low speed, so that a smaller boiler could be used. This latter was outwardly of 'K2' proportions though having considerably less evaporative heating surface. In the 'K2's, however, the large area is due mainly to the use of unusually small tubes, only $1\frac{1}{4}$-in diameter, against $1\frac{3}{4}$-in tubes used in the 'K1', 'K3', and 'K4' classes; for a given smokebox vacuum the 'K4' boiler would steam far more readily than the 'K2'. When first put into service, in the early summer of 1937, the pioneer 'K4', No 3441 *Loch Long*, was working at a boiler pressure of 180 psi. After a short time this was increased to 200 psi and with the latter the engine was able to take loads up to 300 tare tons. Due to weight restrictions piloting was not permitted with the 'K4's.

*Loch Long* proved a marked success, not only taking her rostered maximum load with ease, but doing so on no greater water consumption than that of the 'K2's when hauling their 220-ton trains. In making the through run from Glasgow to Fort William, or vice versa, water was normally taken only once intermediately, at Crianlarich, even with the full 300-ton load, whereas in my experience, on up journeys with 'K2's loaded up to, or near their maximum load of 220 tons, a special stop at times was necessary at Bridge of Orchy for water; and the 'K4's had no more water capacity in their tenders than the 'K2's. With No 3441 *Loch Long* I had a very interesting journey on the 5.45 AM from Glasgow to Fort William, details of which are given in the table on pages 180–1. It was an impressive experience on the footplate and one appreciated particularly how serious was the handicap imposed by the incessant curvature, as revealed by the cut-offs used. On the Ardlui–Crianlarich and Crianlarich–Tyndrum sections – both very winding – cut-off was 32 per cent on the 1 in 60 gradients; north of Bridge of Orchy, however, we made faster climbing on a bank nearly as steep though fairly straight, but on 27 per cent cut-off. Both these cut-offs are in striking contrast to the percentages of 45, 50, and even 60 per cent needed with the 'K2's in the haulage of 220-ton loads. After the successful début of No 3441 *Loch Long* five more of the class were constructed, like No 3441 at Darlington works, and put into service in 1938–9. These latter were painted in passenger colours and received fine Scottish names:

| | | | |
|---|---|---|---|
| 3442 | *The Great Marquess* | 3444 | *Mac Calein Mor* |
| 3443 | *Cameron of Locheil* | 3445 | *Lord of the Isles* |
| | 3446 | *Macleod of Macleod* | |

Engine No 3442 *The Great Marquess* has been preserved, and is now the private property of Viscount Garnock.

The completion of what proved to be Gresley's last design was considerably delayed by the outbreak of war. Although by 1939 a sufficient number of powerful modern locomotives had been built to cover practically all main-line requirements of the LNER a need was expressed for a general utility design, with a fairly high nominal tractive effort, yet at the same time with a sufficiently light axle-loading to permit working over sections where the existing heavy main-line engines were not allowed to run. In adopting a maximum axle-load of 17 tons in the new 'V4' class, Gresley produced a locomotive that could be used over a total of 5,000 route miles, nearly five-sixths of the entire LNER system. The use of the 2–6–2 wheel arrangement led to the 'V4' engines being referred to sometimes as smaller

TABLE 48

COMPARATIVE DIMENSIONS OF LNER 'MOGULS'

| | 'K1' | 'K2' | 'K3' | 'K4' |
|---|---|---|---|---|
| Cylinders | (2) 20 ins × 26 ins | (2) 20 ins × 26 ins | (3) 18½ ins × 26 ins | (3) 18½ ins × 26 ins |
| Coupled wheels (diameter) | 5 ft 8 ins | 5 ft 8 ins | 5 ft 8 ins | 5 ft 2 ins |
| Boiler pressure, psi | 170 | 170 | 180 | 200 |
| Boiler diameter | 4 ft 8 ins | 5 ft 6 ins | 6 ft 0 ins | 5 ft 6 ins |
| Heating surface: | | | | |
| Small tubes | 687 sq ft | 1,131 sq ft | 1,192 sq ft | 871 sq ft |
| Large tubes | 294 sq ft | 396 sq ft | 527 sq ft | 382 sq ft |
| Firebox | 137 sq ft | 152 sq ft | 182 sq ft | 168 sq ft |
| Total | 1,118 sq ft | 1,679 sq ft | 1,901 sq ft | 1,421 sq ft |
| Superheating surface | 303 sq ft | 305 sq ft | 407 sq ft | 310 sq ft |
| Grate area | 24·5 sq ft | 24·5 sq ft | 28·0 sq ft | 27·5 sq ft |
| Nominal tractive effort at 85 per cent boiler pressure | 22,070 lb | 22,070 lb | 30,031 lb | 36,600 lb |

versions of the 'Green Arrows'; actually the general characteristics of the two designs differed considerably. Although the
factor of adhesion was roughly the same in both cases, the boiler
and firebox of the 'V2' were much larger in relation to the nominal tractive effort than in the 'V4', which was designed to put
forth a high drawbar pull for short periods rather than to sus-
tain a big effort continuously. The following were the leading
dimensions of the pioneer 'V4', No 3401 Bantam Cock: cylinders (three) 15-in diameter by 26-in stroke; coupled wheels
5 ft 8 in diameter; total heating surface 1,799·9 sq ft; grate
area 28·7 sq ft; boiler pressure 250 psi; nominal tractive effort
at 85 per cent working pressure 27,420 lb; total weight in
working order (engine only) 70½ tons.

A second locomotive of the 'V4' class was completed shortly
after No 3401 and it seemed that these two were forerunners of
yet another numerous Gresley class. As in the case of the first
two 2–8–2 express engines of class 'P2' there were certain differences in the design of 3401 and 3402, the relative merits of
which were to be investigated. No 3401 had a copper firebox –
a miniature edition of the standard LNER wide type as used on
the 'Pacifics', 2–6–2s and 2–8–2s; on No 3402 a box of similar
proportions was fitted, though built in steel and of completely
welded construction. In view of their widespread use abroad
the trial of steel fireboxes on the LNER was in itself a most
interesting development, and the firebox of No 3402 was in
addition fitted with a thermic syphon. After some experimental
running in East Anglia during which she pulled some very
heavy loads, Bantam Cock joined No 3402 in Scotland. The
latter engine worked on the West Highland line, though, as
might be expected, with her lesser tractive effort, she was not
able to tackle loads of 'K4' magnitude; the maximum rostered
load for a 'V4' was 250 tons, or 50 tons less than a 'K4'.

Before closing the Gresley period brief mention must be
made of the three-cylinder 2–6–2 tank engines of classes 'V1'
and 'V3', first introduced in 1930 and 1936 respectively. They
were neat and handsome engines with characteristic Great
Northern lines, though apart from some experimental running
on the King's Cross suburban services in 1931 they worked

TABLE 49

LNER DUMBARTON–FORT WILLIAM

Load: 286 tons tare, 305 tons full

Engine: 'K4' type 2-6-0 No 3441 Loch Long

Driver: Thompson; Fireman: G. Paterson (Fort William shed)

| Distance miles | | Schedule min | Actual min sec | Speeds mph | Cut-off per cent | Boiler pressure, psi | Steam-Chest pressure, psi |
|---|---|---|---|---|---|---|---|
| 0·0 | Dumbarton | 0 | 0 00 | — | 65 | — | — |
| | Cardross | | 5 50 | 57 | 22 | 195 | 185 |
| 7·1 | Craigendoran Junction | | 9 43 | 15* | 40 | 185 | 175 |
| | | | | 21 | | | |
| 9·3 | Upper Helensburgh | } — | 15 30 | — | | | |
| 0·0 | | } 0 | 0 00 | | 65 | | |
| 6·9 | Garelochhead | | 12 10 | 20* | 32 | 200 | 185 |
| 8·2 | Post 10 | | 14 37 | — | | 200 | 190 |
| 8·6 | Whistlefield | | 15 39 | 25 | 37 | | |
| 9·2 | Post 11 | | 17 28 | 21½ | 40 | | |
| 10·2 | Post 12 | | 20 17 | 20½ | | 190 | 180 |
| 12·2 | Post 14 | | 23 48 | 38 | 32 | | |
| 13·5 | Glen Douglas | | 25 52 | — | 45 | 195 | 10 |
| 17·5 | Arrochar | } 34 | 33 12 | — | 45 | | |
| 0·0 | | } 0 | 0 00 | | | | |
| 8·0 | Ardlui | } 15 | 13 50 | — | 65 | | |
| 0·0 | | } 0 | 0 00 | | | | |

'SHIRES' IN SCOTLAND
*Upper:* No 62704 *Stirlingshire*, formerly No 264, on Crail-Glasgow express near Croy
*Lower:* No 277 *Berwickshire* on Aberdeen-Edinburgh express pounding its way up the 1 in 70 to the Forth Bridge

PACIFIC DEVELOPMENT
*Top:* Gresley 'A3' class No 2500 *Windsor Lad* (1935 series)
*Centre:* The world-famous 'A4' No 4468 *Mallard*
*Bottom:* Peppercorn 'A1' class No 60119 *Patrick Stirling* (1948 design)

EDINBURGH WAVERLEY IN BR DAYS
*Upper:* An 'A4' No 19 *Bittern*, and a Glen 4-4-0 No 2490 *Glen Fintaig* at adjoining platforms

*Lower:* The up 'Queen of Scots' Pullman leaving with 'A3' Pacific No 60037 *Hyperion*

*Upper:* Up Waverley route mail, 2.33 PM Edinburgh to Carlisle, behind
'V2' 2-6-2 No 60816
*Lower:* An 'A3' No 60078 *Night Hawk* on up express goods near
Croxdale

EAST COAST EXPRESSES: PRE- AND POST-GROUPING
*Upper:* 8 AM Newcastle-King's Cross near Low Fell, with NER 'Z' class three-cylinder 4-4-2 No 735

*Lower:* The 'Coronation' of 1937 at high speed near Hatfield with 'A4' engine No 4492 *Dominion of New Zealand*

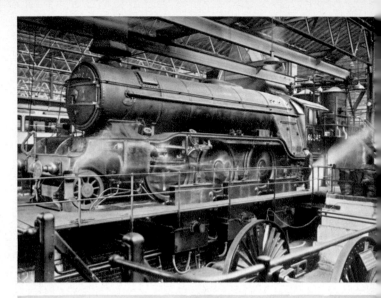

THE 'V2' NO 60845 ON TEST AT SWINDON
*Upper:* Running at high speed on the stationary plant
*Lower:* Controlled road test, with twenty-coach train, passing Hullavington

'V2's IN HEAVY DUTY
*Top:* The pioneer engine No 4770 *Green Arrow* on the 3.40 PM Scotch goods near Harringay (the author on the footplate)

*Centre:* On loan to the Southern: No 60896 leaving Waterloo on the Bournemouth Belle

*Bottom:* On down West of England express passing Crewkerne, at a time when the 'Merchant Navy' class were temporarily withdrawn: engine No 60928

*Top:* One of the ex-GER 'B12' 4-6-0s, No 8519, fitted with ACFI feed-water heater (Hikers)

*Centre:* One of the later 'B1' 4-6-0s No 61379 *Mayflower* at King's Cross

*Bottom:* 'K4' three-cylinder 2-6-0 for the West Highland line: No 3446 *MacLeod of MacLeod*

SPECIAL DUTY IN 1954
The preserved GNR 4-4-2 No 251 with a 'Director' class 4-4-0 No
62663 *Prince Albert* work the 'Farnborough Flyer'
*Upper:* Rounding the curve at Reading West Junction
*Lower:* At Basingstoke shed amid a group of Southern 4-6-0s

PACIFICS IN POST-WAR DAYS
*Top:* Thompson's rebuild of the pioneer Gresley Pacific *Great Northern*
*Upper centre:* The 'A4' No 14 *Silver Link* with valances removed, but
pre-war blue livery restored
*Lower centre:* Thompson 'A2' class No 511 *Airborne*
*Bottom:* Peppercorn 'A2' class No 525 *A. H. Peppercorn*

PEPPERCORN 'A1' PACIFICS AT WORK
*Upper:* Engine No 60138, as originally built and unnamed, with stove-pipe chimney, leaving York with the down 'Flying Scotsman'
*Lower:* No 60131 *Osprey* on the down 'Queen of Scots' Pullman near Stevenage

*Top:* The 'A3' Pacific No 2751 *Humorist* with Kylchap double blast-pipe and chimney: prototype of the final 'A3' development
*Centre:* Sir Nigel Gresley beside the 'A4' engine bearing his name
*Bottom:* The final version of 'A3's with Kylchap exhaust arrangements and small smoke-deflecting plates

*Upper:* Peppercorn 'A1' No 60161 *North British* on loan to Polmadie shed, near Lancaster on the 11.15 PM Birmingham to Glasgow

*Lower:* Peppercorn 'A2' No 60527 *Sun Chariot* on the express fish train from Aberdeen, climbing to the Forth Bridge

FAMOUS EXPRESSES: 1914 AND 1961
*Upper:* GCR. The 3.15 PM Marylebone-Sheffield non-stop near Neasden, with 4-4-0 engine No 433 *Edwin A. Beasley*

*Lower:* The 'Elizabethan' non-stop Edinburgh to King's Cross near Hadley Wood, with 'A4' Pacific No 60009 *Union of South Africa*

PRESERVED 'A4's AT WORK
*Upper: Mallard*, on an LCGB rail tour train at Tiverton Junction, Western Region
*Lower: Sir Nigel Gresley*, climbing Shap at 50 mph with an eleven-coach train

One of the most famous of LNER locomotives: No 4472 *Flying Scotsman*, at King's Cross shed. Driver Sparshatt stands just beneath the nameplate

| Miles | Station | | Time | | | | |
|---|---|---|---|---|---|---|---|
| 0·4 | Post 28 | | 1 42 | | 40 | 190 | 180 |
| 1·4 | Post 29 | | 3 55 | 26 | 32 | — | — |
| 2·4 | Post 30 | | 6 17 | 25 | 32 | 187 | 175 |
| 3·4 | Post 31 | | 8 25 | 33½ | 32 | 190 | 190 |
| 5·4 | Post 33 | | 12 30 | 27 | 32 | — | — |
| 7·4 | Post 35 | | 17 03 | 25½ | 32 | 195 | 185 |
| 8·7 | Crianlarich | 20 } 0 | 19 47 | — | — | 195 | 185 |
| 0·0 | Post 37 | | 0 00 | | 65 | — | — |
| 0·7 | Post 39 | | 1 45 | 39 | 32 | 190 | 175 |
| 2·7 | Post 41 | | 5 23 | 31 | 32 | — | — |
| 4·7 | | | 10 15 | 23½ | 35 | — | — |
| 5·0 | } Tyndrum | 11 } 0 | 11 20 | | | 190 | 190 |
| 0·0 | Post 42 | | 0 00 | | 65 | 200 | 175 |
| 0·7 | Post 43 | | 2 35 | | 65 | 185 | 180 |
| 1·7 | | | 4 56 | 28½ | 45 | | |
| 7·5 | } Bridge of Orchy | 14 } 0 | 14 30 | | 45 | 190 | 185 |
| 0·0 | Post 50 | | 0 00 | 29 | 65 | | |
| 0·2 | Post 52 | | 3 19 | 44½ | 30 | 195 | |
| 3·2 | Post 54 | | 6 22 | 28½ | 25 | | |
| 5·2 | Post 56 | | 9 46 | 31½ | 27 | | |
| 7·2 | Gorton | | 13 52 | 36 | 27 | | |
| 8·7 | | | 16 29 | | 27 | | |
| 15·6 | } Rannoch | 27 } 0 | 27 12 | | — | 195 | |
| 0·0 | Post 66 | | 0 00 | | 65 | | |
| 1·6 | Corrour | 15 | 5 17 | 18 | 35 | | |
| 7·3 | | | 15 22 | | — | | |

\* Service slack.

entirely in the North Eastern and Scottish areas. All three cylinders drove the middle pair of coupled wheels. The three cylinders were combined in a single casting forming the smoke-box saddle and steam passages to the outside-cylinders. The leading dimensions of the 'V1' engines were: cylinders (three) 16-in diameter by 26-in stroke; coupled wheels 5 ft 8 in diameter; valve-travel in full gear $6\frac{1}{16}$; total heating surface 1,609 sq ft; grate area 22 sq ft; working pressure 180 psi. The nominal tractive effort at 85 per cent working pressure was 22,464 lb. The 'V3' class was the same except that the working pressure was 200 psi, and the nominal tractive effort 24,960 lb. There were, in all, 78 of the 'V1' class, and 14 of 'V3'.

# CHAPTER FOURTEEN

# EDWARD THOMPSON

It is no disparagement to the memory of those who followed him to say that the death of Sir Nigel Gresley left a profound gap in the ranks of LNER senior officers. He had been a man of towering stature. His locomotives had brought world-wide fame to his railway, to such an extent that one is apt to forget that from the shareholders' point of view the LNER was the least attractive of all the British railways during the grouping era. Yet such were the achievements of the Gresley locomotives that everyone concerned with the line, right down to the humblest country porter, delighted to bask in the glow that emanated from the daily work of the 'A4's, let alone such a breathtaking feat as that of *Mallard*. Edward Thompson was appointed to succeed Gresley at a very anxious and critical stage of World War II, and the new chief once told me personally how at the time he was appointed, the chairman, Sir Ronald Matthews, told him there was no need to spend time designing new engines; how Gresley's were unbeatable, and if more were needed he was just to use the existing designs.

Sir Ronald Matthews got the shock of his life when Thompson's reply amounted virtually to 'over my dead body'! A long discussion followed, during which time Thompson went to great lengths explaining the difficulties that were being experienced with engines having the three-cylinder conjugated valve gear. Sir Ronald was incredulous, and eventually Thompson made a characteristic gesture. In as many words he said: 'If you don't believe me get an independent authority to examine the position. If I'm wrong my office is at your disposal; if I'm right I require your consent to make radical changes.' Again Sir Ronald was incredulous, and asked if Thompson was really prepared to invite some outsider to examine all the confidential works and drawing-office reports, and make an independent assessment – particularly on the position appertaining to engines fitted with the conjugated valve gear. The latter was of course the very cornerstone of Gresley's designs, both large and small, and to condemn it was to condemn most of what Gresley had done in the past twenty-odd years. But Thompson persisted, and eventually Sir Ronald Matthews agreed to his seeking an independent arbitrator.

The question was, 'who?' It must clearly be an engineer of the very highest status, and so Thompson approached Sir William Stanier, who at that time was away from the LMS, and seconded for special Governmental duties in connexion with the war. Thompson told me how he put his difficulties to Sir William, and how eventually Stanier agreed to make the investigation. Although Thompson confided many details of his early months to me he did not show me a copy of the report. I gathered it was couched in rather non-committal terms. Stanier did not condemn the three-cylinder conjugated valve gear as such, and went no further than to say that he would not use it himself. As Stanier had built many three-cylinder engines for the LMS, the latest of which were the highly successful 'Converted Royal Scots' this could be taken as a reflection on the Gresley arrangement, though really no more than a vaguely indirect one. But it was enough to secure for Thompson the necessary authority to discard it in all new designs on the LNER.

All this had of course been proceeding behind locked doors, as it were, and the first-fruits of this move were not to be seen for some little time. It was to affect mainly the engines of maximum power, though Thompson's very first new design to appear, the 'B1' 4-6-0 of 1942, caused a mild stir among locomotive enthusiasts. One had become so accustomed to all new LNER engines having three cylinders and the conjugated gear that the appearance of this very simple two-cylinder 4-6-0 was at first regarded as something of a retrograde step. For the wartime traffic additional mixed-traffic engines were required for duties for which the Gresley 'V4' 2-6-2 class had been designed. But the 'V4' had been designed mainly against a pre-war background. It involved the use of high-grade, high-tensile steels which, in 1942, were in short supply, and it incorporated the discredited conjugated valve gear. So instead of building on the Gresley prototype, Thompson, by a clever synthesis of existing tools and patterns, produced the 'B1' – an ideal engine for the day. The synthesis consisted of the well-tried 'Sandringham' boiler; the driving-wheel centres from the 'V2', and the cylinders and valve chests from the ex-GNR 'K2' 'Mogul'. The comparison between the Gresley 'V4' and the Thompson 'B1' is shown in the accompanying table:

### GENERAL UTILITY LOCOMOTIVES

| Class<br>Type | 'V4'<br>2–6–2 | 'B1'<br>4–6–0 |
|---|---|---|
| Cylinder number | 3 | 2 |
| Cylinder diameter, ins | 15 | 20 |
| Cylinder stroke, ins | 26 | 26 |
| Coupled wheel diameter, ft ins | 5–8 | 6–2 |
| Total heating surface including super-<br>heater, sq ft | 1819·4 | 2020 |
| Grate area, sq ft | 28·8 | 27·9 |
| Boiler pressure, psi | 250 | 225 |
| Total engine weight, tons | 70·4 | 71·1 |
| Nominal tractive effort, lb | 27,420 | 26,878 |

The 'B1' was, however, no more than a beginning of the production of a new range of standard locomotives, all of which would have 20-in by 26-in cylinders, and work at a pressure of 225 psi. All were to have outside Walschaerts gear with long-lap, long-travel valves, and the prototypes for three out of the remaining four standard types were economically produced by rebuilding an existing design, thus:

| New<br>class | Wheel<br>arrgt | Rebuilt from<br>existing class | Nom. Tract. Eff. lb | |
|---|---|---|---|---|
| | | | Derivative | New class |
| 'O1' | 2–8–0 | From GCR 'O4' | 31,325 | 35,520 |
| 'K5' | 2–6–0 | From GNR 'K3' | 30,030 | 29,250 |
| 'K1' | 2–6–0 | From LNER 'K4' | 36,600 | 32,080 |

The only class of which the prototype had to be built new was the 2–6–4 passenger tank, for which no Gresley counterpart existed. It was, however, a straight tank-engine version of the 'K1'. The plan for future standardization was well thought out, and the prototypes simply produced. Thompson admitted to me his keen admiration of Great Western practice in its use of two-cylinder engines only for all except those of maximum power; but he felt that there was no need to go to what he himself referred to as 'fancy boilers' when he had available all the necessary tools and flanging blocks to make such simply built and good steaming boilers as those of the 'Sandringham' 4–6–0 and the West Highland 'K4'.

Turning now to the big engines, Thompson again stressed the merits of Churchward's practice on his multi-cylindered engines, in so disposing the cylinders that all could have an equal length of connecting-rod, and circumstances permitted him to build the prototype of his new standard 'Pacific' design by rebuilding an existing engine. Gresley's mighty 'P2' 'Mikados' were only six in number. Under the stress of war-time conditions, and in deteriorating standards of maintenance they were reputed to be giving trouble on the Aberdeen route; though what had happened to them since I made my footplate journeys I cannot imagine. As I remarked in an earlier chapter of this book I found them truly superb locomotives. Having the somewhat discredited conjugated valve gear they provided a ready-made set of 'guinea-pigs' for Thompson's new pro-gramme, and in 1943 engine No 2005 *Thane of Fife* was rebuilt as a 'Pacific'. By removing the leading pair of coupled wheels, fitting new cylinders and motion, and substituting a leading bogie for the pony truck, a prototype 'Pacific' was quite ingeniously produced without any alteration to the length of the frame. The boiler remained un-changed, though the striking streamlined front casing was removed.

Although the prototype had been produced, incorporating three sets of valve gear, and equal length of connecting-rods for all three cylinders, the engine looked a horrible makeshift, with an inordinate distance between the rear bogie wheel and the leading pair of coupled wheels. In comparison to the beautifully proportioned designs of Sir Nigel Gresley the rebuild was not 'easy on the eye' quite apart from the surprise and shock the rebuilding itself caused to admirers of Gresley's work. On-lookers from outside, of course, had no conception of what had gone on behind the scenes on the LNER since Thompson's appointment, and while failures of the conjugated valve gear had been known in pre-war years the official announcement that the rebuilding was due to unsatisfactory performance on the Aberdeen road did not have a very convincing ring about it. Surely, it was argued, ample use could have been made of six such powerful engines south of Edinburgh, if it was the curves that were causing heavy maintenance costs. Wartime loads on the East Coast route were of gargantuan proportions, sometimes requiring the double-heading even of 'Pacifics' on the Cockburnspath bank. One can pass over the vapourings of the 'lunatic fringe' of LNER fans, who averred that to alter any-thing that Gresley had created was an act of iconoclasm; but there is no doubt that this rebuilding of the 'P2' engines – for conversion of the five remaining ones quickly followed that of No 2005 – caused much genuine astonishment among loco-motive men in general.

What the maintenance costs of the rebuilt engines turned out to be I have no idea, but the road performance was certainly not improved – quite the reverse. It would have been difficult to imagine it otherwise. The following table of comparative dimensions makes the change clear enough.

### THE 'P2' CLASS REBUILDING

| Class<br>Type | 'P2'<br>2–8–2 | 'A2'<br>4–6–2 |
|---|---|---|
| Cylinders (3) diameter, ins | 21 | 20 |
| Cylinders (3) stroke, ins | 26 | 26 |
| Total evaporative surface, sq ft | 2714 | 2453 |
| Superheater, sq ft | 777 | 680 |
| Boiler pressure, psi | 220 | 225 |
| Adhesion wt, tons | 79 | 66 |
| Nominal tractive effort, lb | 43,462 | 40,318 |

I rode the *Wolf of Badenoch* on the down 'Aberdonian' express early one morning in August 1945 with an enormous train of 575 tons behind the tender. The schedule was considerably easier than in pre-war years, and the engine made a reasonably good showing to Dundee. But after that, with a slightly reduced load, and the dawn bringing on wet and unseasonable weather, the engine became difficult to handle on the wet rails. One missed the extra adhesion of eight coupled wheels, and on sharp ascents like those immediately following the stops at Arbroath and Montrose there was a good deal of slipping. Quite apart from that a most curious error of detail design manifested itself. The exhaust from the front end of the outside-cylinders was taken towards the blastpipe through a cast member bolted on to the cylinder and steam-chest casting, and at the forward end on to the frame. The two jointing faces were at right-angles to each other. To make a job of such an assembly is an awkward enough task at the best of times; but with faces like the frame plates, where there would always be a slight amount of 'breathing' with the motion of the locomotive on the road, steam tightness was virtually impossible. There was continuous leakage of steam from this point, and the continuous 'working' of the joint tended to slack the nuts off the studs. We arrived in Aberdeen with two of the nuts missing altogether and another lying on the splasher over the rear bogie wheel.

Taking all into account one could have accepted the makeshift rebuilt 'P2's, but it soon transpired that this curious wheel spacing was to be the new standard. The last four engines of an order for 'V2' 2–6–2s of Gresley design were built as 4–6–2s in the Thompson style, and then in 1946 there came the biggest shock of all. To provide the prototype for his new express passenger 'Pacific' he took the pioneer Gresley 'Pacific' No 4470 *Great Northern*, and completely rebuilt it as a 6 ft 8 in version of the rebuilt 'P2' class. Now whatever troubles may have beset them during the war years the Gresley 'Pacifics' as a family of engines, 'A1', 'A3', and 'A4' alike, had been an outstanding success, and to locomotive men, as well as the large body of amateur enthusiasts, *Great Northern*, as the first engine of the family, occupied much the same place in their regard and affection as the Stirling eight-footer No 1, as the pioneer British 'Atlantic' No 990 *Henry Oakley*, and as the ever-famous pioneer of the large-boilered Great Northern 'Atlantics' No 251. The pioneer 'Pacific' No 4470 was the culmination of the Great Northern Railway saga, and many people felt that it was almost a foregone conclusion that some day she would be preserved, and exhibited alongside No 1, No 990, and No 251. Imagine, then, the consternation when she was rebuilt out of all recognition, as an addition to the stud of 'makeshifts', and above all, painted in a royal-blue livery similar to, though not quite so elaborate, as that of the Great Eastern in days prior to World War I.

Among locomotive lovers harsh words were used about Thompson and all his works, and comments not greatly watered down appeared in some of the enthusiast journals. Highly critical letters were published even in such journals as the *Railway Gazette*. At the time I was engaged on making a number of footplate journeys in all parts of the country in connexion with a series of articles I had been commissioned to write for *The Engineer*; the scripts of those articles were in due course submitted to Thompson, and in giving his approval he invited me to visit him at Doncaster, so that he could explain to me the policy on which he had been working. It was then that I learned much of the background information contained in this particular chapter. It was no formal visit. I was invited to spend the night at his home, and it was at his own fireside that he told me of the situation regarding the conjugated valve gear, and of how he came to formulate the plan for the range of standard two-cylinder locomotives. I remember him as a charming host; a tall, elegant, scholarly man, but one who was highly sensitive, and it was the criticism of his work in the railway Press that had greatly distressed him, and led to his invitation to me – with the hope that I might help to redress the situation that had arisen.

He felt very strongly and sincerely about the conjugated valve gear, and the following day at Doncaster works a great amount of data had been laid out for me to examine. In the shops I saw several examples of gears that had caused the engines concerned to become total failures on the road. He ended a memorable visit with an invitation to ride on the new 4470 *Great Northern*, which he offered to have put on to any train I liked. The first opportunity I had came some months later when I was going to Scotland to spend Easter riding on the West Highland line. No 4470 was put on the down 'Aberdonian' for me, from King's Cross to Grantham. Although the schedule, in 1946, was not very demanding, the new engine gave an immaculate performance. Following the war years, the

TABLE 50

## THE THOMPSON 'A2' PACIFICS

| Class<br>Year introduced | 'A2/2'<br>1943 | 'A2/1'<br>1944 | 'A2/3'<br>1946 |
|---|---|---|---|
| Cylinders (3) diameter, ins | 20 | 19 | 19 |
| Cylinders (3) stroke, ins | 26 | 26 | 26 |
| Total evap. heating surface, sq ins | 2453 | 2431 | 2461 |
| Superheater, sq ins | 680 | 680 | 680 |
| Grate area, sq ins | 50 | $41\frac{1}{4}$ | 50 |
| Boiler pressure, psi | 225 | 225 | 250 |
| Nominal tractive effort, lb | 40,318 | 36,387 | 40,430 |

Great Northern main-line track had not been restored to its traditionally high standard; but the engine rode very well, and the deficiency at the front end which had been so pronounced on No 2006 was scarcely noticeable at all. Quite apart from track conditions, the splendid alignment of the old GN main line is naturally conducive to good riding. Nevertheless, on sentimental and historical grounds I wished Thompson had chosen a different Gresley 'Pacific' from 4470 for conversion to his new prototype. The irony of it was that the rebuilt 4470 did not prove a prototype at all. She remained an odd engine.

The rebuilt 'P2' class, and the four 'V2's altered at the last minute to 'Pacifics', were classed 'A2', which classification had been blank in the LNER list since the scrapping of the Raven 'Pacifics'. Construction of the new standard 'A2's began in 1946, and these new engines, while having the same wheelbase

and cylinder layout as the interim varieties, differed in having
a double blastpipe and chimney, but the older type of dome
and regulator, as used on the Gresley 'Pacifics' up to but not
including the 2500–2508 batch, built in 1935. These latter had
the 'banjo' type of dome and steam collector. The relative
dimensions of the three varieties of Thompson's 'A2' are
shown in Table 50. I may add that Thompson himself always
referred to those altered from 'V2's, Nos 3696–3699, as 'the
orphans of the storm'. The new engines were named from
the outset. The four 'orphans' were originally nameless, but
later became:

| | | | |
|---|---|---|---|
| 507 | *Highland Chieftain* | 509 | *Waverley* |
| 508 | *Duke of Rothesay* | 510 | *Robert the Bruce* |

The Thompson 6 ft 2 in 'Pacifics' like all modern engines
with a well-designed valve gear, could run very freely. In
Scotland Mr Ronald Nelson once clocked No 506 *Wolf of
Badenoch*, the first of the rebuilds from class 'P2', at a maximum speed of 85 mph on the level, between Dundee and
Arbroath – a most exceptional piece of running in the year
1947. Generally, they rode well, and so far as actual performance is concerned the best run I had with one of them was on
the down 'Heart of Midlothian' express, when No 520 *Owen
Tudor* took over haulage of the train at Peterborough. Because
of checks on the first stage we were a little late in getting away,
but the arrears were immediately and completely wiped out
by a very fine start and climb to Stoke summit. Details of this
run are tabulated in the accompanying log, and some salient
points may be emphasized.

The day was fine, and very hot, and the engine made a very
clean, vigorous start. Cut-off had been reduced to 15 per cent
as early as Werrington Junction, and with a further reduction,
to 12 per cent, this train of 475 tons was worked up to 72 mph
just after Tallington. The boiler was steaming very freely, with
the gauge reading 230–250 psi all the way up to Stoke. Minimum speed on the long 1 in 200 ending near milepost 96 was
62 mph and the last three miles at 1 in 178 were cleared at

$58\frac{1}{2}$ mph – still on 15 per cent. So, leaving Peterborough 4 minutes late we passed Grantham $1\frac{1}{2}$ minutes early. After that we began to get so well ahead of time that signal checks were experienced. Even after the worst of them were over we were still running some 5 minutes early, at Shaftholme Junction, and the fine running that followed on the dead level to Selby was made on 15 per cent with the regulator three-quarters open.

TABLE 51

### BRITISH RAILWAYS: EASTERN REGION
### 3.29 PM PETERBOROUGH–YORK

Load: 13 coaches, 442 tons tare, 475 tons full

Engine: class 'A2/3' 4–6–2 No 60520 *Owen Tudor*

| Distance miles | | Sch. min | Actual min sec | | Speeds mph |
|---|---|---|---|---|---|
| 0·0 | PETERBOROUGH | 0 | 0 | 00 | — |
| 3·1 | *Werrington Junction* | | 5 | 38 | $61\frac{1}{2}$ |
| 8·4 | Tallington | | 11 | 29 | 72 |
| 12·4 | Essendine | | 13 | 44 | 69 |
| 15·8 | Little Bytham | | 16 | 52 | 67 |
| 20·7 | Corby | | 21 | 32 | $62/64\frac{1}{4}$ |
| 23·7 | *Stoke Box* | | 24 | 35 | $58\frac{1}{2}$ |
| 25·6 | Great Ponton | | 26 | 23 | 70 |
| 29·1 | GRANTHAM | 35 | 29 | 35 | $62\frac{1}{2}$ |
| 33·3 | Barkston | $39\frac{1}{2}$ | 33 | 15 | $70\frac{1}{2}$ |
| 39·0 | Claypole | | 37 | 59 | $77\frac{1}{2}$ |
| — | | | sigs | | 40 |
| 43·7 | NEWARK | $49\frac{1}{2}$ | 43 | 20 | 57 |
| 51·0 | Crow Park | | 50 | 30 | 69 |
| 55·5 | Tuxford | | 54 | 47 | 60 |
| — | | | sigs | | — |
| 62·2 | RETFORD | $70\frac{1}{2}$ | 62 | 15 | — |
| 67·5 | Ranskill | | 68 | 03 | 67/56 |
| 73·1 | *Milepost 149½* | | 73 | 45 | $58\frac{1}{2}$ |
| — | | | sigs | | |
| 79·6 | DONCASTER | $95\frac{1}{2}$ | 82 | 25 | — |
| — | | | sigs | | |
| 83·8 | *Shaftholme Junction* | $100\frac{1}{2}$ | 90 | 50 | 10 |
| 86·6 | Moss | | 95 | 14 | 55 |
| 93·4 | Templehirst | | 101 | 26 | 75 |
| | | | sigs | | |
| 98·0 | SELBY | $114\frac{1}{2}$ | 106 | 00 | 25 |
| — | | | checked | | |
| 111·8 | YORK | $132\frac{1}{2}$ | 129 | 35 | |

At York the engine was re-manned, and the new driver used even shorter cut-offs, with full regulator. On this second stage the firing was lighter, and for the fast stretch to Darlington, we were running mostly with pressure below 200 psi. It was not that the engine was in difficulties for steam; it was just that more was not needed. Full regulator and 10 per cent cut-off took us up to 72 mph on the level at Alne, but then the reverser was put to a position indicated on the scale as 'mid-gear', and speed gradually drifted down to 59 mph. Although no more than easy work was required the engine put up quite an impressive performance. The riding was good, and this was altogether a most comfortable and enjoyable trip.

Thompson's stay as chief mechanical engineer was no more than brief. He retired in the autumn of 1946, and with the appointment of Arthur H. Peppercorn as his successor, and with nationalization of the British railways imminent, his carefully worked-out plan for future locomotive standardization was to a large extent stillborn. New 'Pacific' engines were authorized, but Peppercorn immediately discarded one of Thompson's most cherished precepts, by reverting to a more normal wheel spacing, with unequal lengths of connecting-rod for the outside and inside-cylinders, but retaining three sets of valve gear. Thus the peculiar Thompson wheel spacing which was intended to be the future LNER standard for 'Pacific' engines, was confined to no more than twenty-six examples: the six rebuilt 'P2's, the four 'orphans of the storm', the fifteen new engines, Nos 500 and 511 to 524, and the unfortunate 4470 *Great Northern*. No 500 was named *Edward Thompson*, at a little ceremony presided over by Sir Ronald Matthews. It was a pleasing gesture to a man whose motives were to a great extent misunderstood, and who I feel sure acted with deep conviction. But I do wish he had chosen a different Gresley 'Pacific' to rebuild as his prototype express passenger engine!

There is no doubt Thompson's greatest success was the 'B1' 4-6-0. They were strong, willing engines with a fine turn of speed, and in the interchange trials of 1948 showed they could haul a really heavy train at high speed. I must leave the story of this part of their prowess to the next chapter. Large orders for them were placed with outside contractors, and eventually the class numbered 400. I had many runs with them both on the footplate and when travelling passenger. On the footplate they could be very rough and uncomfortable. They had no wedges for taking up play in the axlebox guides when wear developed, and on engines that had amassed a considerable mileage the vibration when running with steam shut off was horrible. At their best they were pleasant engines, and my happiest recollection of footplate work with them is on the Great Central line. At the time I made these runs I could not publish the whole story. There was then a 70-mph speed limit over the whole line, as an aftermath of war conditions of track maintenance. This was frequently exceeded, and on two runs from Leicester to Marylebone we ran up to 82 mph in places. The first of these runs, with engine No 61130, was particularly memorable to me because soon after leaving we ran into the densest fog in which I have ever travelled on the footplate – so dense, indeed, that when we finally arrived in Marylebone station there was a man waving a brazier to show us where the buffer stops were!

I rode the pioneer 'K1' 2–6–0, rebuilt from a 'K4', on the West Highland line, and found her very much a smaller edition of the 'B1' in her action. Unfortunately from the viewpoint of testing performance we were double-headed and with no more than a moderate load shared between the 'K1' and a 'K2' the running data I took had no significance. At this stage I may add that Thompson initiated the rebuilding of several other existing LNER engine designs. The most important of these was that of several 'Sandringham' class 4–6–0s into a two-cylinder variant, classified 'B2'. One of these latter, No 61671 *Royal Sovereign*, was stationed at Cambridge and retained in immaculate condition for Royal Train workings between King's Cross and Wolferton, just as the 'Super-Clauds' 4–4–0s Nos 8783 and 8787 had been retained in pre-war days. Ten of the 'Sandringhams' were rebuilt as class 'B2', but they never superseded the Gresley engines on East Anglian duties, rather working turn and turn about with them. Another Thompson rebuild of which I have never seen any record of performance

was the alteration of one of the ex-Great Central four-cylinder
4–6–0s of the 'Lord Faringdon' class, formerly No 6166 *Earl
Haig*, to the new standard two-cylinder layout. This was a
much more extensive reconstruction, and involved replacing
the original Great Central boiler by a 'B1' standard type. One
would take leave to doubt if such a rebuilding was really worth
the work involved on so relatively old an engine.

We can leave discussion of the Thompson 'O1' standard
2–8–0 until the next chapter, which includes the results of
comparative freight engine running in the interchange trials of
1948. For the present there remain to be mentioned two more
Thompson rebuilds that were intended to form future LNER
standards. The first was the Robinson 'Pom-Pom' – his extremely handsome 0–6–0 goods engine introduced as long
previously as 1901. It was certainly a robust well-proportioned
engine, that could be used, like the ex-Midland '4F' 0–6–0 on
the LMS, as a mixed-traffic engine as well as in light goods
duties. The rebuild was superheated, and the Stephenson's
link motion and valves were altered to have longer laps and
longer valve-travel. Alone among the constituent companies
of the LNER, the engines of the Great Central had suffered
greatly in appearance since grouping. It is a little difficult to
imagine why the very handsome Robinson's chimneys and
dome covers should have been discarded and replaced by
Great Northern type chimneys and woefully truncated dome
covers. It can be safely asserted that such changes were not at
the direction of Sir Nigel Gresley, otherwise similar dese-
crations would have been perpetrated on the North Eastern,
Great Eastern, and North British engines. The initiative in
this regrettable step would appear to have come from within
Gorton works.

The appearance of the 'Pom-Poms' had been ruined long
before Thompson selected them as a future LNER standard. At
the time the LNER passed into national ownership 25 of them
had been converted into the new modernized form, while 149
remained as originally built, save for the changes in the various
boiler mountings.

The final rebuild to be mentioned was also of an old Great

Central design, the Robinson outside-cylindered o–8–o of 1902. This engine was a very handsome engine for a heavy freighter; but Thompson turned it into a tank engine for short-distance work and shunting. No new engines were built either of the o–6–o light goods or the o–8–o shunting tanks.

# CHAPTER FIFTEEN

# NATIONALIZATION—THE INTERCHANGE TRIALS

Although the London & North Eastern Railway itself ceased to exist from January 1st, 1948, one cannot ring down the curtain abruptly upon all that happened afterwards, because in many ways the history of LNER steam locomotives in the ensuing dozen years includes many points of deep significance, particularly in relation to the design features of the Gresley locomotives. The three-cylinder engines, especially the 'Pacifics' and the 'V2's, were still under something of a cloud at the time of nationalization, and the reputation of the 'A4's was not enhanced in the interchange trials of 1948, for reasons to be described later. At the beginning of the year the new Peppercorn 'Pacifics' were coming into service, and it cannot be said that their début was very impressive. Immediately they began to show a most curious trait in their riding: they seemed to pivot on a vertical axis passing through the middle driving axle.

This was something new in Doncaster-built locomotives. The Ivatt 'Atlantics' used to swing about in the most disconcerting way at the rear end but they were noticeably steady at the front. The Gresley 'Pacifics' might suddenly go into this pivoting action, but it was immediately damped out. But the Peppercorns used to keep it up for miles on end. I first struck it on an 'A2', No 60539, working the 5.30 PM from King's Cross between Grantham and York. It was not a very fast train in those days, and on the relatively good track of the GN main line, although quite pronounced and continuous for long periods, it was not such as to appear dangerous. But there we were, pegging our way along at about 60 mph with the front of the engine quietly swinging from side to side one way, while we in the cab were being swung in synchronism the other way. When the project of large-scale locomotive interchange trials was first mooted, only a few weeks after nationalization had

taken place, it was originally suggested that one of the latest
'Pacifics' should represent the Eastern and North Eastern
Regions in the first-line express passenger engine trials. When
it came to the final selection of locomotive, however, the E & NE
were not prepared to put either a Thompson or a Peppercorn
'Pacific' into the arena, and so authority fell back upon a
Gresley 'A4'.

Before coming to the interchange trials themselves details of
the Peppercorn 'Pacifics' must be set down:

## THE PEPPERCORN PACIFICS

All the dimensions are common to both 'A1' and 'A2' classes except
the coupled wheel diameter and the resulting tractive effort. The 'A2's
had single blastpipe and chimneys; the 'A1's had the Kylchap double
blastpipe arrangement:

| | |
|---|---|
| Cylinders (3)             19-in diameter by 26-in stroke | |
| Boiler: Total evaporative heating surface | 2461·4 sq ft |
| Superheater | 680 sq ft |
| Grate area | 50 sq ft |
| Working pressure | 250 psi |
| Coupled wheel diameter | |
|    'A1' class | 6 ft 8 ins |
|    'A2' class | 6 ft 2 ins |
| Nominal tractive effort at 85 per cent bp | |
|    'A1' class | 37,397 lb |
|    'A2' class | 40,300 lb |

Originally the 'A2's had single chimneys of standard Gresley
shape while the 'A1's had double chimneys of the Thompson
stove-pipe form. By comparison with the Doncaster engines
that had preceded them it cannot be said that either class was
particularly handsome, though certainly an improvement upon
the Thompson 'makeshifts'. It was also something of an inno-
vation for the designer's name to be bestowed on the first
engine of his first new class – the 'A2' *A. H. Peppercorn*. This
engine had the melancholy distinction of being the last built
by the LNER itself. The remaining engines of the class were built
by British Railways. Previously Sir Nigel Gresley was the first
locomotive engineer ever to have his name given to an engine
during his own tenure of office. Then it was his hundredth
'Pacific', and only then after those engines had won for the
LNER imperishable fame. The times were certainly changing.

Further evidence of this was shown when the first of the Peppercorn 'A1' 'Pacifics' was named after a prominent trade unionist, who had recently been appointed a member of the new Railway Executive. It is true that W. P. Allen had once been an engine driver, and a Great Northern driver at that; but bringing politics into engine naming can also bring its embarrassments, as the LNER once discovered over the former Great Central 4–6–0 named *Lloyd George*!

Coming to the interchange trials, here I need not be concerned with the circumstances that led to those interesting events, but only with the way the engines of the former LNER fared. For the 'A4' 'Pacifics' it could have been a resounding triumph: a vindication of the design, sweeping aside all the doubts and denigrations that had followed the death of Sir Nigel Gresley. Unfortunately high authority, authority that was not in touch with day-to-day running affairs, insisted that the E & NE representative should be the historic world record breaker *Mallard*. Unfortunately that engine was far from being in good condition at the time, and those responsible at King's Cross 'top shed' pleaded incessantly against this directive. But *Mallard* it had to be, and as those who knew best had feared, she failed on the Western Region even before the preliminary running had been completed. *Seagull* was substituted, and she failed in tests on the Southern Region. *Mallard* took up the running again, and failed a second time; and so a third 'A4' had to be used to finish the tests, No 60034 *Lord Faringdon*.

The drivers, knowing only too well that they had engines below standard, handled them with the utmost care and skill, and one rarely saw the fire and dash that had characterized 'A4' performance in former days. As it turned out, these engines had the lowest basic coal consumption of any of the large express passenger classes; but much of it was achieved by running that could not be called anything but mediocre when the work of these engines in pre-war years was recalled. Some observers felt that the 'A4's had passed their prime and could no longer repeat their pre-war feats; but only a few weeks after the conclusion of the interchange trials I rode No 60030 *Golden Fleece* from King's Cross to Grantham and recorded some magnificent running, quite up to the old standards. For the record I have tabulated one interesting run made by an 'A4' on a 'foreign' line during the interchange trials: one with *Mallard* from Salisbury to Exeter. In view of the recent exploits of the now-privately owned No 4498 *Sir Nigel Gresley* it would have been extremely interesting to see what an 'A4' could have done with the 530-ton test trains between Crewe and Carlisle, had the schedules been smart and the line free from checks. But the schedule time of the down 'Royal Scot' then allowed as much as 183 minutes for the 141 miles from Crewe to Carlisle, and so many speed restrictions were in force for track repairs, that on one occasion the 'A4' 'Pacific' No 60034 *Lord Faringdon* took 203 minutes for the trip!

The main line of the Southern, and particularly that west of Salisbury, had been little affected by the maintenance difficulties that had beset so many famous British routes in the war years and in the period of austerity that followed, and in contrast to the conditions elsewhere *Mallard* was able to run in magnificent style on the down 'Atlantic Coast Express'. The late R. E. Charlewood gave me details of this run, and it was one of the fastest ever made over that route with such a load – a route traditionally the scene of very fast running, from the days of Dugald Drummond on the London & South Western Railway. The work grew progressively finer as the train forged its way westwards, and the culmination was a truly magnificent ascent of Honiton bank, entering the tunnel at $33\frac{1}{2}$ mph after 5 miles of continuous ascent at 1 in 80.

The 'B1' 4–6–0s, competing against Stanier 'Black-Fives', Great Western 'Halls', and Bulleid West Country 'Pacifics', put up an excellent show. On the rival routes from London to Manchester, on trains making many intermediate stops, there was not much chance for display of their prowess in sustained express running; but the working of the Wolverhampton–Penzance express on the Western Region, in each direction between Plymouth and Bristol, was a different matter altogether, and a performance I personally logged on the up service, with engine No 61251 *Oliver Bury*, was of a quality such as to make the Great Western 'Castle' class look to their laurels, let alone the competing 'Hall' 4–6–0 in the actual interchange trials. This run, tabulated herewith, is without doubt the finest performance I have ever personally noted with a 'B1', and its outstanding features require special mention and emphasis. A

TABLE 52

SOUTHERN REGION: SALISBURY–EXETER

1948 Interchange Trials

Load: 481 tons tare, 505 tons full

Engine: class 'A4' 4–6–2 No 22 *Mallard*

| Distance miles | | Actual min sec | | Speeds mph |
|---|---|---|---|---|
| 0·0 | SALISBURY | 0 | 00 | — |
| 2·5 | Wilton | 5 | 08 | — |
| 8·2 | Dinton | 11 | 25 | — |
| 12·5 | Tisbury | 15 | 47 | — |
| 17·5 | Semley | 21 | 13 | 48 |
| 21·6 | Gillingham | 25 | 06 | 69 |
| 23·9 | *Milepost* 107½ | 27 | 11 | 58 |
| 28·4 | TEMPLECOMBE | 31 | 16 | 73 |
| 29·9 | *Milepost* 113½ | 33 | 10 | 42½ |
| 34·5 | Sherborne | 37 | 40 | 75 |
| 39·1 | YEOVIL JUNCTION | 41 | 39 | 68½ |
| 42·7 | *Milepost* 126¼ | 45 | 19 | 50 |
| 47·9 | Crewkerne | 50 | 18 | 66 |
| 49·7 | *Milepost* 133¼ | 52 | 51 | 36 |
| 55·9 | Chard Junction | 58 | 31 | 76½ |
| 61·0 | Axminster | 62 | 20 | 82 |
| 64·2 | Seaton Junction | 64 | 48 | 73½ |
| 69·0 | *Milepost* 152½ | 70 | 46 | 33½ |
| 70·0 | *Milepost* 153½ | 72 | 45 | 30 |
| 71·2 | Honiton | 74 | 10 | — |
| | | | | 70 |
| 75·8 | SIDMOUTH JUNCTION | 79 | 24 | |
| | | p.w.s. | | — |
| 3·7 | Whimple | 7 | 43 | — |
| 7·4 | Broad Clyst | | | 67½ |
| 11·1 | *Exmouth Junction* | 15 | 07 | |
| 12·2 | EXETER | 18 | 11 | |

further table shows the details of the overall performance of the engine throughout from Plymouth to Bristol, though the inclusion of the earlier stage of the run, with only the Cornish portion of the train, of 249 tons tare, very much reduced the overall coal consumption as measured in pounds per train mile. Apart from the brief, though strenuous efforts needed on the Hemerdon and Dainton banks the engine was working under easy steam throughout from Plymouth to Exeter.

TABLE 53
WESTERN REGION: EXETER–BRISTOL
1948 Interchange Trials
Load: 450 tons tare, 490 tons full
Engine: class 'B1' 4–6–0 No 61251 *Oliver Bury*

| Distance miles | | Actual min | sec | Speeds mph |
|---|---|---|---|---|
| 0·0 | EXETER | 0 | 00 | — |
| 1·3 | *Cowley Bridge Junction* | 3 | 43 | — |
| 3·4 | Stoke Canon | 6 | 54 | — |
| 7·2 | Silverton | 11 | 31 | 55 |
| 8·4 | Hele | 12 | 52 | 52½ |
| 12·6 | Cullompton | 17 | 19 | 58 |
| 14·8 | Tiverton Junction | 19 | 59 | 47 |
| 16·6 | Sampford Peverell | 22 | 01 | 56 |
| 19·9 | *Whiteball Box* | 26 | 27 | 31 |
| — | | p.w.s. | | 30 |
| 23·7 | Wellington | 31 | 01 | 81 (max) |
| 28·8 | Norton Fitzwarren | 35 | 08 | — |
| 30·8 | TAUNTON | 37 | 49 | |
| 4·7 | *Cogload Junction* | 6 | 58 | 62/58 |
| 11·5 | BRIDGWATER | 13 | 54 | 65 |
| 14·0 | Dunball | 16 | 12 | 67 |
| 17·8 | HIGHBRIDGE | 19 | 42 | 66 |
| 25·1 | *Uphill Junction* | 26 | 18 | 69/62 |
| 32·8 | Yatton | 33 | 01 | 70 |
| 36·7 | Nailsea | 36 | 25 | 68 |
| 38·8 | Flax Bourton | 38 | 27 | 54 |
| 42·9 | Parson Street | 42 | 32 | |
| 44·8 | BRISTOL | 47 | 32 | |

It was another matter entirely from Exeter northwards, and although somewhat naturally the performance could not be compared with the maximum efforts of Great Western 'Castles' it was very much above the standards of average 'Castle' work at that time. The horsepower output quoted in the table of test performances of the 'B1's on various parts of British Rail-

ways during the 1948 trials, achieved in the final ascent from
Tiverton Junction to Whiteball summit, was the highest of any
standing to the credit of the 'B1's. The running along the level
of the Somersetshire coast was also excellent, with 'even time'
achieved in 36 miles from the Taunton start, and a sustained
speed of 69 to 70 mph on the level with this 490-ton load.

TABLE 54
WESTERN REGION TEST: JULY 9th, 1948
1.35 PM PLYMOUTH–BRISTOL

| | |
|---|---|
| Load tons tare | |
| Plymouth to Exeter: | 249 tons |
| Exeter to Bristol: | 450 tons |
| Booked running time | 165 min |
| Actual running time | 164·4 min |
| Work done, hp hours: | 1648 |
| Coal lb per mile: | 48·18 |
| Coal lb per dhp hr: | 3·71 |
| Coal lb per sq ft of grate area per hr: | 80·1 |
| Water: gall per mile: | 32·5 |
| lb water per lb of coal: | 6·76 |
| Average dhp (under power) | 771 |

There was also some very interesting work on the Highland
line. Here the train services and loadings were so arranged that
it was only on the down test runs with the 4 PM express out of
Perth that assistance had to be provided on any of the severe
inclines. The maximum unassisted load from Blair Atholl up to
Dalnaspidal was 255 tons for a Stanier 'Black-Five' 4-6-0. The
test train had a scheduled tare load of 350 tons between Perth
and Aviemore, and so that the unassisted effort of the train
engines could be recorded in the dynamometer car rear-end
assistance was provided up 'The Hill', instead of a pilot in front
as customary with trains making a station stop at Dalnaspidal.
There was considerable divergence from scheduled times on the
Highland line. Both the Southern 4-6-2 and the LNER 'B1' ran
considerably harder than the booked times demanded, whereas
the local enginemen with the Stanier 4-6-0 ran in their normal
style. The relative figures for fuel and water consumption do
not, therefore, compare like for like; but from the accompanying tables it will be seen that despite the harder effort her crew

were making the results from the 'B1' compared favourably
with those from the Stanier 'Black-Five'.

Too much significance must not be attached to these results.
The Stanier 'Black-Fives' are by common consent one of the
most generally successful engine classes ever to have taken the
road in Great Britain, yet during the interchange trials they
made a relatively poor showing on almost every route they
worked. It seemed as if, to use a colloquialism, the drivers
were 'coal dodging'; but even so, despite indifferent running –
particularly on the London–Manchester tests – the coal consumption figures were not flattering to the design as a
whole.

TABLE 55

COAL CONSUMPTION COMPARISONS

| Engine | Route | lb per train mile | lb per dhp-hour |
|---|---|---|---|
| GW 'Hall' | Western | 46·9 | 4·11 |
| | Eastern | 46·75 | 3·84 |
| LNE 'B1' | Western | 46·9 | 3·96 |
| | Eastern | 41·8 | 3·32 |
| | LM | 33·7 | 3·34 |
| | Scottish | 49·5 | 4·01 |
| LMS class '5' | Western | 39·2 | 3·39 |
| | Eastern | 40·49 | 3·29 |
| | LM | 38·15 | 3·71 |
| | Scottish | 48·28 | 3·90 |
| 'West Country' 4–6–2 | Western | 52·97 | 4·28 |
| | Eastern | 50·29 | 3·90 |
| | LM | 43·33 | 3·80 |
| | Scottish | 63·24 | 4·77 |

Some horsepower outputs of the various 'B1's engaged are
given in a separate table, while an extract from the official
report gives some interesting details of the working of the
engines.

Little need be said about the freight engine trials. Slow
hard-slogging goods workings, while requiring plenty of brute

## Table 56
## SOME 'B1' TEST PERFORMANCES 1948

| Engine No | Region | Location | Direction | Load tons tare | Gradient 1 in | Speed mph | Equiv dhp | Cut-off % | Boiler pressure, psi | Steam-Chest pressure, psi |
|---|---|---|---|---|---|---|---|---|---|---|
| 61251 | Western | Burlescombe | Up | 450 | 115 | 42·5 | 1341 | 35 | 225 | 205 |
| 61251 | Western | Wellington bank | Down | 418 | 175 | 47·0 | 1336 | 30 | 225 | 205 |
| 61163 | Eastern | Rothley (gc) | Up | 374 | 176 | 57·7 | 1278 | 25 | 220 | 205 |
| 61163 | Eastern | Oughty Bridge | Down | 372 | 120 | 36·7 | 1202 | 33 | 210 | 195 |
| 61251 | LM | Peak Forest | Up | 312 | 90 | 28·5 | 994 | 38 | 217 | 208 |
| 61292 | Scottish | Slochd | Down | 261 | 70 | 29·2 | 1030 | 45 | 200 | 170 |
| 61292 | Scottish | Dalanraoch | Down | 353* | 70 | 32·9 | 1138 | 35 | 220 | 200 |
| 61292 | Scottish | Carr Bridge | Down | 261 | 60 | 25·7 | 1110 | 40 | 220 | 200 |
| 61292 | Scottish | Eteridge | Up | 354 | 95 | 32·4 | 1225 | 40 | 215 | 200 |

* Engine banking in rear.

TABLE 57

# WORKING OF MIXED-TRAFFIC ENGINES

EASTERN REGION 'B1' CLASS

*Bristol–Plymouth route*
*July 6th–9th inclusive*

Engine worked in 15–20 per cent cut-off on easier stretches, maximum 55 per cent, full regulator on the steeper banks.

*Marylebone–Manchester route*
*June 1st–4th inclusive*

Engine steamed freely with a maximum boiler pressure of 215 psi. Worked in 25 per cent cut-off on the easier sections and generally in 35 per cent on the steeper gradients with the regulator full open, the drop in pressure between boiler and steam-chest was in the region of 15 psi. Although rail conditions were not ideal, the recorded drawbar pulls showed no tendency to slipping.

*St Pancras–Manchester route*
*June 15th–18th inclusive*

Steaming very fair, boiler pressure fluctuating between 190 and 225 psi, and difficulty was occasionally experienced in recovering from the lower pressure. Water-level was generally not maintained on banks.

On June 16th on the up trip, poor steaming was experienced between Bedford and Leagrave. Minimum pressure on this occasion was 185 psi with $\frac{1}{4}$ glass water.

Exhaust generally clear. Engine free running.

Mainly worked in the following cut-off and regulator positions:

25–35 per cent, $\frac{1}{2}$–$\frac{2}{3}$ reg. $\left\{ \begin{array}{l} \text{steam-chest pressure} \\ \text{145–210 psi} \end{array} \right\}$ rising gradients

22–28 per cent, $\frac{1}{2}$ reg. $\left\{ \begin{array}{l} \text{steam-chest pressure} \\ \text{157–190 psi} \end{array} \right\}$ level

22–25 per cent, $\frac{1}{4}$–$\frac{1}{2}$ reg. $\left\{ \begin{array}{l} \text{steam-chest pressure} \\ \text{85–180 psi} \end{array} \right\}$ falling gradients

Riding generally fair, but when running fast at short cut-offs, and when coasting, a considerable lateral oscillation of short amplitude and period developed. Knock in trailing boxes also apparent at short cut-offs.

*Perth–Inverness route*
*July 20th–23rd inclusive*

Engine steamed freely except in the early stages of the first run.

As the safety valves commenced to blow at a pressure of 220 psi, the boiler was, in general, kept down to an average of 205–215 psi.

On steep grades the engine was generally worked with full regulator opening and in cut-offs of 30–40 per cent, the pressure drop to the cylinders varying between 15 and 25 psi. On this route, where the engine is either working hard or coasting downhill at speed, it was not possible to notch up above 25 per cent cut-off.

strength in the form of nominal tractive effort, are not such as to bring out the finer points of detail design. The freight variants of several notable locomotive families of indifferent reputation have achieved a far greater longevity than the passenger engines – in particular the Webb four-cylinder compounds of the LNWR. The express passenger 'Jubilee' and 'Alfred the Great' classes, and the mixed-traffic 4-6-os, were discredited at a very early stage in their respective careers, whereas the o 8 o coal engines, with exactly the same characteristics of front-end design as the others, were retained in first-line duty to such an extent that sixty of them were still in service as compounds in 1922. In the interchange trials of 1948 the differences in performance recorded with the various 2-8-o engines was in any case no more than marginal. What would have been interesting to know was the relative differences in maintenance charges between the Swindon and neo-Swindon boilers of the GW and the LMS engines, and the far simpler parallel boiler, with round-topped firebox, of the Doncaster-designed 'O1'.

Some time after nationalization a 'B1' 4-6-o, No 61353, was put through a complete series of trials on the new stationary testing plant at Rugby, and subsequently in controlled road tests at constant steaming rates on the Settle and Carlisle line. These tests were far removed from the uncertainties and inconsistencies surrounding dynamometer car testing on service trains. In strictly controlled conditions the performance of the locomotive can be subjected to ruthless analysis, and the details of some of these tests quoted herewith are enough to establish the 'B1' as a mixed-traffic engine of the highest all-round ability, and economical performance. A fine run, with a load of 405 tons, gave the following result between Appleby and Aisgill – pass to pass:

| Distance | | Time | |
| miles | | min | sec |
| --- | --- | --- | --- |
| o·o | Appleby | o | oo |
| 2·4 | Ormside | 2 | 30 |
| 7·5 | Crosby Garrett | 9 | 10 |
| 10·7 | Kirkby Stephen | 13 | 55 |
| 17·5 | Aisgill | 26 | 10 |

The intermediate fluctuations of speed were:

|  | *mph* |
|---|---|
| Ormside | 68 |
| Griseburn Box | 40 |
| Smardale Viaduct | 50 |
| Birkett Tunnel | 32 |
| Mallerstang | 39 |
| Aisgill Summit | 30 |

The cut-offs used, always in conjunction with full regulator, varied from a minimum of 27 per cent at Ormside to 40 per cent at traditionally the worst place on the route, passing through Birkett tunnel. The constant steaming conditions were:

| Water rate (feed from tender) | 18,020 lb per hr |
|---|---|
| Coal rate | 2,537 lb per hr |

The coal was best Yorkshire Hards from South Kirkby Colliery, having a calorific value of 13,950 Btu per pound.

# CHAPTER SIXTEEN

# NORTH EASTERN FREIGHT

For more than thirty years after grouping locomotives of the former North Eastern Railway were responsible for practically all the local freight workings in the North Eastern Area. The term 'local' had a definite significance north of the Humber, because a large proportion of the freight mileage in the area consisted of relatively short hauls. Along the seaboard of Northumberland and Durham were numerous small ports, and to these the North Eastern brought coal for shipment in small colliers engaged in a coastwise trade. Along this coast the ports were mostly situated at river estuaries, and there were to be seen the high galleries, or 'staithes', on to which the coal trains were propelled. From the high level the wagons were emptied in tipplers feeding chutes to the ships' bunkers. While the Stockton & Darlington Railway, connecting the Bishop Auckland coalfields with Tees-side was the pattern, and always the greatest of this form of traffic, the same pattern could also be seen on the Wear, on the Tyne, and at Blyth.

At the time of the grouping the North Eastern had considerably the largest stock of locomotives of any of the constituents of the LNER, contributing 2,143 out of the group total of 7,392. Of those 2,143 only 299 were of passenger tender types, with 72 'Atlantics', 186 miscellaneous 4–4–os, 2 'Pacifics', and 39 very elderly 2–4–os. Against these modest totals there were 230 of the o–8–o type; a swarm of 752 o–6–os; 434 tank engines of the o–6–o and o–6–2 types, and 103 mixed-traffic 4–6–os of the various 'S' classes. The North Eastern earned its handsome dividends in freight haulage, and much of this was of a humdrum, unspectacular, but money-spinning kind. The old North Eastern engines stayed on the job for very many years after grouping, and in the early 1950s, when the old name had become that of a Region of British Railways I was able to footplate on Worsdell and Raven engines still hard on their old jobs from sheds like Blaydon, Blyth, and West Auckland.

The North Eastern entered the LNER group with no fewer than 86 of the old Fletcher main-line goods engines. These never received a new classification in the 'J' series, but remained as the '398' class. They were being withdrawn fairly rapidly, and the class was extinct by 1928. Another early class was the McDonnell NER class '59'. There were 44 of them, and they had all been scrapped by the end of 1930. The mainstay of the intermediate goods traffic were the Worsdell and Raven classes, as follows:

TABLE 58

| LNER class | NER class | Designer | First built | Wheel dia ft | ins | Number at grouping |
|---|---|---|---|---|---|---|
| J21 | C1 | T. W. Worsdell | 1886 | 5 | 1 | 201 |
| J24 | P | W. Worsdell | 1894 | 4 | 7 | 70 |
| J25 | P1 | W. Worsdell | 1898 | 4 | 7 | 120 |
| J26 | P2 | W. Worsdell | 1904 | 4 | 7 | 50 |
| J27 | P3 | W. Worsdell and Sir V. Raven | 1906 | 4 | 7 | 105 |

Classes 'C1', 'P', and 'P1' all had small boilers, while 'P2' and 'P3' had boilers with the very large diameter, for a 0–6–0, of 5 ft 6 ins. The last 25 of class 'P3' were superheated when built, and another 10 engines of the class were built after grouping. In the first fifteen years of grouping this fine stud of 556 engines had been reduced only by 126, by withdrawal of 84 of class 'J21', 14 of 'J24', and 28 of class 'J25'. The large-boilered classes were still intact in 1952, when the oldest of them was forty-eight years old!

I had an interesting experience on one of these engines on a typical working from North Blyth. The engine in question was one of the very last built, No 2384, dating from 1923, and fitted with a superheater. With a brake van attached we went out tender first past Cambois Colliery and then westwards to join the passenger line to Newbiggin at Marchey's House just before reaching North Seaton. Thence we pushed on, in the

face of an icy wind (!) to Ashington; then passing on to the
metals of the Ashington Colliery Railway we drove northwards to Ellington Colliery, abreast of the East Coast main line
between Longhirst and Widdrington stations. This outward
run, of about six miles, was made in just half an hour. On
arrival at Ellington our load was not quite ready, and some time
was spent in marshalling; but after a stay of only half an hour
we restarted for North Blyth with a substantial train of twenty
20-ton hopper wagons, five 10 tonners, and the 20-ton brake
van – a load of approximately 700 tons behind the tender.
Over a route including several sharp rising gradients the engine
handled this load most competently, without one single slip.
On the grade past the colliery workings at Ashington she was
going hard, with the lever one notch from full gear – about
60 per cent cut-off – and the regulator full open. Naturally
the exhaust was loud and fierce, but she was dead on her beat,
and boiler pressure was well sustained. In spite of adverse signals, which nearly stopped us at Ashington station, we passed
Marchey's House Junction, 4·6 miles from the start, in 22¾
minutes; but immediately afterwards we were stopped at
Winning Colliery Crossing. In general the coal trains got a
fairly clear road and followed each other in close succession –
all worked by 'P3' class engines. Short though it was this out-
and-home trip was a most interesting example of latter-day
working of the class, though when first introduced the 'P2' and
'P3' engines took a big share in the long-distance mineral
workings, and in the main-line freight traffic.

The 'C1' class, like many another vintage 0-6-0 one can
recall, like the Great Western 'Dean Goods', and the LNWR
'Cauliflowers', did a good deal of branch-line passenger working in their later years, and I had a delightful run with two of
them over the fascinating mountain route from Penrith to Darlington – now, alas, closed, and the track lifted. We had a load
of only three coaches; but 90 tons behind the tender was a
train not to be despised over a line so heavily graded. We had
engine No 65047 (British Railways numbering) as far as Kirkby
Stephen, and then No 65110. Both these engines had then
been superheated, with 204·5 sq ft of heating surface in the

elements out of a total of 1,062·6 sq ft. Furthermore, in re-building they had been fitted with piston-valves $8\frac{3}{4}$-in dia-meter. Another interesting point was that the driver who had No 65047 from Penrith to Kirkby Stephen afterwards trans-ferred to Carlisle Upperby shed, and the next time I met him on the footplate the conditions could not have been more con-trasting, for it was in the 'white collar' atmosphere of a Brush Type '4' Diesel, running from Crewe to Carlisle.

The cabs of the old North Eastern 'C1' class 0–6–0s were not so roomy as one might have imagined. Like the passenger engines with large coupled wheels they had a tall and wide platform each side, as if casing the rear coupled wheels of a 6 ft 9 in or 7-ft engine, and space between those boxed-in platforms was limited. I rode perched up high on the left-hand side, the fireman's, with my legs dangling in the direct line of the fire. This might have been still more uncomfortable but for the hooded 'surround' fitted to the fire door of North Eastern engines. Stopping at all stations there was no chance for Driver Horsfield to show off the paces of his engine. The gradients are not difficult, and between stations we had speeds up to 57 mph. The 25·2 miles from Penrith to Kirkby Stephen were covered in 52 minutes, inclusive of seven intermediate stops, none of which, however, lasted more than 60 seconds.

At Kirkby Stephen we changed engines and got a newly overhauled and beautifully clean engine in No 65110. I cer-tainly treasure the memory of my ride on this splendid little engine, for it took me over a route that is not merely closed, but is now completely dismantled. The main climb over the Pennines could be a real killer. In $9\frac{1}{2}$ miles from Kirkby Stephen the line rose a clear 720 ft over the bleakest and most exposed moorland country imaginable. Apart from a single half-mile past Barras, the gradient was never easier than 1 in 72 and there were 6 miles continuous at 1 in 60. Up this gradient, in the serene air of a still, cloudless evening, we started away with the setting sun flashing on the glossy paintwork of our engine. Driver Bound put the lever into the fourth notch back from full gear, about 25 per cent cut-off, and opened the regu-lator just short of halfway point. The little engine got away beautifully, and in the first two miles of ascent, on the 1 in 72, speed rose quite smartly to 28½ mph. Boiler pressure was maintained just short of the maximum, and the steady, even exhaust beat told of a front end in first-rate fettle. Above Merrygill signal-box, now on the 1 in 60, the lever was put forward one notch, increasing the cut-off to 30 per cent and speed dropped back slightly to a steady 24–25 mph. All the time we were mounting the open hillside, heading north-east, till we came to a shoulder of the fells, swung round in a south-easterly direction, and saw, far ahead of us yet, the incredibly light and almost fairy-like structure of Belah viaduct. The evening sun was glinting on the ironwork, and the effect seen against the piled-up moorland country to the south was very beautiful.

Uphill we forged our way. On such a gradient a load of no more than 90 tons could not be regarded as a feather-weight. Although the nominal tractive effort of these engines was more than 19,000 lb the boilers were small, and it was the heating surface more than anything else that governed the performance. In such calm and favourable weather conditions No 65110 was not in any way extended; but I could well imagine that those high exposed moorlands could have been a holy terror in the winter storms. Belah viaduct was under repair, and we came on to it doing no more than 5 mph. At close quarters one could hardly appreciate its fine proportions and remarkable construction; the track was double line throughout, and that in itself took away some of the thrill of crossing an exceptionally high viaduct. Once over the viaduct No 65110 was put to it hard, with lever in fourth notch back, and regulator half open, and we accelerated quite smartly to 26 mph on the 1 in 60 gradient. I kept looking back for a final glimpse of Belah viaduct; but it was hidden by a ridge in the moorland and could not be seen again from this side. Soon we were entering Barras station, 6·3 miles from Kirkby Stephen, climbed in 16½ minutes start to stop, including the slack over the viaduct.

It was now almost 9.30 PM and as we got away, and for a while heading almost due north, I watched the sun going down over the most northerly and highest ranges of the Pennines. We ourselves were now well over 1,000 ft up, and a gentle wind was coming in cool from the west. Climbing better than ever on the continuous 1 in 59 we were soon turning due east, and heading for a shallow trough in the hills which marked the summit of the line. The country up there was almost harsh in its bleakness, but No 65110 went pedalling away, and approached the final cutting at 27 mph. So we came up to Stainmore, 1,370 ft above Ordnance datum, and only just short of the highest summit level in England. The Princetown branch of the Western Region secures this distinction by the narrow margin of 3 ft. The 3 miles up from Barras had been climbed in 7 minutes 22 seconds and now we were setting off down the 1 in 68 towards Bowes. The lever was put forward in the second notch from full gear, 45 per cent cut-off, and regulator eased back to the drifting position; the track was good, and our little engine was soon galloping along in style. Several times the speed had to be checked down by the brakes, but intermediately we had several runs at 50 mph and once a maximum of 55 mph. Despite the absence of a leading bogie the engine rode well, and took the curves like a lady – in fact she was positively luxurious after a 'B1' on which I had ridden earlier that same day. In all the 7·4 miles from Stainmore down to Bowes took $10\frac{1}{2}$ minutes pass to stop. Downhill we continued, heading at one time direct for the sunset as we took the wide curve at Lartington, and so in the gathering dusk we came to Barnard Castle. With the line continuing downhill all the way into Darlington, I had decided to bring my footplate work to an end.

Making now a transition from the smallest to the largest of the North Eastern freight locomotives I had some interesting experiences with the Raven three-cylinder 0–8–0s of class 'T3', which became LNER class 'Q7'. After the end of World War II all the fifteen engines of this class were stationed at Tyne Dock for working the iron-ore trains up to Consett, and on No 63465 formerly No 624 I made a trip on the footplate. We had a maximum load train, 22 hopper wagons, and a brake van, representing an estimated load of about 690 tons behind the tender, and after taking banking assistance up the sharp grade from Tyne Dock, No 63465 took this heavy train single-headed to Stella Gill; then, of course, we were banked in rear up the tremendous climb to Annfield Plain. We were stopped by signal at Pontop Crossing to allow two passenger trains on the Sunderland–Newcastle line to cross, after which we got away in fine style on the gradually rising gradients. We covered the 9 miles from Pontop Crossing to a stop abreast of milepost 11½ in 47 minutes, inclusive of a 7 minute stop for water at Washington, and a signal stop just prior to this junction. Our running average speed was 14 mph, with a maximum of 23 mph on level track. The engine was in very good trim, steaming freely, and with a good even beat. She was worked in one notch from full gear, 65 per cent cut-off, and between Pontop Crossing and Stella Gill the first port of the regulator sufficed, except for a short spell on the 1 in 135–104 gradient near Harraton.

But it was on restarting from Pelaw Junction, with another 'Q7', No 63471, in rear, that the really thrilling part of the journey began. From this point up to Annfield East the ruling gradient is 1 in 50; there are short stretches of 1 in 35 and 1 in 42, and for 35 minutes on end we blazed away with the main regulator practically full open, and the cut-off in 65 per cent. Against this hard slogging the boiler steamed magnificently. Pressure was never below 160 psi and for the most part it was above 170, and sometimes blowing off. We maintained a full glass of water, and indeed it seemed as though the engine would have sustained the effort indefinitely. The mileposts on this line relate to a zero at Ouston Junction, on the Team Valley line, and between posts 1 and 7¼ we averaged 11·7 mph on these terrific gradients. There was one specially thrilling piece on the climb; we had been pounding up the 1 in 52 above Beamish station at 9–10 mph when we came to a pronounced easing of the gradient for nearly half a mile at West Stanley. But there was no easing. Both engines were allowed to charge away, 'flat-out', to nearly 30 mph, and the roar of the three-cylinder exhaust was indescribable. There was good reason for such tactics for a stretch of 1 in 35 follows, and we climbed it without falling below 14 mph. It was also at this precise moment that the engine blew off! But by now Annfield was in

sight; the worst of the climbing would soon be at an end, and
the bank engine would drop off. Over the easier gradients onwards to Leadgate we averaged 18 mph and finally came to a
stand at Carr House East Box, just short of Consett station in
51½ minutes from South Pelaw Junction, 11·3 miles. One could
not have wished for a finer example of North Eastern freight
engine performance.

My footplate work with the 'T2' class, LNER 'Q6', was confined to a single run with a heavy freight train down the steep
descent from Blackhill, near Consett, to Blaydon. It required
no output of power from the engine, but considerable skill
from the driver in controlling this heavy train, without the aid
of continuous brakes on a continuously steep descending gradient. We ran tender first, and from the high stance in the cab
got an excellent view of the line ahead. The engine itself was a
hard-riding old harridan, on which one was very conscious of
heavy revolving parts, massive coupling-rods, huge balance
weights in the wheels, banging their way along. The 'Q6' class
was designed for slow, hard-slogging freight work, and they
did it admirably, with a notable absence of mechanical failure
in very long terms of service between visits to works for overhauls. They were ugly old things, but they engendered an
affection from faithful service, and it is good to know that one
of them has been saved from the scrap heap and is in the safe
keeping of the North Eastern Preservation Society.

The various 4–6–0 mixed-traffic engines were used mostly
on the main-line freights, bound for other lines, and I had a
fine trip with one of the 'S3' three-cylinder engines, LNER class
'B16', from Dringhouses Yard, York, to Mexborough West
Junction where we handed over a heavy train to the Great
Central section. The engine on which I rode, No 61426 in the
BR numbering, was one retaining the original front end, with
three sets of Stephenson's link motion. I joined the engine at
York running sheds, and we went 'light engine' down to
Dringhouses to pick up our train; this was made up to 43
actual vehicles 'equal to 58' under the system of reckoning
freight-train loads, and representing about 700 to 750 tons
gross weight behind the tender. None of these vehicles had

continuous brakes in operation. The engine was worked by Driver Marshall and Fireman Doughty of York, with Inspector C. Fisher also on the footplate.

Driver Marshall eased the long train gently out of the yard, and we had been moving for just 2 minutes before he opened the regulator out to a position about two-fifths over on the quadrant. The reverser was set at $2\frac{1}{2}$ notches from mid-gear – about 35 per cent cut-off – and the engine began to work in earnest, with a smooth, even, and relatively quiet beat. These engines had right-hand drive, and even though the characteristic North Eastern tool boxes were absent there was not too much room in the cab. The riding was very easy and comfortable, however, and I noticed at once that although engines with outside admission are prone to steam leakage at the front end there was very little from No 61426. Any leakage was likely to show on a morning of such sharp frost. We passed Chaloners Whin Junction, now remotely controlled from York, and went pegging away steadily down the one-time York and North Midland line. Signals were all clear, we passed Copmanthorpe at 27 mph, and with the engine steaming steadily and well we reached 30 mph and held it on the continuing dead level, through Bolton Percy and Church Fenton. The North Eastern men usually ran with about three-quarters of a glass of water over relatively easy roads, as it lessened the chances of priming and consequent trouble with cover leakage at the valves.

Beyond Church Fenton we sighted an adverse distant signal; but after shutting off steam speed had fallen only to 23 mph when we got the 'right-away' once more, and No 61426 had recovered to 26 mph at Milford Junction. The gradients were then slightly rising, and the regulator was opened a little wider. These engines were fitted with the Lockyer balanced double-beat regulator, which permitted of very good graduation of the steam supply when starting. The designer, Mr N. Lockyer, was for some years locomotive works manager at Darlington, and his type of regulator was used on the majority of Sir Vincent Raven's engines for the NER. By this time we were nearing Burton Salmon; we overhauled a slower goods, worked by an 'O4' 2-8-0, and passing through the station at 27 mph, we turned from the main line of the York and North Midland on to the Knottingly line. From the flat country south of York we were coming into a more undulating and delightful landscape, with the trees devoid of leaves but partaking of that rich brown that precedes the spring. The engine was not pressed, and occasional slight rising gradients made themselves felt; speed was down to 23 mph when we entered the short tunnel before the crossing of the River Aire at Brotherton, but on emerging we saw the distant for Ferrybridge 'on'.

Using his steam brake Driver Marshall quickly reduced the speed still further, for Ferrybridge is about the last place on this route that one would *choose* to make a stop with a heavy freight train. Immediately beyond there comes a bank of 2½ miles, graded at 1 in 153, and drivers usually liked to take something of a run at it. But there was no chance of a run today. As we crawled up to Ferrybridge station we saw the cause of the check; a northbound train was approaching from the Knottingly line, and the signalman at the junction was making sure she was almost at a stand before he set the road for us to cross her path on to the Swinton and Knottingly joint line. Then at last the signals were pulled off, and from a speed of about 5 mph we had to attack the bank. There was frost on the rails, and once or twice the engine slipped a little in getting hold of the train again. The northbound train from the Knottingly line was worked by a 'Q6' 0-8-0 – an old NER 'T2', 'one of the engines that won the war', Inspector Fisher remarked as we passed her by. I have heard the same praise applied to the 'V2's by York men.

No 61426 was now really opened out. Cut-off remained the same, but the regulator handle was put three-quarters over on the quadrant, and the exhaust developed into a real bark. We gathered speed in grand style, and were soon doing 20 mph. The regulator was then eased back, and on the curve through Pontefract we fell off to 18¾ mph; but we rallied to 20½ mph before the top of the 1 in 153 was reached, and then the regulator was closed altogether. Downhill we coasted, over a picturesque piece of line; speed rose to 34 mph, and with the Ackworth signals clear Driver Marshall opened the regulator very slightly, to take up any slack couplings, before he opened up in earnest for another 2 miles of 1 in 151 ascent. This route is a continuous switchback on a ruling gradient of 1 in 150, and needs careful enginemanship with a heavy train. On this second ascent the regulator was opened to two-fifths shortly after Ackworth, and to about five-eighths when speed had dropped to 21 mph. This took us over the summit at a minimum of 18½ mph. The general average we were making, of 30 to 35 downhill and 20 to 25 uphill, struck me as very uniform and an excellent speed to be holding with a heavy loose-coupled freight over so sharply undulating a road; on the footplate the riding was exceptionally smooth, with no suspicion of surging due to running in, or taking up the couplings. On passing each summit Driver Marshall made a very slight application of the steam brake; it steadied the train, and also had the effect of warming up the brake cylinders in case of an adverse distant signal requiring a heavier application.

But we were getting an absolutely clear road, and I could study the performance of the engine and the driver's artistry in handling her, without any interruption. On the 1 in 151 descent to Moorthorpe speed was allowed to rise to 33½ mph and from this we passed on to the last ascent where only one mile is as steep as 1 in 152. The regulator was not opened beyond two-fifths this time, and we carried the summit easily at 16½ mph. We had now entered the region of the South Yorkshire coalfield; evidence of underground subsidence was to be seen in one of the bridges over the line on which the arches were supported by wooden centrings. We coasted downhill through Bolton-on-Dearne, with speed rising to 29 mph, and then brakes were applied for the slowing at Dearne Junction where we were to branch away from the joint line to take the spur to the Great Central proper at Mexborough West. I *did* feel a very slight surging from behind as we slowed down; but the driver had the train under perfect control, and at no time was it necessary to use the hand brake on the tender.

So we passed dead slow round the curve to Mexborough West Junction, and stopped in 90 minutes 20 seconds from our start at Dringhouses Yard. Our average speed of 22·7 mph for this run of 34·1 miles was a very good one over an undulating road, particularly as downhill speeds were so rigidly restricted. The engine had steamed well throughout, although the coal had included some very poor stuff.

Such are a few of my personal experiences with the freight engines of the former North Eastern Railway. Many of these runs were made in the early 1950s, when the Worsdell and Raven engines were still on their old jobs, thirty years after grouping took place. One could not wish for a finer testimony to their design than this.

# CHAPTER SEVENTEEN

# PERFORMANCE SINCE 1950

In the years of austerity that followed nationalization of the railways in 1948 train services were to a large extent in the doldrums. Anything in the nature of high speed was frowned upon, as having an adverse effect upon the track; and on the other side of the coin, the state of the track in many parts of the line was such as to make high speed in the style of the late 1930s positively unsafe. From 1950 onwards there was a strong revival on the East Coast route proper, though it was saddening to enthusiasts for the old Great Central that an overall limit of 70 mph was imposed. This of course took a good deal of the sparkle out of the running, as compared with pre-war days. One feature of much interest was the observance of the working of locomotives over routes previously foreign territory to them. One of the most interesting of these was the use of Peppercorn 'A1' 'Pacifics' over the West Coast route between Glasgow and Crewe, and in later years some 'A3's were stationed at Leeds Midland shed for the double-home turns between there and Glasgow St Enoch.

A notable addition to the locomotive stock of the North Eastern Region of British Railways came in a batch of the Riddles austerity 2–8–0s, built specially for war service. This, of course, lies outside the province of LNER steam; but these engines proved so acceptable, and rendered such excellent trouble-free service that they became the principal freight engine class in North Eastern England, and the older NER engines were at last displaced from the heaviest main-line duties. A profound change also came over the Great Eastern line from 1951 with the introduction of the 'Britannia' 'Pacifics'. Other than in these two areas, however, the engines of the former LNER saw steam out. There were one or two other incursions such as 2–6–4 tanks of LMS design working on the fast Newcastle–Middlesbrough locals and the ubiquitous

Stanier 'Black-Five' 4–6–0s between Edinburgh and Perth via
the Forth Bridge, taking some turns on the Newcastle and
Carlisle line, and on the West Highland. Another point of some
interest was to observe how the 'Pacifics' of Thompson and
Peppercorn design shaped in really fast running, when the
track restrictions of the immediate post-war period were
gradually removed.

A commentary upon British locomotive practice in general,
taken over the period from 1900, would most certainly emphasize the smallness of the majority of our engine power, particularly in respect of boilers and fireboxes, resulting from the
availability up to 1939 of ample quantities of good-quality
bituminous coal. Fireboxes were small; grate areas in excess of
30 sq ft were rare, and even on railways where big engines had
been built they were, with one exception, few in numbers. The
exception was of course the LNER, where the big-engine policy
of Sir Nigel Gresley had paid such handsome dividends in the
form of ample engine power during the war years. Furthermore, whatever Thompson and Peppercorn did with the
design of the front end, they retained the Gresley boiler in all
the new big engines built from 1945 onwards. By the time the
authorized programmes of new construction were complete
the successors to the LNER had no fewer than 202 'Pacifics' at
their disposal, plus 184 large-boilered 2–6–2s of the 'Green
Arrow' class.

It is worth while taking a brief survey of that remarkable
stud. The weak spot in the development that had taken place
during the Gresley, Thompson, and Peppercorn régimes was
that none of these engines were permitted to run on the Great
Eastern line. 'V2's from Doncaster worked over the former
GN & GE joint line as far south as March, but for the express
passenger services in East Anglia itself nothing larger than the
Gresley 'Sandringhams' or the Thompson 'B1's was available.
Gresley 'A3' 'Pacifics', mostly in very poor condition, were at
work on the Great Central line, others had been the regular
power over the Waverley route in Scotland, from the Carlisle
end, for many years, but on the East Coast route proper, on all
sections between King's Cross and Dundee one found 'A1',

'A2', 'A3', and 'A4' 'Pacifics' in almost indiscriminate use. The Copley Hill turns were mostly worked by Peppercorn 'A1's; Peppercorn 'A2's were in the majority north of Dundee, while the then-celebrated top link at Haymarket shed, Edinburgh, with picked engines allocated to regular crews, included 'A1', 'A3', and 'A4' engines. This link worked to Glasgow, to Perth, and to Dundee, in addition to taking the Anglo-Scottish expresses as far as Newcastle.

Before coming to the 'Pacifics' there are some interesting runs to be set on record with the smaller engines. A criticism of the 'Sandringham' class 4-6-os to which I have referred earlier was their tendency to ride roughly as mileage between overhauls mounted up. I had been very fortunate in my footplate experiences of these engines until one August day in 1955 when I had a pass to ride the engine of the 'Easterling', nonstop from Liverpool Street to Beccles. As will be seen from the accompanying log, the schedule of this train was not unduly sharp, with 71 minutes to passing Manningtree, 59·5 miles, compared with 70 minutes allowed to the 'Hook Continental' of Holden 4-6-o days, and 82 minutes to Ipswich, 68·7 miles, compared with 73 minutes of the 'Broadsman' in steam days. With a load of slightly under 300 tons gross all would have been plain sailing and doubtless a bit humdrum to record; but we had quite a number of checks, first from a Southend train, from which we got clear at Shenfield, and then from a Clacton train which we caught up in the approaches to Colchester. In recovering the time thus lost our enterprising driver and fireman put up some really fast work, and passed Ipswich in a net time very little longer than that of the 'Broadsman'.

We got a thoroughly bad start out of London. Following a permanent way check to 20 mph at Ilford, we had evidently closed up on the preceding train and although with the aid of the four-aspect colour-light signals our driver was able to regulate his speed to avoid a series of drastic slowings, we were close enough behind the other train to see the aspects changing from yellow to double yellow in successive signals, and it was not until nearing Romford that at last we sighted a green. This respite was very slight, however, for we had a single yellow at

Harold Wood, bringing us down to 35 mph and went right up Brentwood bank with nothing less restrictive than double yellows. It was good in such circumstances to top the bank at $33\frac{1}{2}$ mph and to pass Shenfield no more than a minute late.

Then we got away to good purpose, and made fast time until nearing Marks Tey, where we caught up the Clacton train and were slowed to 5 mph. No 61669 was a lively engine with

TABLE 59

LIVERPOOL STREET–BECCLES

Load: 282 tons tare, 295 tons full

Engine: class 'B17' 4–6–0 No 61669 *Barnsley*

| Distance miles | | Sch. min | Actual min sec | Speeds mph |
|---|---|---|---|---|
| 0·0 | LIVERPOOL STREET | 0 | 0  00 | — |
| 4·0 | STRATFORD | 9 | 8  28 | — |
| 7·3 | Ilford | | 12  43 | 52 |
| | | | sigs continually | |
| 20·2 | Shenfield | 31 | 31  58 | — |
| 23·6 | Ingatestone | | 35  28 | 69 |
| 29·7 | CHELMSFORD | 40 | 41  05 | 62/57 |
| 38·6 | Witham | 49 | 49  12 | 77 |
| 44·1 | *New Hall Box* | | 53  47 | $64\frac{1}{2}$ |
| | | | sigs | |
| 51·7 | COLCHESTER | 62 | 65  48 | — |
| 56·0 | Ardleigh | | 70  56 | 60 |
| 59·5 | MANNINGTREE | 71 | 74  05 | 76 |
| — | *Belstead* | | — | $56\frac{1}{2}$/71 |
| 68·7 | IPSWICH | 82 | 83  15 | slack |
| 72·3 | Westerfield | 87 | 89  01 | 42 |
| 76·0 | Bealings | | 92  54 | 67 |
| 79·0 | WOODBRIDGE | 95 | 96  28 | 30* |
| 84·5 | Wickham Market | 103 | 102  35 | 56 |
| 88·1 | *Snape Junction* | | 105  53 | 72 |
| 91·1 | SAXMUNDHAM | 110 | 109  00 | 50 |
| 93·0 | *Milepost 93* | | 111  13 | 43 |
| 95·4 | Darsham | | 113  51 | 71 |
| 96·5 | *Milepost 96½* | | — | 58 |
| 100·7 | HALESWORTH | 122 | 118  40 | 72 |
| 102·3 | *Milepost 102¼* | | 120  08 | $50\frac{1}{2}$ |
| | | | sigs | 10 |
| 104·6 | Brampton | | 123  41 | |
| 107·2 | *Beccles Bank Box* | | 128  18 | |
| 109·2 | BECCLES | 133 | 130  53 | |

\* Speed restriction.   Net time: 120 minutes.

plenty of speed and 'go' in her, but though tolerably comfortable and steady when steaming she became very harsh when
steam was shut off. The driver had used 35 per cent cut-off
up Brentwood bank, and after Shenfield the reverser position
was varied between 15 and 25 per cent, with regulator about
three-quarters open.

We passed Colchester about 4 minutes late at much reduced
speed; but the combined effect of the two series of checks had
been a loss of at least 8 minutes in running so that our net time
for the 51·7 miles from Liverpool Street was 58 minutes. The
engine was in first-rate fettle at the front end, and responded
vigorously to full regulator and 30 per cent cut-off from Colchester. The rise at 1 in 141–123–144 to Parsons Heath Box
was mounted at a sustained 47½ mph, we passed Manningtree
at 76 mph and cleared the rise to Belstead summit, after 2 miles
at 1 in 157, at 56½ mph. This good work regained us nearly
3 minutes between Colchester and Ipswich and we passed
through the latter station in 83¼ minutes from Liverpool Street,
just over a minute late, but in no more than 75¼ minutes net.
The most interesting part of the journey was still to come,
however, for less than a mile from Ipswich we were to take
the right-hand turn at East Suffolk Junction to follow the
sharply-graded coastal route to Yarmouth.

Although running through a country that could in no circumstances be called hilly, or difficult, this line was constructed
very cheaply and with the minimum of earthworks, following
the lie of the land, and including some extraordinarily severe
gradients. None of them is of any appreciable length, but
numerous miles and half-miles at such inclinations as 1 in 95,
89, 80 and even a mile at 1 in 75 can be most troublesome if a
driver has the ill-luck to be checked at the foot of one of them.
Fortunately, the speed restrictions are few, and the worst one,
through Woodbridge, is succeeded by a short distance of almost
level track.

The worst bank is the very first, from East Suffolk Junction
up to Westerfield, where a length of 2 miles at 1 in 111–150
immediately succeeds the severe slack over the Junction. Here,
with 30 per cent cut-off, No 61669 sustained 42 mph. Follow-

ing the slack through Woodbridge we covered the 22 miles from Melton to milepost 102¼ at an average of exactly 60 mph. The line is, in the aggregate, rising over this length with four marked climbs, at 1 in 95 to Wickham Market, and at 1 in 89 after Saxmundham, at 1 in 85 after Darsham, and finally 2 miles at 1 in 81–97 to post 102¼.

Only once on this stretch did we fall below 50 mph, and this was after observing the moderate speed restriction through Saxmundham, which naturally hampered the climbing of the 1 in 89 that immediately follows. Full use was made of the down grades, with speeds of 72 mph before Snape Junction, 71 at Darsham, and 72 before Halesworth. We were now getting comfortably ahead of time and at Brampton we were checked by signal to 10 mph; but the minutes in hand were more than enough to offset this hindrance, and we reached Beccles 2 minutes early. Net time for this run of 109·2 miles was, as near as I can judge, exactly 2 hours, showing a net average speed of 54·6 mph.

Another run, for details of which I was indebted to Mr T. Pearson, shows the remarkable speed capacity of the 'B1' class engines in favourable conditions. The Great Northern main line was always the recognized speedway of the entire LNER system, but by way of a change from 'Pacific' working it is interesting to see what the Immingham drivers could do on the through King's Cross–Grimsby trains. In general the 'B1's were not so free-running as the 'Sandringhams' – possibly a reflection on their very 'hard' riding under light steaming conditions; but this was certainly an exception.

Up the heavily graded start out of the terminus things were taken quietly, and speed had risen to no more than 33 mph when Finsbury Park was passed. But excellent work was done up to Potters Bar, and the acceleration to 47½ mph at the summit would have involved an output of about 1,200 edhp. This was a fine effort for an engine of class '5' capacity, and some brilliant running was to follow. The permanent way check near Woolmer Green was a severe one, and cost about 3 minutes; again, however, the engine was put to it hard in recovering speed, and the summit of the long descent into the Ouse valley, at Stevenage station, was topped at 59½ mph. Then came some of the freest running ever seen with a 'B1'. Speed rose to 88 mph at Arlesey, and fast time was made on to Tempsford over the more nearly level grades after Biggleswade. This gave a fine average speed of 75·8 mph over the 24·1 miles from Hitchin to Offord.

TABLE 60
### KING'S CROSS–PETERBOROUGH
Load: 378 tons tare, 410 tons full
Engine: class 'B1' 4–6–0 No 61190

| Distance miles | | Sch. min | Actual min sec | | Speeds mph |
|---|---|---|---|---|---|
| 0·0 | KING'S CROSS | 0 | 0 | 00 | — |
| 2·6 | Finsbury Park | | 8 | 02 | 33 |
| 5·0 | Wood Green | | 11 | 30 | 52 |
| 9·2 | New Barnet | | 16 | 40 | 46 |
| 12·7 | Potters Bar | 20 | 21 | 13 | 47½ |
| 17·7 | HATFIELD | 27 | 26 | 12 | 66 |
| | | | p.w.s. | | 22 |
| 28·6 | Stevenage | | 39 | 40 | 59½ |
| 31·9 | HITCHIN | 42 | 42 | 29 | 78 |
| 35·7 | Three Counties | | 45 | 15 | 88/78 |
| 41·1 | Biggleswade | | 49 | 07 | 80½ |
| 44·1 | Sandy | 52 | 51 | 26 | 76 |
| 47·5 | Tempsford | | 54 | 10 | 74 |
| 51·7 | St Neots | | 57 | 47 | 66/72 |
| 58·9 | HUNTINGDON | (pass | 65 | 30 | special |
| | | (65 | 67 | 00 | stop |
| 62·0 | *Milepost 62* | | 73 | 00 | 43 |
| 67·4 | *Connington South* | | 78 | 03 | 81½ |
| 69·4 | Holme | | 79 | 32 | 79 |
| | | | p.w.s. | | |
| 75·0 | *Fletton Junction* | | 85 | 31 | |
| 76·4 | PETERBOROUGH | 92 | 88 | 05 | |

By this time the train was running nicely ahead of schedule, with something in hand for the further permanent way check that was to come near Yaxley. A special stop was necessary at Huntingdon, to which point the net time from King's Cross was 62½ minutes start to stop. After a stand of 1½ minutes the engine was put to it more vigorously than ever. On the continuous rise of 1 in 200 to milepost 62 speed rose to 43 mph –

rate of acceleration rarely surpassed by southbound East Coast
expresses starting southwards from Grantham – and then
came another burst of high speed, with a maximum of 81½ mph
near Holme. Despite the concluding check the 17·5 miles from
Huntingdon to Peterborough took only a shade over 21 minutes, and the overall time from King's Cross, two checks and
special stop included, was only 88 minutes against 92 minutes
booked. On such form the run from King's Cross, if unchecked, could have been made comfortably in 79 minutes – an
excellent example of 'B1' performance, and a fine effort by
driver and fireman.

Next come two runs on the 'South Yorkshireman' leaving
Marylebone at 4.50 PM, both heavily loaded and both 'Pacific'
hauled. One's thoughts inevitably go back to the old 4.55 PM of
pre-war days, and to such runs as that made by the 'Director'
class 4–4–0 *Jutland*, as described in Chapter Two of this book,
when Aylesbury was passed in just over 45 minutes. In those
days of austerity after the war one could not get really going
until after Aylesbury, and the start-to-stop allowance of 71 minutes for the run of 65·2 miles was quite strenuous compared
with the 62 minutes of the old 4.55 PM down, pass to stop,
having regard to the imposition of the 70-mph limit throughout. After the checks in the early stages both engines climbed
splendidly over the Chilterns; *Flying Scotsman* accelerated
from 30 mph through Rickmansworth to 32 mph on the 1 in
105 gradient until checked down to 22 mph by signals. *Galtee
More* sustained 31 mph throughout. Despite the comparative
easiness of the schedule such were the initial delays that both
engines failed to keep the 57 minutes' allowance to Aylesbury,
37·9 miles, taking 59 minutes 19 seconds and 59 minutes 1 second respectively.

From Aylesbury both runs are tabulated. *Flying Scotsman*
had a clear road throughout, and by dint of some excellent
work on the long stretches of 1 in 176 passed Charwelton
33·6 miles in 38 minutes 41 seconds. The minimum speed of
55 mph at Helmdon was quite remarkable with a 445-ton train.
The engine was held in severely on the racing descent from
Catesby tunnel to Braunston, but after accelerating to exactly

the 70-mph limit after Rugby there was another good climbing performance to Lutterworth. There was a momentary maximum of 77 mph at the conclusion, but it was followed by a very cautious run into Leicester. *Galtee More* did even better, and

TABLE 61

AYLESBURY–LEICESTER

| Run No<br>Engine 4–6–2 No<br>Engine Name<br>Load tons E/F | | | 1<br>60103<br>*Flying Scotsman*<br>413/445 | | 2<br>60049<br>*Galtee More*<br>419/450 | |
|---|---|---|---|---|---|---|
| *Distance*<br>*miles* | | *Sch.*<br>*min* | *Actual*<br>*min sec* | *Speeds*<br>*mph* | *Actual*<br>*min sec* | *Speeds*<br>*mph* |
| 0·0 | AYLESBURY | 0 | 0 00 | — | 0 00 | — |
| 6·1 | Quainton Road Junction | | 8 55 | 55 | 8 22 | 61/58 |
| 8·8 | *Grendon Jcn* | | 11 45 | — | 11 09 | 63½ |
| — | | | — | 68 | p.w.s. | 15 |
| 10·8 | Calvert | | 13 35 | 65 | 13 10 | — |
| 16·5 | FINMERE | | 21 23 | 46/64 | 21 11 | 50/66 |
| 21·3 | Brackley | | 26 48 | 60 | 26 20 | 60 |
| 24·5 | Helmdon | | 30 13 | 55 | 29 44 | 55½ |
| 29·4 | *Culworth Jcn* | 32 | 34 43 | 71 | 34 12 | 71 |
| 31·2 | WOODFORD | 34 | 36 16 | 62 | 35 48 | 64 |
| | | | — | — | p.w.s. | 20 |
| 33·5 | Charwelton | | 38 41 | 58 | 39 23 | 43 |
| 40·5 | Braunston | | 45 50 | 65 | 46 34 | 68 |
| 45·2 | RUGBY | | 50 20 | 59/70 | 51 03 | 60/70 |
| 48·8 | *Shawell* | | 53 38 | 60 | 54 18 | 63½ |
| 52·0 | Lutterworth | | 57 07 | 54/63 | 57 33 | 56/62½ |
| 55·9 | Ashby | | 61 08 | 55 | 61 20 | 58½ |
| 60·4 | Whetstone | | 64 54 | 77 | 65 15 | 70 |
| 64·1 | *Leicester South Goods* | | 67 00 | — | 68 35 | — |
| 65·1 | LEICESTER | 71 | 69 38 | — | 70 07 | — |

despite a permanent way check to 15 mph before Calvert produced even faster hill-climbing times to Woodford Halse. The net time on this fine run with only the slightest excess over the 70 mph limit was 67 minutes.

What the old Gresley 'Pacifics' of the old 'A1' class – then rebuilt to 'A3' – could do in the way of high speed when given their heads is shown by the accompanying log taken in the summer of 1958 with the engine *Tracery*, No 2558, as she was in Gresley days. In early grouping days we used to regard the old 43 minutes' timing from Darlington to York as something to be attempted only with loads of less than 300 tons, even with 'Pacifics'. The rebuilding of the 'A1' class with long-lap valves greatly increased their speed worthiness, and that old schedule

TABLE 62

DARLINGTON–YORK

Load: 372 tons tare, 400 tons full

Engine: class 'A3' 4–6–2 No 60059 *Tracery*

| Distance miles | | Sch. min | Actual min sec | Speeds mph |
|---|---|---|---|---|
| 0·0 | DARLINGTON | 0 | 0 00 | — |
| 2·6 | Croft Spa | | 4 11 | 58 |
| 5·2 | *Eryholme* | 6 | 6 47 | 61 |
| 10·4 | Danby Wiske | | 11 09 | 78 |
| 14·1 | NORTHALLERTON | 14 | 14 04 | 76 |
| 17·5 | Otterington | | 16 39 | 84 |
| 21·9 | THIRSK | 20 | 19 41 | 87 |
| 25·1 | *Milepost 19* | | 21 57 | 85 |
| 28·1 | Pilmoor | | 23 59 | 86 |
| 31·1 | *Milepost 13* | | 26 06 | 89 |
| 33·0 | Alne | 29 | 27 20 | 88 |
| 38·6 | Beningbrough | | 31 14 | 85/86 |
| 40·9 | *Milepost 3¼* | | 32 53 | 83 |
| 42·5 | *Skelton Box* | 36 | 34 09 | |
| — | | | sigs | |
| 44·1 | YORK | 39 | 39 15 | |

Net time: 37½ minutes.

was tackled successfully with loads up to 500 tons. But there is a world of difference between running those 44·1 miles in 43 minutes and making the kind of speed shown in the accompanying table. *Tracery* averaged 86·3 mph for 23½ miles of little easier than level track, and made a net start-to-stop average speed of 70·6 mph with a 400-ton train.

The Peppercorn 'A1's were excellent heavy-load engines, and a run I had one winter's night on the up 'Heart of Midlothian' express was a typical example of their work. Engine No 60129 *Guy Mannering* was on the job, with a gross load of

475 tons behind the tender. We made a brilliant start, passing Croft Spa, 2·6 miles out, at 56 mph; Northallerton was passed in 15 minutes 37 seconds at 70 mph, and the average over the ensuing 24·5 miles to Beningbrough was exactly 76 mph, with a maximum of 80 mph at Thirsk. We were checked in the approach to York, but stopped nevertheless in 43 minutes 17 seconds from the Darlington start. The net time was 41¾ minutes. This was a typical rather than an exceptional run for an 'A1' in the middle 1950s. At that time they were still addicted to that disconcerting swing, which I experienced in full measure on No 60159 *Bonnie Dundee* between Carlisle and Carstairs.

In 1951 Polmadie shed, Glasgow, was short of 'Pacifics', and arrangements were made to transfer some 'A1's temporarily from Haymarket. They were used principally on the Glasgow–Crewe double-home jobs, and having a footplate pass for the 3.46 PM down from Carlisle I was extremely interested when *Bonnie Dundee* turned up from the south nearly a quarter of an hour late. This is the second engine of this name to figure prominently in this book; but anything less like that rock-steady 'Rolls-Royce' of a North British 'Atlantic' that I rode in 1935 than this wild, swinging 'Pacific' would be hard to imagine. We left Carlisle 14 minutes late, with a load of 365 tons, and got a bad start with a dead stand for signals at Floriston. Instead of crossing the Border at about 70 mph we had to fight against the long 1 in 200 ascent from the Solway Firth and gradually accelerated to 54½ mph at the summit marked roughly by milepost 14½. Our immediate start from Carlisle had, however, been so smart that despite the signal stop our time to this summit point was only 20¾ minutes.

Then we really had it! The gentle snaking action that I had experienced in a mild form on both 'A1' and 'A2' varieties of Peppercorn 'Pacifics' on the Great Northern main line, now developed into a violent swinging about the centre point of the chassis. Whereas the Great Northern 'Atlantics' used to fling their rear ends from side to side, their front ends were quite steady; on the Peppercorn 'Pacifics' the front end was swinging as much as the rear – but the opposite way! With all due respect to those who had the responsibility for it, the Caledonian

permanent way was not one of the best in Great Britain, and as
we tore down towards Kirtlebridge rounding curve after curve,
with speed rising to 72 mph and the engine swinging violently
I was, for the first time in my footplate experience, genuinely
apprehensive. Only once subsequently have I had the same

TABLE 63
CARLISLE–SYMINGTON
Load: 346 tons tare, 365 tons full
Engine: class 'A1' 4–6–2 No 60159 *Bonnie Dundee*

| Distance miles | | Actual min   sec | Speeds mph |
|---|---|---|---|
| 0·0 | CARLISLE | 0    00 | — |
| 4·1 | Rockcliffe | 5    43 | 64½ |
| 6·1 | Floriston | 8    33 | sig. |
|  |  | 8    55 | stop |
| 8·6 | Gretna Junction | 13    17 | — |
| 13·0 | Kirkpatrick | 19    05 | 54½ |
| 16·7 | Kirtlebridge | 22    52 | 72 |
| 20·1 | Ecclefechan | 25    55 | 63½ |
| — | *Castlemilk* | — | 60 |
| 25·8 | LOCKERBIE | 31    05 | 71/67 |
| 28·7 | Nethercleugh | 33    36 | 70½ |
| 31·7 | Dinwoodie | 36    28 | 60 |
| 34·5 | Wamphrey | 39    21 | 66/74 |
| 39·7 | BEATTOCK | 43    44 | 65 |
| 45·0 | *Milepost* 45 | 50    15 | 38 |
| 47·0 | *Milepost* 47 | 53    42 | 34 |
| 49·7 | *Summit* | 58    27 | 35 |
| 52·6 | Elvanfoot | 61    32 | 66 |
| 57·8 | Abington | 66    46 | easy |
| 63·2 | Lamington | 71    35 | 74 |
| 66·9 | SYMINGTON | 75    35 |  |

Net time: 70½ minutes.

feeling of alarm, and that was on a diesel-hydraulic, in the
early days of the 'Warships', at 95 mph.

It can well be imagined how unpleasant the riding was on
No 60159, for after breasting Castlemilk summit the driver,
who was anxious to make up as much lost time as possible,
eased right down on the curves approaching Lockerbie where
ordinarily he would have been going at a tearing pace, and

accelerating very rapidly. He did not open the regulator again until we were into the straight beyond Lockerbie, and the engine was riding less violently. Nevertheless we passed Beattock, 39·7 miles, in 43¾ minutes – a very good time seeing that the Floriston signal stop had cost us a good 5 minutes in

TABLE 64

CARLISLE–EDINBURGH (WAVERLEY)

Load: 346 tons tare, 365 tons full

Engine: class 'A2' 4–6–2 No 60522 *Straight Deal*

| Distance miles | | Sch. min | Actual min sec | Speeds mph |
|---|---|---|---|---|
| 0·0 | CARLISLE | 0 | 0 00 | — |
| 1·3 | *Canal Junction* | 4 | 3 53 | — |
| 6·6 | Lyneside | | 9 53 | 64½ |
| 9·6 | LONGTOWN | 13 | 12 52 | 57/60 |
| 11·9 | Scotch Dyke | | 15 15 | 56/62 |
| | | | sigs | |
| 14·1 | Riddings Junction | | 17 43 | 32 |
| 16·6 | Penton | | 22 35 | 36 |
| 21·1 | Kershopefoot | | 28 38 | 60½ |
| | | | p.w.s. | 33 |
| 24·2 | NEWCASTLETON | 31 | 32 50 | 52 |
| 28·8 | Steele Road | | 40 18 | 32/28 |
| 32·3 | Riccarton Junction | 47 | 47 27 | 31 |
| 34·5 | *Whitrope* | 52 | 51 40 | 29½ |
| — | | | — | 56 (max) |
| 45·4 | HAWICK | 68 | 66 59 | |
| 4·3 | Hassendean | | 7 18 | 48 |
| 7·6 | Belses | | 10 55 | 61½ |
| 12.2 | St Boswells | 16 | 16 08 | |
| 3·4 | Melrose | 6 | 5 55 | |
| 3·7 | GALASHIELS | 7 | 5 58 | |
| 3·7 | Bowland | | 7 53 | 46 |
| 6·8 | Stow | | 11 47 | 52 |
| 10·9 | Fountainhall | | 16 38 | 50 |
| 14·4 | Heriot | | 21 08 | 46 |
| 15·6 | *Falahill* | 23 | 22 42 | 45 |
| 25·2 | *Hardengreen Junction* | 36 | 33 38 | 61 (max) |
| | | | p.w.s. | — |
| 29·1 | *Niddrie South Junction* | 41 | 38 45 | — |
| 30·5 | Portobello | 43 | 41 05 | — |
| | | | sigs | |
| 33·5 | EDINBURGH (WAVERLEY) | 49 | 51 04 | — |

running. As a motive power unit No 60159 was excellent, but as a vehicle she was horrible. We climbed Beattock bank in good style and after the initial impetus was expended the speed settled down to a steady 35 mph, with the engine working in 30 per cent cut-off, with the regulator full open. The complete 10 miles of the bank took 14 minutes 43 seconds, thus passing the summit in 58 minutes 27 seconds from Carlisle. We made an easy descent of the Clyde valley, not exceeding 74 mph, and here, by way of contrast, the engine rode reasonably well. Symington, 66·9 miles, was reached in 75 minutes 35 seconds against 80 minutes scheduled.

Over the neighbouring Waverley route Gresley 'Pacifics' provided the usual power on the principal expresses, but Sir James Colyer-Fergusson logged an interesting run when the morning St Pancras–Edinburgh express, then known as 'The Thames-Forth Express', was worked by a Thompson 'A2', and, moreover, one belonging to York shed. This route is a very difficult one, being so infested with curves as to preclude any speeds much in excess of 60 mph on the favourable stretches, and so heavily graded as to involve very hard work elsewhere. The run is tabulated. There was a signal check at the foot of Penton bank with its $3\frac{1}{2}$ miles of 1 in 100; but the main effort is required from Newcastleton, where the gradient is 1 in 75 for 10 miles to Whitrope. Here the speed lay between 28 and 31 mph. The variations were caused more by the curves in the line than by fluctuations in the effort put forth by the engine. The second main ascent, from Galashiels to Falahill, is generally on easier gradients, varying between 1 in 99 and 1 in 200, though some very short level strips intermediately make the average speed somewhat easier. The engine kept good time throughout, until the severe delays outside Waverley caused the last 3 miles to occupy all but 10 minutes.

The next step is to approach Edinburgh by the East Coast route, and this leads us on to some much higher standards of speed. I have tabulated herewith two very fast runs on the 'Talisman' – the first with a Gresley 'A3' and the second with a Peppercorn 'A1', *Bonnie Dundee* once again. Judging by the speeds achieved I fancy she must have been a somewhat

TABLE 65

## NEWCASTLE–EDINBURGH

| Run No<br>Engine No<br>Engine Name<br>Engine Class (4–6–2)<br>Load tons E/F | | 1<br>60043<br>Brown Jack<br>'A3'<br>311/325 | | 2<br>60159<br>Bonnie Dundee<br>'A1'<br>306/320 | |
|---|---|---|---|---|---|
| Distance<br>miles | Sch.<br>min | Actual<br>min sec | Speeds<br>mph | Actual<br>min sec | Speeds<br>mph |
| 0·0 NEWCASTLE | 0 | 0 00 | — | 0 00 | — |
| 5·0 Forest Hall | | 8 06 | 53 | 9 03 | 45/63 |
| 9·9 Cramlington | | 12 32 | 69 | 14 09 | 60 |
| 13·9 Stannington | | 15 33 | 85½ | 17 35 | 77 |
| 16·6 MORPETH | 20½ | 18 10 | 40* | 20 24 | 35* |
| 23·2 Widdrington | | 23 59 | 77 | 26 58 | 71/68 |
| 28·5 Acklington | | 27 51 | 87 | 31 10 | 81½ |
| 34·8 ALNMOUTH | 37 | 32 35 | slack | 36 21 | 66* |
| 39·4 Little Mill | | 36 31 | 66 | 40 35 | 59 |
| 46·0 Chathill | | 41 26 | 92½ | 45 46 | 89 |
| 51·6 BELFORD | 52 | 45 15 | 87 | 49 37 | 84¾ |
| 58·6 Beal | | 49 50 | 95 | 54 24 | 90 |
| 63·5 Scremerston | | 53 06 | 73 | 57 58 | 71 |
| 66·9 BERWICK | 69½ | 56 44 | 40* | 61 24 | 50* |
| 72·5 Burnmouth | | 63 56 | 53 | 67 53 | 57¾ |
| 78·1 Reston Jcn | 82 | 69 04 | 71½ | 72 59 | 72½ |
| | | — | | sigs | 5 |
| 83·1 Grantshouse | 87 | 73 55 | 60¼ | 80 34 | |
| | | sigs | — | sig stop | |
| 87·9 Cockburnspath | | 78 16 | — | 90 58 | |
| | | sigs | 45 | — | |
| 95·2 DUNBAR | 97 | 86 26 | | 98 47 | |
| 101·0 East Linton | | 92 27 | 63 | 103 42 | 73½ |
| | | — | | p.w.s. | 20 |
| 106·6 DREM | 107 | 97 14 | 77 | 110 56 | 64 |
| 114·9 Prestonpans | | 104 07 | 69/76 | 117 36 | 85½ |
| | | sigs | — | sigs | |
| 121·4 Portobello | 120 | 112 24 | — | 124 59 | |
| | | sig stop | — | — | |
| 124·4 WAVERLEY | 126 | 122 04 | — | 130 19 | |
| Net times min | | 112½ | | 115½ | |

\* Speed restrictions.

reformed character so far as her riding was concerned. Both runs involved some very fine locomotive work, and equally some very bad operating. *Brown Jack* was away from Newcastle $11\frac{1}{2}$ minutes late, but was so splendidly driven as to pass Berwick just over a minute *early*. Even after a succession of checks the train was only a minute late through Portobello, but time was lost, as usual, then, in the immediate approach to Waverley station. *Bonnie Dundee* was 4 minutes late away from Newcastle, and 4 minutes early at Berwick. Then Scottish Region ran true to its current form, and involved the train in a number of serious delays so that the eventual arrival was $8\frac{1}{4}$ minutes late.

The 'A3' *Brown Jack* made a most brilliant start out of Newcastle, clearing Cramlington summit at 69 mph, and reaching $85\frac{1}{2}$ mph before the Morpeth slowing. The maximum of 87 mph at Acklington viaduct was again unusual, and after Alnmouth, and the clearing of the $4\frac{1}{2}$ miles of Longhoughton bank at the remarkable minimum speed of 66 mph, there was some tremendous running on the coastal stretch, with a top speed of 95 mph near Beal. By comparison with such an effort the 'A1', *Bonnie Dundee*, although running very well, was almost pedestrian, at any rate until Little Mill had been passed; but then they hit up some fine speed, and by a rather faster passage through Berwick gained a little on the 'A3' between the latter station and Reston Junction. After that the checks on both runs were crippling, though *Bonnie Dundee* got in a maximum of $85\frac{1}{2}$ mph near Prestonpans. Although the 'A3' claims the principal honours with the remarkable net time of $112\frac{1}{2}$ minutes both were fine runs.

Last of all in this miscellany of LNER engine performance, in the years since 1950, comes the working of the 'A3's from Leeds Midland shed, on the double-home turns to and from Glasgow. The Midland express drivers at Leeds had, over the years, amassed a wealth of varied experience with all sorts and conditions of engines. On the Carlisle road many of them had done their firing on Midland compounds, and the '999' class '4' simple 4–4–0s. Then, from 1930 onwards, the principal turns were for a time given over to North Western 'Claughton' class 4–6–0s, which could take considerably heavier loads than the Midland 4–4–0s without pilot assistance. Then came the various Stanier types, followed by the rebuilt 'Royal Scots', and still later, one or two of the new 'Britannia' 'Pacifics' were tried out. The introduction of diesels on the East Coast route made a number of the Gresley 'Pacifics' redundant at Gateshead, and it was a batch of these engines that was transferred to the Midland shed at Leeds. In a very short time these engines were generally voted the best they had ever had for the Glasgow jobs. This was remarkable because in most cases the engines transferred from Gateshead had amassed considerable mileages since last overhaul, and they were all very far from new engines.

In the autumn of 1960 I enjoyed a splendid run on the footplate of engine No 60036 *Colombo*, non-stop from Leeds to Carlisle on 'The Thames–Clyde Express', details of which are set out in the log on page 238. The load was not heavy for a Gresley 'Pacific', but Driver Gibbs and Fireman Chambers gave us a beautiful piece of running, and converted a late start of 6 minutes into an arrival 4 minutes early. The line out of Leeds includes much curvature, quite apart from the severely restricted lengths at Shipley and Keighley, and no time had been regained on passing Skipton, despite some smart intermediate running. But the engine was put to it with great vigour up the steeply rising gradients from Skipton and although we had a short engineering slack for drainage near Gargrave 2½ minutes had been regained when we ran through Hellifield, at 60 mph. We then drifted down the grade to Settle Junction not exceeding 63 mph, but at the latter point, where the long ascent to Blea Moor begins, the engine was opened well out, with regulator full open and cut-off in 25 per cent.

The controls remained unchanged throughout the 14 miles of ascent, almost entirely at 1 in 100. Speed was held consistently at 43 to 45 mph and it was only when we were crossing Batty Moss viaduct, and Blea Moor was in sight, that the effort was slightly relaxed, and speed fell to 38 mph at the very top of the climb. By then, however, we were slightly ahead of time,

TABLE 66
## LEEDS–CARLISLE
'The Thames–Clyde Express'
Load: 317 tons tare, 335 tons full
Engine: class 'A3' 4–6–2 No 60036 *Colombo*

| Distance miles | | Sch. min | Actual min sec | | Speeds mph |
|---|---|---|---|---|---|
| 0·0 | LEEDS | 0 | 0 | 00 | — |
| 3·3 | Kirkstall | | 6 | 57 | 56 |
| 7·6 | Apperley Bridge | | 11 | 49 | 53/54½ |
| 11·0 | *Shipley: Bingley Junction* | 15 | 16 | 00 | 20* |
| 13·8 | Bingley | | 20 | 15 | 50/55 |
| 17·0 | KEIGHLEY | | 23 | 52 | 50* |
| 23·1 | Cononley | | 28 | 35 | 70 (max) |
| 26·2 | SKIPTON | 33 | 32 | 35 | 30* |
| 28·6 | *Delaney's Siding* | | 35 | 16 | 57 |
| — | | | p.w.s. | | 20 |
| 29·9 | Gargrave | | 36 | 43 | — |
| 34·9 | *Milepost 230* | | 43 | 21 | 53 |
| 36·2 | HELLIFIELD | 47 | 44 | 38 | 60 |
| 39·5 | *Settle Junction* | 51 | 47 | 42 | 64 |
| 41·4 | Settle | | 49 | 41 | 57 |
| 47·4 | Horton | | 57 | 07 | 44/47 |
| 52·2 | Ribblehead | | 63 | 27 | 43 |
| 53·5 | *Blea Moor* | 73 | 65 | 14 | 38 |
| 58·4 | Dent | | 71 | 35 | 54 |
| 61·6 | Garsdale | | 75 | 05 | 66 |
| 64·6 | *Aisgill* | 86 | 78 | 12 | 54 |
| 71·5 | Kirkby Stephen | | 84 | 33 | 73 |
| 74·7 | Crosby Garrett | | 87 | 40 | 62 |
| 79·8 | Ormside | | 92 | 03 | 75 |
| 82·2 | APPLEBY | 103 | 94 | 15 | 63 |
| 85·1 | Long Marton | | 96 | 42 | 75 |
| — | | | p.w.s. | | 30 |
| 89·6 | Culgaith | | 101 | 27 | 75 |
| 94·6 | Little Salkeld | | 105 | 55 | easy |
| 97·7 | LAZONBY | | 108 | 57 | |
| 102·9 | Armathwaite | | 114 | 24 | 69 |
| 109·1 | Cumwhinton | | 120 | 11 | easy |
| 112·1 | *Petteril Bridge Junction* | | 123 | 40 | |
| 113·0 | CARLISLE | 136 | 126 | 28 | |

Net time: 124 minutes.          * Speed restrictions.

and after we emerged from Blea Moor tunnel, at 54 mph the
cut-off was reduced to 15 per cent and the regulator partly
closed. The rest was easy. For much of the descent to Carlisle
the regulator was in the drifting position. It was slightly
opened on the approach to each tunnel to avoid any chance of
'blow-back'; but we were to finish very quietly and reach
Carlisle in 126 minutes 28 seconds from Leeds. What could
have been done in the way of a fast overall time with such
engines was shown some three years later, when with an
RCTS special the 48·3 miles from Aisgill to Carlisle were
covered, with an 'A4', in 42 minutes 12 seconds pass to stop.
Then the average speed over the 40·9 miles from Mallerstang
Box to Cumwhinton (31 minutes 17 seconds) was 78·4 mph.
*Colombo*'s average on my footplate trip was a modest 63·6 mph.

# CHAPTER EIGHTEEN

# 'PACIFICS' IN EXCELSIS

Alone among the British railways the LNER had consistently pursued the 'big engine' policy, and in the post-war years the East Coast route, throughout from King's Cross to Aberdeen, was essentially and almost exclusively a line of 'Pacifics'. In the previous chapter I have given a miscellany of interesting runs on many parts of the line. The present chapter presents the 'Pacifics' at their most brilliant – 'Pacifics' in Excelsis. It is important, however, to appreciate the essential differences in the work of the various designs. Once Thompson had retired the Gresley faction began to raise their heads ever higher. With maximum train-loads diminishing, and scheduled speeds increasing, the need for boilers with 50 sq ft of grate area began to recede. I have always remembered the words of a North Eastern running man in those post-war years, in respect of the two main groups of 'Pacifics'. He said: 'The "A4"'s are the greyhounds of the stud, but if you have to take 600 tons on a dirty night, given me an "A1" every time'. Against this, of course, 600-ton loads were getting fewer and fewer, and with the grades of coal most usual on the East Coast route requiring to be burned on a thin fire, one could reach a point, in light steaming where coal was being used on an 'A1' merely to keep the firebars covered. I have never seen any comparative figures, but it has always been understood that the Peppercorn 'A1's were considerably heavier on coal than the 'A4's when engaged on strictly comparable work.

Gradually the Gresley engines began to regain their old pre-eminence, and when the time came for the restoration of the summer non-stop trains between King's Cross and Edinburgh there was never any question of using engines other than the Gresley 'A4's. Within my own experience the 'A1's did their best work on the Leeds Pullman trains, which loaded to considerably heavier formations than those normally worked, prior

## TABLE 67
### EASTERN REGION: KING'S CROSS–LEEDS
The 'Queen of Scots' Pullman
Load: 11 cars, 430 tons tare, 450 tons full
Engine: class 'A1' 4–6–2 No 60123 *H. A. Ivatt*

| Distance miles | | Sch. min | Actual min sec | | Speeds mph |
|---|---|---|---|---|---|
| 0·0 | KING'S CROSS | 0 | 0 | 00 | |
| 2·6 | Finsbury Park | | 6 | 46 | |
| 5·0 | Wood Green | | 10 | 06 | 54 |
| 12·7 | Potters Bar | | 19 | 46 | 45½ |
| 17·7 | HATFIELD | 27 | 24 | 49 | 67/58½ |
| 23·5 | *Woolmer Green* | | 30 | 22 | 60 |
| 31·9 | HITCHIN | 40 | 37 | 47 | 76/90 |
| — | | | sigs | | 66 |
| 41·1 | Biggleswade | | 44 | 46 | 83½ |
| — | | | p.w.s. | | 35 |
| 58·9 | HUNTINGDON | 62 | 60 | 56 | 71 |
| 62·0 | *Milepost 62* | | 63 | 44 | 62 |
| — | | | p.w.s. | | 55 |
| 69·4 | Holme | | 70 | 15 | 77½ |
| — | | | sigs | | 10 |
| 76·4 | PETERBOROUGH | 78½ | 77 | 27 | — |
| 79·5 | *Werrington Junction* | | 82 | 08 | 59 |
| 88·6 | Essendine | | 90 | 07 | 73½ |
| 97·1 | Corby Glen | | 97 | 31 | 64/69 |
| 100·1 | *Stoke Box* | | 100 | 16 | 64½ |
| 105·5 | GRANTHAM | 107½ | 104 | 33 | 82/66 |
| — | | | p.w.s. | | 50 |
| 115·4 | Claypole | | 113 | 21 | 85 |
| 120·1 | NEWARK | 120 | 117 | 06 | 60 |
| 127·4 | Crow Park | | 123 | 31 | 72½ |
| 131·3 | Dukeries Junction | | 126 | 51 | 66 |
| — | | | sig stop | | |
| 138·6 | RETFORD | 137 | 138 | 16 | |
| — | | | sig stop | | |
| 156·0 | DONCASTER | 159 | 156 | 17 | |
| 160·0 | Carcroft | | 161 | 53 | 64/61 |
| 164·7 | South Elmsall | 167½ | 166 | 16 | 63½ |
| 167·9 | Hemsworth | | 169 | 21 | 61 |
| 171·9 | Hare Park | 175 | 173 | 06 | 76 |
| — | | | sigs | | 25 |
| 175·9 | WAKEFIELD | 179 | 178 | 26 | — |
| 180·2 | Ardsley | 186 | 185 | 12 | 37/43 |
| 185·8 | LEEDS CENTRAL | 195 | 192 | 53 | |

Net time: 176½ minutes.

to World War II. I have tabulated details of a good run recorded from the footplate by Mr Ronald I. Nelson, with the engine so happily named after the former Great Northern locomotive engineer. The driver was Cartwright, of Copley Hill shed, but one fears that in his enthusiasm and desire to show off the paces of his engine to the visitor he ran harder than was really necessary, and that some of the signal checks were largely self-inflicted. It will be seen that after passing Newark 3 minutes early, and then being stopped dead by signal twice, he was still able to get through Doncaster $2\frac{3}{4}$ minutes early.

Quite apart from the timekeeping there were several demonstrations of fine locomotive capacity, particularly in the fast climb from Peterborough to Stoke summit, with its time of 18 minutes 8 seconds over the 20·6 miles from Werrington to the top, and its minimum speed of $64\frac{1}{2}$ mph after the final 3 miles rising at 1 in 178. On this section the engine was working in 25 per cent cut-off with regulator full open. The Peppercorn and the Thompson engines had the same general working characteristics as the Gresleys, in that drivers worked them in 15 per cent cut-off, or even less, whenever possible, and used a wide, if not necessarily full open regulator. At the same time in studying this Pullman run it must be admitted that the load of 450 tons would not have been considered very heavy for a Gresley 'Pacific' of less tractive power, in days before the war, when the 'standard' load for the principal East Coast trains was at least '15' – twelve of the heaviest bogies and a triplet articulated dining-car set, having in all a tare weight of about 485 tons. The task set to the Peppercorn 'Pacifics', on the 'Queen of Scots', comparing tractive effort for tractive effort was much the same as when the Great Northern 'Atlantics' were on the job, and hauling seven-car trains totalling about 290 tons gross behind their tenders. The schedule was the same.

Reverting now to the Gresley 'Pacifics', one of the most enjoyable runs out of many I had on the 'A3's during the last twenty years of their existence was one afternoon when I had a footplate pass to ride the down 'Flying Scotsman', from Newcastle to Edinburgh. This was a job for the celebrated

Haymarket top link, in which a select band of 'Pacifics', some 'A4's, some 'A3's, and one specially favoured 'A1', was allocated to regular drivers. There were two crews to each engine, and although the running of individual trains reflected the personalities of the various drivers and their firemen, the performance of the link as a whole, in its timekeeping, its economy, and its freedom from failure must surely have been second to none among enginemen and locomotives continuously engaged in heavy and fast duties. A train worked by this link was practically ensured of a good run, and quite apart from a number of trips I have made on the footplate I have logged in full detail many more runs from the train on occasions when the engine crews were not aware I was recording their work. It made no difference. The dependability of the link was proverbial.

On this particular afternoon no prior arrangements had been made, and it was therefore all the greater pleasure to find that our engine was to be none other than the world record breaker of 1935, *Papyrus*, though then carrying her BR number 60097 instead of the more familiar 2750. Her driver was one of the three brothers Smith, backed up by a perfect artist of a fireman in Angus Wylie. In these days when steam working is outmoded one sometimes hears remarks about the indignity of men having 'to shovel coal for a living'. If it were nothing more than coal heaving I would agree; but to watch a fireman like Wylie at work, anticipating his driver's needs, never wasting a pound of coal or steam, suiting his control of the boiler feed and the actual firing to the fluctuations in demands of the road and the schedule, and withall keeping the footplate – and himself! – clean, was a complete abnegation of the idea of indignity. The traditions of steam on the footplate die hard, and I know of many engineers, trained in locomotives, and who have subsequently obtained positions of great distinction in their profession, who can rarely miss the chance of a glimpse of 'auld lang syne' on the footplate. Then it is not a desire to take the regulator or the reverser, but to have the pleasure once again of putting a dozen shovelfuls round the box.

Table 68 on page 244 shows the exploits of *Papyrus* that

spring afternoon, when Ralph Smith and Angus Wylie gave such an immaculate display. They left Newcastle on time, with 142 minutes in which to reach Edinburgh. This was not an unduly hard task, even with a load of 510 tons, but through some

TABLE 68

NE & SCOTTISH REGIONS:
NEWCASTLE–EDINBURGH
'The Flying Scotsman'
Load: 477 tons tare, 510 tons full
Engine: class 'A3' 4–6–2 No 60096 *Papyrus*

| Distance miles | | Actual min sec | | Speeds mph |
|---|---|---|---|---|
| 0·0 | NEWCASTLE | 0 | 00 | |
| — | | sig stop | | |
| 1·7 | Heaton | 6 | 50 | |
| 5·0 | Forest Hall | 12 | 51 | 39 |
| 9·9 | Cramlington | 18 | 31 | 58/54½ |
| 13·9 | Stannington | 22 | 21 | 70 |
| 16·6 | MORPETH | 25 | 15 | slack |
| 20·2 | Longhirst | 29 | 30 | 66 |
| — | | p.w.s. | | 40 |
| 28·5 | Acklington | 38 | 49 | 69 |
| 34·8 | ALNMOUTH | 44 | 42 | 65 |
| 39·4 | Little Mill | 50 | 01 | 48½ |
| 46·0 | Chathill | 56 | 05 | 75 |
| 51·6 | Belford | 61 | 02 | 63½ |
| 58·6 | Beal | 66 | 53 | 76 |
| 63·5 | Scremerston | 71 | 18 | 55/60 |
| 65·7 | Tweedmouth Junction | 73 | 50 | 50 |
| 66·9 | BERWICK | 75 | 24 | — |
| 72·5 | Burnmouth | 83 | 08 | 41/46 |
| — | | — | | 62½ |
| 78·2 | Reston Junction | 88 | 58 | 57½ |
| 83·2 | Grantshouse | 94 | 58 | 49 |
| 87·9 | Cockburnspath | 99 | 40 | 72/59 |
| 95·2 | DUNBAR | 106 | 25 | 62½ |
| 100·9 | East Linton | 112 | 13 | 60 |
| 106·6 | DREM JUNCTION | 117 | 32 | 69/61½ |
| 114·9 | Prestonpans | 125 | 10 | 67 |
| 118·3 | *Monktonhall Junction* | 128 | 39 | |
| 121·4 | Portobello | 133 | 35 | |
| — | | sigs | | |
| 124·4 | EDINBURGH | 139 | 48 | |

Net time: 134 minutes.

conflicting local traffic movement we were stopped at Heaton and lost 4 minutes at the very outset. After that there was a steady recovery of time and we eventually arrived in Edinburgh 2 minutes early. The engine was run with the regulator full open, for all the hard and fast work. The boiler pressure was kept around 205 to 215 psi and the cut-off varied from the usual 15 per cent for all the fast running south of the Border, to 20–25 per cent along the Lothian coast, where the gradients, though undulating are in the aggregate slightly adverse between Dunbar and Prestonpans. One could not take advantage of the favourable stretch onwards to Portobello, because of slight civil engineering restrictions.

Some of the most impressive work, from the viewpoint of locomotive power output, followed the crossing of the Royal Border Bridge, and on the ascent to Grantshouse summit, in the Lammermoor hills. The ascent is at first 1 in 190, and Smith gave the engine 37 per cent cut-off immediately we were through Berwick. Wylie had for several minutes been building up in readiness for this, and despite the heavy demands for steam, with the engine gradually accelerating this 510-ton train to 46 mph on the gradient, the boiler pressure showed a tendency to rise, while the water-level remained quite steady. The one break in the climbing took us rapidly up to $62\frac{1}{2}$ mph near Ayton, and on the continuous 1 in 200 gradient from Reston Junction to the summit we settled down to a steady 49 to 50 mph. This stretch of line includes much curvature, and with our long train this undoubtedly caused some variation in the rolling resistance of the stock. Cut-off was gradually increased from 20 per cent at Reston to 32 at the summit. In other circumstances this might be considered a large increase, but in the last miles Wylie was easing the firing a little to avoid blowing off when steam would be shut off completely for the descent of Cockburnspath bank. We thus topped Grantshouse summit with only 195 psi 'on the clock', and the driver was having to use a longer cut-off to maintain speed.

In post-war years the introduction of the Tees–Tyne Pullman service was a tolerable substitute from the passenger point of view, for the loss of the 'Silver Jubilee'. The schedules were

not so fast, but with 'A4' 'Pacifics' in generally good condition
and a load not exceeding eight cars there was often some
exciting running. Business was taking me frequently to North
Eastern England in the early 1950s, and the down Pullman,
leaving King's Cross at 4.45 PM, was a very convenient service.
It was always worked by the King's Cross top link, and for a
time they too had regular engines. At 'top shed', as it was always
known in the London area, certain footplate names became as
much household words as Jimmy Swan, the McLeod brothers,
Willie Bain, and others in the Haymarket top link. At King's
Cross there was no greater personality than Ted Hailstone, and
it was perhaps fitting that he should have had *Silver Link*. To
say that he was a born engineman would be an understatement.
His father was an express driver on the Midland, at Trafford
Park, and had the compound 4–4–0 No 1013 for many years,
and his brother was on the Great Western, stationed at West-
bury. In the course of travelling I came to know Ted Hailstone
well, and when the opportunity came to make a footplate run
on the down Tees–Tyne Pullman I was able to arrange things
so as to travel when he was on, with *Silver Link*, of course.

It proved to be a very exciting trip, in more senses than one.
To Peterborough, as shown in the accompany log, it was the
kind of running one would expect on the 'Silver Jubilee' or the
'Coronation' in pre-war days, though on this Pullman train
with a distinctly heavier load. Quite apart from the high speeds
on the level and downhill there was some splendid work uphill,
when the engine was well warmed up, as evidenced by the
climb from Huntingdon to the summit point at milepost 62 –
all climbing on 1 in 200. The net time to passing Peterborough
was about 63 minutes against the $63\frac{1}{2}$ minutes allowed to the
pre-war streamlined trains. We were going well after Peterborough when around Tallington the driver sensed that something was wrong. We stopped at Essendine to find that the
right-hand driving axlebox was hot. A stop of less than 2
minutes sufficed to get a message forward to Grantham, asking
for a fresh engine, and we continued, at no more than moderate
speed, to cover the remaining 16·9 miles in $21\frac{1}{4}$ minutes. I
learned afterwards that the failure was due to a maintenance

TABLE 69

# EASTERN REGION: KING'S CROSS–ESSENDINE
## (Run on the Tees–Tyne Pullman)
### Load: 8 cars, 323 tons tare, 345 tons full
Engine: No 60014 *Silver Link*    Driver: E. Hailstone (King's Cross)

| Distance miles | | Sch. min | Actual min sec | Speed mph |
|---|---|---|---|---|
| 0·0 | KING'S CROSS | 0 | 0 00 | — |
| 2·6 | Finsbury Park | | 6 27 | — |
| 5·0 | Wood Green | | 9 14 | 64½ |
| 9·2 | New Barnet | | 13 18 | 62½ |
| 10·6 | Hadley Wood | | 14 36 | 63½ |
| — | | | p.w.s. | |
| 12·7 | Potters Bar | | 17 05 | 20 |
| — | | | sigs | — |
| 17·7 | HATFIELD | 28 | 22 52 | 68 |
| 20·3 | Welwyn Garden City | | 25 15 | 65 |
| 22·0 | Welwyn North | | 26 44 | 70½ |
| 23·5 | *Woolmer Green* | | 28 01 | 68½ |
| 26·7 | *Langley Junction* | | 30 33 | 82 |
| 28·6 | Stevenage | | 32 00 | 77⅛ |
| — | | | — | 85 |
| — | | | sigs | — |
| 31·9 | HITCHIN | 40 | 35 04 | 30 |
| 35·7 | Three Counties | | 39 43 | 67 |
| 41·1 | Biggleswade | | 44 02 | 88 |
| 44·1 | Sandy | | 46 06 | 83 |
| 47·5 | Tempsford | | 48 23 | 90 |
| 51·7 | St Neots | | 51 15 | 85 |
| — | | | eased | 91 |
| 56·0 | Offord | | 54 23 | 67 |
| 58·9 | HUNTINGDON | 62 | 56 46 | 75 |
| 62·0 | *Milepost 62* | | 59 20 | 72 |
| 63·5 | Abbots Ripton | | 60 32 | 84 |
| — | | | p.w.s. | 40 |
| 69·4 | Holme | | 65 32 | 70½ |
| — | | | — | 76½ |
| 72·6 | Yaxley | | 68 10 | 75 |
| — | | | — | 77½ |
| 75·0 | *Fletton Junction* | | 70 03 | slowing |
| 76·4 | PETERBOROUGH | 78½ | 72 25 | 5 |
| 79·5 | *Werrington Junction* | | 78 11 | 63 |
| 84·8 | Tallington | | 82 40 | 77½ |
| 88·6 | Essendine | | 86 40 | — |

Engine developed hot right-hand driving box.
Examined at Essendine; left there at 88 minutes 25 seconds, and reached Grantham in 109 minutes 35 seconds.
Net time to Essendine stop: 77 minutes.

TABLE 70

# E & NE REGIONS: GRANTHAM–DARLINGTON
## (The Tees–Tyne Pullman)
### Load: 8 cars, 323 tons tare, 345 tons full
### Engine: class 'V2' 2–6–2 No 60853
### Driver: E. Hailstone (King's Cross)

| Distance miles | | Sch. min | Actual min sec | Speeds mph |
|---|---|---|---|---|
| 0·0 | GRANTHAM | 0 | 0 00 | — |
| 4·2 | Barkston | | 7 40 | 64½ |
| | | | p.w.s. | 40 |
| 9·9 | Claypole | | 14 16 | 69 |
| 14·6 | NEWARK | 12½ | 18 35 | — |
| — | *Muskham troughs* | | — | 66½ |
| 21·9 | Crow Park | | 24 54 | 76 |
| — | *Dukeries Junction* | | — | 62½ |
| 26·4 | Tuxford | | 29 07 | 66 |
| 28·5 | *Milepost 134* | | 31 04 | 64 |
| — | *Grove Road Crossing* | | — | 78 |
| 33·1 | RETFORD | 29½ | 34 58 | 65 |
| — | *Canal Box* | | — | 60 |
| 36·2 | Sutton Box | | 37 57 | 68 |
| 38·4 | Ranskill | | 39 52 | 74 |
| 42·2 | Bawtry | | 43 07 | 66 |
| 44·0 | *Milepost 149½* | | — | 63½ |
| 45·8 | Rossington | | 46 25 | 69½ |
| — | | | p.w.s. | — |
| 47·7 | *Black Carr Junction* | | 48 20 | 30 |
| — | | | sigs | 30 |
| 50·5 | DONCASTER | 51½ | 52 45 | — |
| 52·6 | Arksey | | 55 41 | 55½ |
| 54·7 | *Shaftholme Junction* | 56 | 57 55 | 61 |
| 57·5 | Moss | | 60 35 | 65 |
| 60·5 | Balne | | 63 14 | 68 |
| 61·8 | Heck | | 64 24 | 66/68 |
| 64·3 | Templehirst | | 66 35 | 75 (max) |
| 68·9 | SELBY | 69 | 70 30 | slack |
| 73·0 | Riccall | | 75 18 | 63 |
| 75·6 | Escrick | | 77 40 | 68 |
| — | | | | 75 (max) |
| 78·5 | Naburn | | 80 07 | slack |
| 82·7 | YORK | 84½ | 85 30 | — |
| 0·0 | | 0 | 0 00 | |
| 1·0 | *Milepost 1* | | 2 55 | — |
| 1·6 | *Skelton Junction* | | 3 54 | — |
| 5·5 | Beningbrough | | 8 06 | 67 |

TABLE 70 *(continued)*

| Distance miles | | Sch. min. | Actual min  sec | Speeds mph |
|---|---|---|---|---|
| 9·7 | Tollerton | | 11  46 | 71½ |
| 11·2 | Alne | | 13  01 | 72½ |
| 13·4 | Raskelf | | 14  49 | 75 |
| 16·1 | Pilmoor | | 17  02 | 73 |
| 18·0 | Sessay | | 18  36 | 74 |
| 22·2 | Thirsk | | 21  55 | 82 |
| 26·6 | Otterington | | 25  13 | 79 |
| 30·0 | Northallerton | | 27  52 | 75 |
| 33·7 | Danby Wiske | | 30  49 | 77½ (max) |
| — | | | p.w.s. | |
| 38·9 | *Eryholme Junction* | | 37  04 | 54 |
| 41·5 | Croft Spa | | 39  38 | 65 |
| — | | | sigs | — |
| 44·1 | DARLINGTON | 41 | 43  50 | — |

Net times: Grantham–York 81 minutes    York–Darlington 41 minutes
Time regained by engine north of Newark: 8 minutes

error in which the wrong grade of lubricating oil had been used on the particular bearing.

The best Grantham could give us in exchange was a somewhat run-down 'V2'. She rode well, and steamed freely, but the valve setting was very much adrift. The beat was wildly syncopated; but once Hailstone found she would stand punishment he flogged her in merciless fashion all the way. He used full regulator and long cut-offs. It would be no use quoting the actual readings on the reverser scale, because from the irregularity of the beat there was obviously a marked inequality of the work done in the three cylinders. The starts were slow, but once fairly on the move we ran well. The continuous roar of the exhaust was extraordinary, and caused many men at the lineside to turn to see what was coming. As will be seen from the log we made some fast times, and a tremendous effort was put forth to try and keep the sharp 41-minute allowance for the 44·1 miles from York to Darlington. But for the checks I think we should have successfully done this. By this resolute running nearly 8 minutes of lost time were regained between Newark and Darlington.

Table 71
## E & NE REGIONS:
## DARLINGTON–KING'S CROSS
(The Tees–Tyne Pullman)
Load: 8 cars, 320 tons tare, 335 tons full
Engine: class 'A4' 4–6–2 No 60029 *Falcon*

| Distance miles | | Actual min sec | | Speeds mph |
|---|---|---|---|---|
| 0·0 | DARLINGTON | 0 | 00 | — |
| 5·2 | *Eryholme Junction* | 7 | 16 | 62½ |
| 14·1 | NORTHALLERTON | 14 | 23 | 78 |
| 17·5 | Otterington | 16 | 56 | 85 |
| 21·9 | Thirsk | 19 | 55 | 88½ |
| 28·0 | Pilmoor | 24 | 10 | 86 |
| 32·9 | Alne | 27 | 31 | 89 |
| 38·6 | Beningbrough | 31 | 24 | 88 |
| 44·1 | YORK | 39 | 35 | sig |
| | | 41 | 09 | stop |
| 53·8 | Riccall | 52 | 42 | 69 |
| 57·9 | SELBY | 56 | 52 | slack |
| 62·5 | Templehirst | 61 | 58 | 64 |
| 69·3 | Moss | 67 | 45 | 75 |
| 76·3 | DONCASTER | 74 | 04 | 55 |
| 79·1 | *Black Carr Junction* | 77 | 02 | 65 |
| 82·8 | *Milepost* 149½ | 80 | 46 | 56 |
| 84·6 | Bawtry | 82 | 30 | 73 |
| | | sigs | | 50 |
| 93·7 | RETFORD | 90 | 57 | — |
| 98·3 | *Milepost* 134 | 95 | 42 | 56 |
| 104·9 | Crow Park | 101 | 11 | 82 |
| — | | slack | | 61 |
| 112·2 | NEWARK | 107 | 29 | 64½ |
| 116·9 | Claypole | 111 | 40 | 72 |
| 122·6 | Barkston | 116 | 37 | 64 (min) |
| 126·8 | GRANTHAM | 120 | 22 | 75 |
| 132·2 | *Stoke Box* | 124 | 59 | 65½ |
| 135·2 | Corby Glen | 127 | 17 | 88 |
| 140·1 | Little Bytham | 130 | 25 | 103½ |
| 143·7 | Essendine | 132 | 37 | 87 |
| 147·5 | Tallington | 135 | 17 | 86½ |
| 150·4 | *Helpston Box* | 137 | 29 | 80½ |
| 152·8 | *Werrington Junction* | 139 | 20 | slack |
| 155·9 | PETERBOROUGH | 143 | 17 | — |
| 162·9 | Holme | 151 | 01 | 76 |
| 168·8 | Abbots Ripton | 155 | 57 | 64 |
| 173·4 | HUNTINGDON | 159 | 58 | |

TABLE 71 (*continued*)

| Distance miles | | Actual min sec | Speeds mph |
|---|---|---|---|
| 176·3 | Offord | 162   15 | 65 |
| 180·6 | St Neots | 165   37 | 77/75 |
| 184·8 | Tempsford | 168   48 | 85 |
| — | | p.w.s. | 25 |
| 191·2 | Biggleswade | 174   13 | — |
| 196·6 | Three Counties | 181   07 | 69 |
| 200·4 | HITCHIN | 184   24 | 67 |
| 203·7 | Stevenage | 187   25 | 66½ |
| 207·3 | Knebworth | 190   28 | 72½ |
| — | | sigs | — |
| 214·6 | HATFIELD | 197   27 | — |
| — | | p.w.s. | 5 |
| 219·6 | Potters Bar | 204   27 | |
| 227·3 | Wood Green | 214   25 | 65 (max) |
| 229·8 | Finsbury Park | 216   57 | |
| 232·3 | KING'S CROSS | 221   42 | |

Actual time York start to passing Hatfield, 170·5 miles: 156 minutes 18 seconds.

My southbound trip on the Tees–Tyne Pullman train was another memorable experience. But as I have described the personal side of the journey in some detail on various earlier occasions, including the section over which, at Inspector Dixon's invitation, I drove the engine myself, I must concentrate on two particular features that have a significant bearing upon the working of the 'A4' class engines in general. The first was the 85–90 mph spin on the level between Northallerton and York, and the second was the manner in which we reached the maximum speed of 103½ mph near Little Bytham. The running between Darlington and York was precisely the standard of work for which the 'A4's were designed – running at, or near 90 mph on level track in easy and economical conditions. And here *Falcon* averaged 87 mph for 21 miles working in 15 per cent cut-off, with the regulator about three-quarters open. The steam-chest pressure was around 200 psi, against a boiler pressure of 230 to 235 psi. The riding of the engine at this continuous high speed was easy and elegant, and altogether

I felt that here was a demonstration of 'A4' working at its most
immaculate.

The next thing about this run is the memory of my own
driving of this fine engine. The schedule did not demand such
fast work as that just described; but I found the controls easy
to adjust, and 15 per cent cut-off with the regulator eased back
to give 160 to 170 psi steam-chest pressure gave me a steady
75 mph on the level between Templehirst and the approach to
Doncaster. Naturally, however, everything else on this run
pales before the experience south of Grantham when we attained
the highest speed I ever noted on the footplate of a steam locomotive, 103½ mph. Again the cut-off was 15 per cent, but
Driver Hoole had pushed the engine to a very rapid acceleration from Stoke summit, and had it been necessary we could
clearly have attained a much higher maximum. We were going
so fast by Little Bytham that the engine had to be checked
down. The milepost averages from 98 to 89 were:

|         |     *mph*            |
|---------|---------------------|
| 98 to 97 | 87·8               |
| 97 to 96 | 88·9               |
| 96 to 95 | 92·3               |
| 95 to 94 | 94·8               |
| 94 to 93 | 97·5               |
| 93 to 92 | 100·0              |
| 92 to 91 | 102·7 (then eased) |
| 91 to 90 | 98·7               |
| 90 to 89 | 96·0               |

After this great spurt we continued in good, though less spectacular style, and eventually arrived in King's Cross 8 minutes
early.

This was a grand demonstration of the capacity of the 'A4'
Pacifics, in 1954. Something even more significant in that same
year was the acceleration of the London–Edinburgh non-stop
to a level 6½-hour run, and I was able to travel on the up train
shortly after the introduction of the new schedule. With all
allowance for the fact that the engines used were specially picked
units the performance on that non-stop train was always one of
the greatest things ever achieved with steam traction – not
only on the LNER line, nor in Great Britain, but in the whole

world. Steaming, coal consumption, the skill of the drivers and firemen all played their part; but especially one must pay tribute to the lubrication system of the Gresley 'Pacifics'.

The log tabulated was a typical performance with the engine *Golden Fleece*, beautifully driven by Paterson of Haymarket, and then Tappin of King's Cross. To me one of the most interesting features was the descent from Stoke to Peterborough. Inspector Jenkins invited me to go through the corridor tender and spend some time on the footplate, and I was thus able to see at first hand the way in which this very fast running occurred almost incidentally in the course of a 6½-hour non-stop run. There was no attempt at anything spectacular on this occasion. Tappin took *Golden Fleece* easily and comfortably up to Stoke, with speed falling to 53 mph, and then merely allowed the engine to make her pace downhill to Werrington. With the utmost nonchalance – if I may apply a human simile to this noble engine – she swept up to 96 mph, and averaged all but 90 mph over the 12·3 miles from Corby Glen to Tallington. The effect of all the incidental checks had been offset by our sustained fine running, and Hatfield was passed just over 2 minutes early. At that point, inclusive of all checks, the speed had averaged 62½ mph, and with the ample recovery time remaining we stopped in King's Cross 4¾ minutes early. Up to that point we had a net gain of 13 minutes on schedule. No finer tribute to the Gresley 'Pacifics' could be found than the regular performance on this train, of which this run of mine was no more than typical.

It was nevertheless not only the Gresley engines that produced an occasional maximum speed of 100 mph and over, and I have three most interesting examples in which the newer engines were involved. Two were all the more creditable in that they were made in everything but propitious circumstances. The first was on up 'Morning Talisman' in November 1958, which by that time was diagrammed for a diesel. This locomotive failed at York, and a Peppercorn 'A1' was hastily substituted. It was doubly fortunate that so resolute and expert a driver as R. Turner of King's Cross was on the job, and that so expert a recorder as Ronald I. Nelson was a passenger to log

TABLE 72
### EAST COAST ROUTE: 'THE ELIZABETHAN'
Load: 11 coaches, 403 tons tare, 425 tons full
Engine: class 'A4' 4-6-2 No 60030 *Golden Fleece*
Drivers: Paterson (Haymarket), Tappin (King's Cross)

| Distance miles | | Sch. min | Actual min sec | | Speeds mph |
|---|---|---|---|---|---|
| 0·0 | WAVERLEY | 0 | 0 | 00 | — |
| 3·0 | Portobello | 5 | 4 | 39 | — |
| — | | | pitfall | | — |
| 6·1 | *Monktonhall Junction* | 10 | 8 | 46 | — |
| 13·2 | Longniddry | | 16 | 46 | 62 |
| 17·8 | DREM | 19 | 21 | 00 | 70/77 |
| 23·5 | East Linton | | 25 | 35 | 69 |
| — | | | p.w.s. | | 15 |
| 29·2 | DUNBAR | 29 | 32 | 22 | 61½ |
| 31·3 | *Oxwellmains* | | 34 | 35 | 56 |
| 33·8 | Innerwick | | 37 | 04 | 67 |
| 41·2 | Grantshouse | 44 | 45 | 46 | 38½ |
| 46·2 | Reston Junction | 49 | 50 | 30 | 76½ |
| 51·9 | Burnmouth | | 55 | 07 | 66/81 |
| 56·4 | *Marshall Meadows* | 58 | 58 | 58 | — |
| 57·5 | BERWICK | 60 | 60 | 10 | 15* |
| 60·9 | Scremerston | | 64 | 31 | 61½ |
| 65·8 | Beal | | 68 | 23 | 82½ |
| 72·8 | Belford | 74½ | 73 | 57 | 66 |
| 78·4 | Chathill | | 78 | 53 | 72½ |
| 81·4 | Christon Bank | | 81 | 22 | 71½/61 |
| 85·0 | Little Mill | | 84 | 41 | 66/75 |
| 89·6 | ALNMOUTH | 90 | 88 | 32 | slack |
| 92·5 | Warkworth | | 91 | 24 | 64 |
| 95·9 | Acklington | | 94 | 24 | 70½ |
| 104·2 | Longhirst | | 101 | 27 | 75 |
| 107·8 | MORPETH | 107 | 104 | 46 | 30* |
| 110·5 | Stannington | | 108 | 34 | 60 |
| 114·5 | Cramlington | | 112 | 47 | 54½ |
| 119·4 | Forest Hall | | 117 | 17 | 69 |
| 123·8 | Manors | | 122 | 28 | — |
| 124·4 | NEWCASTLE | 125 | 124 | 08 | * |
| 125·0 | *King Edward Bridge Junction* | 127 | 125 | 56 | — |
| 128·2 | Lamesley | | 129 | 54 | 61 |
| — | | | sigs | | — |
| 132·6 | Chester-le-Street | | 135 | 52 | — |
| — | | | p.w.s. | | — |
| 138·4 | DURHAM | 141 | 144 | 40 | — |
| 142·6 | Croxdale | | 150 | 17 | 68/62 |
| 147·5 | Ferryhill | 151½ | 155 | 01 | 64 |

TABLE 72 (*continued*)

| Distance miles | | Sch. min | Actual min sec | Speeds mph |
|---|---|---|---|---|
| 150·2 | Bradbury | | 157 28 | 78 |
| 155·0 | Aycliffe | | 161 15 | 63* |
| 160·4 | DARLINGTON | 163½ | 165 44 | 82 |
| 163·0 | Croft Spa | | 167 38 | 84 |
| 165·6 | *Eryholme* | 168 | 169 33 | 77½ |
| 170·8 | Danby Wiske | | 173 27 | 82 |
| 174·5 | NORTHALLERTON | 175½ | 176 21 | 75 |
| 182·3 | Thirsk | 182 | 182 16 | 82 |
| 188·4 | Pilmoor | | 187 00 | 77 |
| 193·3 | Alne | 191 | 190 47 | 80/79 |
| 199·0 | Beningbrough | | 195 04 | 82 |
| 202·9 | *Skelton Box* | 198½ | 198 18 | — |
| 204·5 | YORK | 201½ | 200 03 | * |
| 206·5 | *Chaloners Whin Junction* | | 202 53 | — |
| 214·2 | Riccall | | 210 17 | 73½ |
| 218·3 | SELBY | 216½ | 214 15 | * |
| 222·9 | Templehirst | | 219 21 | 64 |
| 229·7 | Moss | | 225 37 | 73½ |
| 232·5 | *Shaftholme Junction* | 232½ | 227 56 | 69 |
| 236·7 | DONCASTER | 237 | 231 48 | 60 |
| 239·5 | *Black Carr Junction* | | 234 30 | 64½ |
| 243·2 | *Milepost 149½* | | 238 00 | 58½ |
| 245·0 | Bawtry | | 239 40 | 74 |
| 254·1 | RETFORD | 254 | 248 51 | * |
| 258·7 | *Milepost 134* | | 253 03 | 51½ |
| 265·3 | Crow Park | | 258 50 | 82 |
| — | | | p.w.s. | 40 |
| 272·6 | NEWARK | 270½ | 265 36 | 55 |
| 277·3 | Claypole | | 270 18 | 64½ |
| 283·0 | Barkston | 279½ | 275 48 | 56 |
| 287·2 | GRANTHAM | 283½ | 280 10 | 62½ |
| 292·6 | *Stoke Box* | | 285 44 | 53 |
| 295·6 | Corby Glen | | 288 30 | 76 |
| 300·5 | Little Bytham | | 292 02 | 92/96 |
| 304·1 | Essendine | | 294 20 | 93/95 |
| 307·9 | Tallington | | 296 46 | 90 |
| — | | | p.w.s. | 40 |
| 316·3 | PETERBOROUGH | 208½ | 305 28 | 20* |
| 323·3 | Holme | | 313 13 | 75 |
| — | | | p.w.s. | 40 |
| 329·2 | Abbots Ripton | | 319 22 | 50 |
| 333·8 | HUNTINGDON | 325½ | 323 58 | 79 |
| 336·7 | Offord | | 326 14 | 70* |
| 341·0 | St Neots | | 329 52 | 68 |
| 345·2 | Tempsford | | 332 21 | 79 |

TABLE 72 (*continued*)

| Distance miles | | Sch. min | Actual min. sec | | Speeds mph |
|---|---|---|---|---|---|
| 348·6 | Sandy | | 335 | 56 | 75 |
| 351·6 | Biggleswade | | 338 | 17 | 76½ |
| 354·1 | *Langford Bridge* | | 340 | 20 | 70 |
| 357·0 | Three Counties | | 342 | 46 | 75 |
| 360·8 | HITCHIN | 348½ | 346 | 01 | 63 |
| 364·1 | Stevenage | | 349 | 33 | 52½ |
| 367·7 | Knebworth | 355 | 353 | 29 | |
| 370·7 | Welwyn North | | 356 | 09 | 72 (max) |
| 375·0 | HATFIELD | 362 | 359 | 46 | |
| — | | | | p.w.s. | |
| 380·0 | Potters Bar | 370 | 366 | 23 | |
| — | | | | sigs | |
| 387·7 | Wood Green | | 377 | 01 | |
| 390·1 | Finsbury Park | | 380 | 24 | |
| 392·7 | KING'S CROSS | 390 | 385 | 10 | |

Net time: 369 minutes.          * Speed restrictions.

the running. To cut a long and exciting story short they left York 26¼ minutes late by the booked passing time, and passed Finsbury Park only 2 minutes late, with a comfortable 5 minutes left in which to make a completely punctual arrival in King's Cross. Unfortunately they were stopped by signal outside, and arrived 2½ minutes late.

As the accompanying log shows there was some very hard running throughout, including such speeds as 85 mph on the level near Moss, 92½ mph at Carlton, a minimum of 68 mph at Stoke summit, and 73 mph at Stevenage. But the outstanding feature was the maximum speed of 100½ mph at Essendine – one of the earliest examples of a 'three-figure' maximum with an LNER 'Pacific' of other than Gresley design. It came in the course of a long sustained effort when there would not have been any particular attempt to secure a spectacular maximum. The net time on this very fine run, 158¼ minutes, showing an average speed of 71·5 mph from start to stop, was only 1¼ minutes over the 'Coronation' on schedule of 1937, but instead of being run by new engines specially selected and groomed for the job, it was made by a hastily requisitioned substitute for a failed diesel.

TABLE 73
## YORK–KING'S CROSS
The Up 'Morning Talisman'
Load: 308 tons tare, 325 tons full
Engine: class 'A1' 4–6–0 No 60140 *Balmoral*

| Distance miles | | Sch. min | Actual min sec | | Speeds mph |
|---|---|---|---|---|---|
| 0·0 | YORK | 0 | 0 | 00 | |
| 4·2 | Naburn | | 6 | 36 | 61 |
| 9·7 | Riccall | | 11 | 10 | 77 |
| 13·8 | SELBY | 14½ | 14 | 52 | slack |
| 18·4 | Templehirst | | 19 | 17 | 73 |
| 25·2 | Moss | | 24 | 30 | 85 |
| 32·2 | DONCASTER | 36 | 30 | 03 | 56 |
| 36·9 | Rossington | | 34 | 20 | 69½ |
| — | | | sigs | | 20 |
| 49·6 | RETFORD | 52 | 47 | 28 | 65/69 |
| 54·5 | *Milepost* 133¾ | | 51 | 48 | 66 |
| 61·8 | Carlton | | 57 | 08 | 92½ |
| 68·1 | NEWARK | 68 | 61 | 35 | 80½ |
| 78·5 | Barkston | | 69 | 34 | 68 |
| 82·7 | GRANTHAM | 85 | 73 | 07 | 72 |
| 88·1 | *Stoke Box* | 90 | 77 | 42 | 68 |
| 96·0 | Little Bytham | | 83 | 10 | 99 |
| 99·6 | Essendine | 98 | 85 | 20 | 100½ |
| 103·4 | Tallington | | 87 | 42 | 94 |
| — | | | sigs | | 10 |
| 111·8 | PETERBOROUGH | 111 | 95 | 45 | slack |
| 118·8 | Holme | | 103 | 03 | 81 |
| 124·7 | *Abbots Ripton* | | 107 | 38 | 71 |
| — | | | p.w.s. | | 20 |
| 129·3 | HUNTINGDON | 128 | 113 | 50 | |
| 136·5 | St Neots | | 119 | 34 | 76 |
| 140·7 | Tempsford | | 122 | 40 | 86½ |
| — | | | p.w.s. | | 30 |
| 152·5 | Three Counties | | 133 | 23 | 83 |
| 156·3 | HITCHIN | 149 | 136 | 13 | 77 |
| 159·6 | Stevenage | | 138 | 52 | 73 |
| 167·9 | Welwyn Garden City | | 145 | 03 | 90 |
| 170·5 | HATFIELD | 166 | 146 | 51 | — |
| 175·5 | Potters Bar | 172 | 150 | 53 | 72½ |
| — | | | p.w.s. | | — |
| 185·7 | Finsbury Park | 186 | 161 | 49 | — |
| — | | | sig stop | | |
| 188·2 | KING'S CROSS | 193 | 169 | 12 | |

Net time: 158¼ minutes.

Another most experienced compiler of logs, Mr J. L. Lean, recorded a splendid run on the 5.10 PM Newcastle to King's Cross in May 1960, with 'A1' No 60133 *Pommern*. I have tabulated the section of this journey from Retford to Hitchin, in which 106·7 miles were covered in 101 minutes 59 seconds or 96½ minutes net. Again there was a 'three-figure' maximum

TABLE 74

RETFORD–HITCHIN

Load: 308 tons tare, 315 tons full

Engine: class 'A1' 4–6–2 No 60133 *Pommern*

| Distance miles | | Actual min   sec | Speeds mph |
|---|---|---|---|
| 0·0 | RETFORD | 0    00 | — |
| 4·9 | *Milepost* 133¾ | 7    20 | 56 |
| 12·2 | Carlton | 12    33 | 88 |
| 18·5 | NEWARK | 17    56 | 63/74 |
| 28·9 | Barkston | 26    38 | 72 |
| 33·1 | GRANTHAM | 30    25 | 65 |
| 38·5 | *Stoke Box* | 35    24 | 58 |
| 46·4 | Little Bytham | 41    18 | 96 |
| 50·0 | Essendine | 43    27 | 102 |
| 53·8 | Tallington | 45    51 | 95 |
| 62·2 | PETERBOROUGH | 53    24 | 18 |
| — | | p.w.s. | 28 |
| 79·7 | HUNTINGDON | 73    51 | 65 |
| 86·9 | St Neots | 80    17 | 65 |
| 95·5 | Sandy | 87    44 | 71 |
| — | | p.w.s. | 28 |
| 106·7 | HITCHIN | 101    59 | |

Net time: 96½ minutes.

down Stoke bank. Mr Lean clocked one quarter-mile at 103 mph, but I think the maximum probably did not exceed 102 mph. This was not an emergency occasion but a regular steam working although by 1960 steam was very much on the decline, and the engine was probably not in the superb condition of the 'Coronation' stud in 1937–8–9. In this account of LNER steam it is a pleasure to set on record these notable examples of very fast running by the 'A1' class.

A still more remarkable case of 100 mph running by a

Peppercorn engine occurred one morning on the up 'West
Riding' express, when a nine-coach train was being worked by
an 'A2', No 60526 *Sugar Palm*. The friend who logged this
run is an engineer who has had a good deal to do with experimental work and recording in a professional capacity, and I
mention this particularly to indicate that I have every confidence in the accuracy of his recording in this instance. There
was no prior talk with the driver, in fact after boarding the
crowded train at Doncaster he was more exercised in finding a
seat than in communicating with the engineman. In the early
stages the run was a pretty hopeless fight against delays, and
my friend could well have given up keeping a log had it not
been apparent from the tremendous accelerations from checks
that the men on the footplate meant real business. In the early
stages note should be taken of the maximum speeds of 74 mph
at Ranskill and 88 mph descending from Tuxford to the Trent
valley. The engine, moreover, was in poor shape. To quote my
friend: 'The loco had a dreadful beat – more appropriate to a
Gresley engine at its worst. The surging could be felt in the
first coach at starting.'

Grantham saw the last of the crippling series of checks that
had persisted since Bawtry. On passing Grantham 103 minutes
remained in which to make a punctual arrival in King's Cross
and still there remained permanent way checks in store at
Werrington Junction, near Tempsford, at Oakleigh Park, and
Finsbury Park. The first of these four involved the troughs,
and a special stop would be necessary at Peterborough to top
up the tender tank. Yet such was the vigour and enterprise of
the driving and firing that with no better tool than a run-down
Peppercorn 'A2' the train passed Finsbury Park with $5\frac{3}{4}$
minutes left in which to reach King's Cross on time. In other
words, by all ordinary reckonings the job was in the bag. Unfortunately signal checks supervened, and the actual arrival
was $3\frac{3}{4}$ minutes late.

From the exasperating signal check at Grantham itself *Sugar
Palm* was accelerated rapidly up to Stoke, topping the summit
at 58 mph; then the descent was terrific. My friend tells me
that he clocked the first '100' just south of Little Bytham, and

TABLE 75    DONCASTER–KING'S CROSS
Load: 314 tons tare, 335 tons full
Engine: class 'A2' 4–6–2 No 60526 *Sugar Palm*

| Distance miles | | Actual min sec | Speeds mph |
|---|---|---|---|
| 0·0 | DONCASTER | 0 00 | — |
| 4·7 | Rossington | 8 00 | 58 |
| — | | p.w.s. | 5 |
| 12·1 | Ranskill | 17 30 | 74 |
| 17·4 | RETFORD | 22 00 | — |
| — | | p.w.s. | 25 |
| — | *Markham Summit* | — | 51 |
| 24·1 | Tuxford | 30 34 | 72/88 |
| | | sig stop | |
| — | | p.w.s. | 20 |
| 35·9 | NEWARK | 46 20 | 45 |
| — | | p.w.s. | 35 |
| 40·6 | Claypole | 52 46 | 69 |
| — | | sigs | 20 |
| 46·3 | Barkston | 60 40 | 55/63 |
| — | | sigs | 25 |
| 50·5 | GRANTHAM | 66 05 | — |
| 55·9 | *Stoke Box* | 72 23 | 58 |
| 58·9 | *Corby Glen* | 74 56 | 80 |
| 63·8 | *Little Bytham* | 78 10 | 99 |
| 67·4 | Essendine | 80 20 | 102 |
| 71·2 | Tallington | 82 41 | 95 |
| — | | p.w.s. | 20 |
| 79·6 | PETERBOROUGH    arr. | 93 30 | water |
| — | dep. | 97 46 | stop |
| 86·6 | Holme | 106 12 | 80/72 |
| 97·1 | HUNTINGDON | 114 13 | 93 |
| 104·3 | St Neots | 119 05 | 82 |
| 108·5 | *Tempsford* | 122 01 | 93 |
| — | | p.w.s. | 30 |
| 111·9 | Sandy | 126 32 | 53 |
| 114·9 | Biggleswade | 129 13 | 72 |
| 119·0 | Arlesey | 132 34 | 80 |
| 124·1 | HITCHIN | 136 31 | 75 |
| 127·4 | Stevenage | 139 20 | 71 |
| — | | | 85½ |
| 138·3 | HATFIELD | 147 42 | 72/75 |
| 143·3 | Potters Bar | 151 46 | 73 |
| 146·8 | New Barnet | 154 28 | 82½ |
| — | | p.w.s. | 20 |
| 151·0 | Wood Green | 158 16 | 77 |
| — | | p.w.s. | 10 |
| 153·4 | Finsbury Park | 163 11 | — |
| | | sig stop | |
| 156·0 | KING'S CROSS | 172 40 | |

Net time: 133 minutes.

from milepost 90¼ successive quarter-miles gave speeds of 101, 102¼, 101, 101, 100, 100, 100, 103¼, 100, 100, 102¼, 102¼, 100, 101, 97, 97. By way of comment he adds: 'The "103¼" may have been due to a short rail, but I think this evidence supports a maximum of "101"'. On the strength of such data I would almost be inclined to claim 102, as fully half a mile was clocked at this speed south of Essendine, but my friend's more modest claim of 101 mph is well authenticated. The average speed between Little Bytham and Essendine was 99·9 mph.

At Peterborough no time was wasted over taking water, and some magnificent running followed, including a maximum speed of 93 mph at both Huntingdon and Tempsford, and a remarkable recovery from the 30 mph permanent way check south of the latter place. The average speed of 75·5 mph over the 28·4 miles from Biggleswade to Potters Bar was perhaps the finest feat of the entire run, having regard to the predominantly adverse nature of the intervening gradients. The up 'Coronation', with a load almost identical to that hauled by *Sugar Palm*, used to be allowed 32 minutes for the 41·2 miles from Huntingdon to Hatfield. On this recent run the time was 33 minutes 29 seconds inclusive of a permanent way check that cost at least 3 minutes. Over the complete 105·5 miles from Grantham to King's Cross the 'Coronation' allowance was 86½ minutes pass to stop; my friend estimates that the net time on his run with the 'West Riding' was 83 minutes. Again I would emphasize that the pre-war schedule was maintained by brand-new, prized, and carefully serviced 'A4's but the recent run was with a run-down 'A2'.

# CHAPTER NINETEEN

# A FINAL APPRAISAL

On looking back to the steam era on the railways of Britain, and particularly to the time since the grouping of 1923, the LNER stands out immediately as one of the most colourful and exciting of the old railways. In the first seventeen years of the grouping era Sir Nigel Gresley gradually assumed a position of positively towering stature over his fellow CMEs. By comparison Collett, after the blaze of glory surrounding the introduction of the 'King' class engines, retired more or less into seclusion at Swindon. On the Southern, Maunsell, from the viewpoint of steam locomotive practice, was fighting a rearguard action against the advance of electric traction, while on the LMS Stanier was then little more than over the threshold, and entering upon the truly great stage of his career.

For Gresley, apart from the episode of the water-tube boilered compound 4-6-4 No 10000, the years between 1927 and 1939 were one continual success, with each individual triumph more spectacular than the last. It is no wonder that railway enthusiasts rallied to the LNER in their thousands; the exploits of 'A1', 'A3', and 'A4' 'Pacifics', and of the giant 2-8-2s occupied so much space in railway journals, and figured in so much discussion and correspondence in enthusiast societies, that a partisan whose loyalties remained firmly elsewhere complained bitterly that the title of the Stephenson Locomotive Society might well be changed to the Gresley Locomotive Society. Unwittingly or not, Sir Nigel Gresley had acted as a truly magnificent publicity agent for his company, and the exploits of famous locomotives acted as a tonic to staff and shareholders, during a long sustained period of depression, when practically nothing in the way of dividends was forthcoming and an extremely tight hold was kept on the purse strings.

The war curtailed the development of some of the later

Gresley projects, among them the giant 4–8–2 express passenger engine, and then after Sir Nigel's death in 1941 there came
the Thompson episode. I have written enough of this earlier in
the book; but in retrospect it had one very salutary effect upon
the study of Gresley's work. It made us all look at it much
more searchingly, and more critically, and better able to
appreciate the value of the work K. J. Cook did when he arrived
at Doncaster, fresh from Swindon.

Despite all that has happened since, Gresley still personifies
LNER steam. The impact of the Thompson and Peppercorn
'Pacifics' was really very small in relation to their numbers, and
the 'B1', the only really significant product of the post-1941
era, was after all no more than a synthesis of Gresley standard
parts. It is, of course, most unlikely that Gresley, if he had
lived, would have produced the 'B1' himself, although one
must not forget that in his second rebuild of the Ivatt 'Atlantic'
No 3279 he put on two 20-in by 26-in cylinders. For new
design, however, he virtually discarded the two-cylinder engine
with outside-cylinders in 1918 when he built the first engine
with a conjugated valve gear – the 2–8–0 No 461. The various
inside-cylinder types 'N2', 'N7', 'J38', and 'J39' stood outside
the main line of development.

As Edward Thompson stressed so forcibly to me, Gresley's
main programme was built around the three-cylinder layout
with conjugated valve gear, and so with few exceptions the
whole stud remained to the end of their days. Peppercorn
showed no desire to follow up the Thompson rebuildings of
the 'B17's, as 'B2', or of the 'K3's as 'K5'. Then with the
'K4's, even though there were originally only six of them –
like the 'P2's – it was only one of them that was rebuilt to form
the prototype of the new class 'K1'. The remaining five finished
their days as three-cylinder engines just as Gresley built them.

On his translation from Swindon to Doncaster K. J. Cook
applied the Great Western practice of optically lining up the
frames and the cylinder centre lines as each of the 'Pacifics'
went through the works for general overhaul, and the greater
accuracy of erection enabled the running gear to be assembled
to much tighter clearances than had hitherto been possible;

and with tighter initial clearances the rate of wear was very much reduced. Slogger in the pin joints of the conjugated valve gear which had been the bugbear of all the Gresley three-cylinder engines was much slower in developing, and the characteristic Gresley 'ring' of the connecting- and coupling-rods largely vanished. Instead the engines ran with the silence of sewing-machines. Another change was the fitting of an adaptation of the Great Western de Glehn type of inside big-end.

In due course all the 'A4's were equipped with the Kylchap double-blastpipe exhaust arrangement which Gresley himself had fitted to the four engines 4468, 4901, 4902, and 4903, while the 'A3's were modernized to the Kylchap exhaust arrangement fitted by Gresley on No 2751 *Humorist*.

With the greater precision of repair work and the fitting of the Kylchap exhaust arrangement throughout, the whole stud of Gresley three-cylinder 'Pacifics' – 112 strong – was given a new lease of life, and except on the London–Edinburgh non-stops, 'A3's and 'A4's were used almost indiscriminately on the hardest East Coast duties. Although they had been improved in detail these 'A3's and 'A4's were essentially Gresley 'Pacifics' and as such they saw steam out on the most famous of the East Coast trains. Even this was not their last bow, for some were drafted to the Caledonian route between Glasgow and Aberdeen, while the most striking transition of all was that of a batch of 'A3's to Leeds (Whitehall Junction shed) to work the double-home turns to Glasgow St Enoch over the Midland and G & SW route. But I have written enough to establish the Gresley 'Pacifics' in their rightful place in history, and it is time to conclude.

In concluding, however, I must refer once again to some very famous LNER steam locomotives that are still on the active list, though now under private ownership, the 'Pacifics' No 4472 *Flying Scotsman* and 4498 *Sir Nigel Gresley*. Both have done some great work, and I am ending this saga of LNER Steam by reference to two runs, in 'foreign parts', on which some very fine performances were achieved. The first is the high-speed run from Swindon to Paddington made by No 4472 with the up

'Panda Pullman' on November 13th, 1965, on which the schedule was that of the pre-war Cheltenham Flyer: 65 minutes start to stop for the run of 77·3 miles. There was, however, a big difference in the working conditions, for while the Cheltenham Flyer had no speed restriction, and could be run at 85 to 90 mph throughout, a limit of 80 mph was placed upon the *Flying Scotsman*. It meant running her at the limit speed for the whole journey, but so splendidly was the engine working that she needed holding in, rather than pressing to achieve this result. A log of the journey is shown herewith.

TABLE 76
WESTERN REGION:
SWINDON–PADDINGTON
'The Panda Pullman'
Load: 195 tons gross
Engine: No 4472 *Flying Scotsman*
Driver: R. Williams; Fireman: D. Wyllis (Southall)

| Distance miles | | Sch. min | Actual min sec | Av. Speed mph |
|---|---|---|---|---|
| 0·0 | SWINDON | 0 | 0 00 | — |
| 5·8 | Shrivenham | | 7 12 | — |
| 10·8 | Uffington | 10½ | 11 02 | 78·3 |
| — | | | p.w.s. | |
| 16·9 | Wantage Road | | 17 10 | 59·6 |
| 24·2 | DIDCOT | 20½ | 22 40 | 79·6 |
| 41·3 | READING | 33½ | 35 40 | 79·0 |
| 68·2 | Southall | 54½ | 54 12 | 87·0 |
| 74·0 | *Milepost* 3¼ | | 59 24 | 67·0 |
| 76·3 | Westbourne Park | 61 | 62 02 | 52·2 |
| 77·3 | PADDINGTON | 65 | 66 03 | |

Net time: 64½ minutes.

The second run was a magnificent performance by *Sir Nigel Gresley* over the Crewe–Carlisle main line of the former LNWR. I was not a passenger myself on this occasion, but I was furnished with a very complete log by Mr H. G. Ellison. With the agreement of Mr B. W. C. Cooke, editor-in-chief, I am quoting verbatim the description of this run that I wrote in the *Railway Magazine* for February 1968.

I do not think there would be a more fitting conclusion to the story of LNER steam power than a reference to a performance of such superb quality.

The train went out of Crewe in a style enough to make some of the Liverpool 'electrics' look to their laurels, for in just over 10 minutes from the dead start *Sir Nigel Gresley*, with his load of 385 tons, was travelling at 96 mph! Once out from 'under the wires', however, the pace had to be moderated to suit the reduced speed limit of the non-electrified line. Even so to reach Warrington, 24 miles, in 22 minutes 40 seconds was a most exhilarating start. On the ensuing section from Warrington to Preston, the train was beset by checks, and so took 40 minutes 5 seconds for this distance of 27 miles. Then they set out on the non-stop run to Carlisle, for which the ultra-cautious time of 118 minutes had been laid down to a working stop at Carlisle No 13 Box, 88·6 miles.

The immediate start out of Preston can never be very brisk, and the engine was taken gently over the labyrinth of crossings until the Blackpool lines had veered away to the left. Then the acceleration was to some purpose, and the speed soared to 84 mph on the level at Garstang. Then came two permanent way checks, one at Scorton intermediate signals, and the second at Lancaster No 1 Junction. The two together cost about 8½ minutes in running and the engine was not pressed to a very rapid acceleration from Lancaster; the speed rose only from 61 to 64 mph along the level between Hest bank and Carnforth. But after passing the latter station the engine was magnificently opened up to make an average speed of all but 63 mph right up to Shap summit. From the accompanying log it will be seen that the sharp rise to milepost 9½ was cleared at 59 mph and then the speed rose to all but 80 mph on the level before tackling Grayrigg bank. The time of 12 minutes 7 seconds for the 12·6 miles from Milnthorpe to Grayrigg must be something of a record with a gross load of 385 tons although of course the climbing on the upper part of the bank does not match the classic effort

TABLE 77
LONDON MIDLAND REGION:
10.48 CREWE–CARLISLE
'The Border Limited'; October 28th, 1967
Load: 351 tons tare, 385 tons full
Engine: class 'A4' 4–6–2 No 4498 *Sir Nigel Gresley*
Driver: Bert Stuart; Fireman: Neil Cadman (Crewe)

| Distance miles | | Sch. min | Actual min sec | | Speeds mph |
|---|---|---|---|---|---|
| 0·0 | PRESTON | 0 | 0 | 00 | — |
| 1·3 | *Oxheys* | | 4 | 28 | 43 |
| 4·7 | *Barton* | | 8 | 13 | 65 |
| 7·4 | *Brock* | | 10 | 29 | 78 |
| 9·5 | Garstang | 12 | 12 | 00 | 83/84 |
| — | | | p.w.s. | | — |
| 12·7 | *Scorton* | | 16 | 07 | 15* |
| 15·3 | *Bay Horse* | | 19 | 28 | 58 |
| 18·0 | *Oubeck* | | 22 | 00 | 70 |
| — | | | p.w.s. | | — |
| 19·9 | *Lancaster No 1* | | 27 | 15 | 20* |
| 21·0 | LANCASTER | 24 | 28 | 52 | 52 |
| 24·1 | Hest Bank | | 32 | 19 | 61 |
| 27·3 | CARNFORTH | 31 | 35 | 16 | 64/70 |
| 29·5 | *Yealand IBS* | | 37 | 17 | 62 |
| 30·5 | *Milepost 9½* | | 38 | 16 | 59 |
| 32·7 | *Burton No 2* | | 40 | 13 | 74 |
| 34·5 | *Milnthorpe* | | 41 | 37 | 79 |
| 36·4 | *Hincaster site* | | 43 | 11 | 71 |
| 38·0 | *Sedgwick IBS* | | 44 | 31 | 68/70 |
| 40·1 | OXENHOLME | 46 | 46 | 27 | 63 |
| 42·0 | *Peat Lane IBS* | | 48 | 13 | 61 |
| 43·5 | *Hay Fell site* | | 49 | 50 | 57 |
| 45·2 | *Lambrigg Crossing* | | 51 | 38 | 56 |
| 47·1 | *Grayrigg* | | 53 | 44 | 52 |
| 48·9 | *Low Gill* | | 55 | 30 | 58* |
| 51·0 | *Dillicar IBS* | | 57 | 33 | 68 |
| 53·1 | Tebay | 68 | 59 | 21 | 73/69 |
| 54·5 | *Tebay North IBS* | | 60 | 34 | 67 |
| 55·5 | *Milepost 34½* | | 61 | 30 | 60 |
| 56·0 | *Milepost 35* | | 62 | 02 | 55 |
| 56·1 | *Scout Green Crossing* | | 62 | 12 | 54 |
| 56·5 | *Milepost 35½* | | 62 | 35 | 53 |
| 57·0 | *Milepost 36* | | 63 | 09 | 52 |
| 57·5 | *Milepost 36½ (Wells)* | | 63 | 44 | 50 |
| 58·0 | *Milepost 37* | | 64 | 21 | 48 |
| 58·5 | *Milepost 37½* | | 64 | 59 | 47 |
| 58·7 | *Shap Summit* | 80 | 65 | 13 | — |

TABLE 77 (*continued*)

| Distance<br>miles | | Sch.<br>min | Actual<br>min   sec | Speeds<br>mph |
|---|---|---|---|---|
| — | | | p.w.s. | — |
| 60·7 | Shap | | 68   38 | 20* |
| 63·9 | *Thrimby Grange* | | 75   00 | 60* |
| 68·0 | *Clifton* | | 79   22 | 55* |
| 72·2 | PENRITH | 94 | 83   54 | 50* |
| 74·5 | *Milepost 53½* | | 86   04 | 68 |
| 77·0 | Plumpton | 99 | 88   02 | 84 |
| 79·3 | *Calthwaite* | | 89   38 | 88 |
| 82·7 | *Southwaite* | | 92   06 | 78 |
| 85·2 | *Wreay* | | 94   07 | 70* |
| 86·8 | *Brisco* | | 95   29 | 74 |
| 88·6 | CARLISLE No 13 home | 118 | 97   43 | — |

Net time to Citadel Station: 86½ minutes.    * Speed restrictions.
IBS = Intermediate block signal.

of the Stanier 4–6–2 LMS No 6244, *King George VI*, with the
wartime 10·05 from Euston, when, with a 475-ton train, the
speed was 59 mph sustained at Lambrigg and 57 mph over
the summit. Nevertheless, this performance of 4498 was a
grand effort, and judging from the brilliant acceleration that
followed from Low Gill, was in no way beyond the continuous steaming capacity of the boiler.

Then came Shap itself with a phenomenal ascent, and an
average speed over the four miles of 1 in 75 ascent between
mileposts 33½ and 37½ of 54½ mph. Making careful allowance
for the loss in kinetic energy of engine and train by the
deceleration during this period, it would appear that the
average equivalent drawbar horsepower over this four miles
of ascent was around 2,550. This was an exceptional piece of
work in every way and one of the finest Shap ascents ever
recorded with steam. The occasion was splendidly docu-
mented photographically by Mr W. B. Greenfield whose
result is reproduced in this book. The photograph is, however, much more than a mere record of a 'train in motion'.
It reveals in the clearness of the exhaust, and the slight wisp
of steam from the safety valves, that the working of the

engine was absolutely ideal – a wonderful piece of work every way.

There was a permanent way slack just after Shap summit, and speed was severely restrained thereafter until Penrith had been passed. Then *Sir Nigel Gresley* was allowed to run and there was a brilliant finish, with a top speed of 88 mph near Calthwaite. The train was stopped, by order, at Carlisle No 13 home signal, but Mr Ellison estimates a net time of 86½ minutes to Citadel station.

# *INDEX*

# THE MOST SOUGHT AFTER SERIES IN THE '70's

These superb David & Charles titles are now available in PAN, for connoisseurs, enthusiasts, tourists and everyone looking for a deeper appreciation of Britain than can be found in routine guide books.

**BRITISH STEAM SINCE 1900** W. A. Tuplin 45p
An engrossing review of British locomotive development – 'Intensely readable' – COUNTRY LIFE. Illustrated.

**THE SAILOR'S WORLD** T. A. Hampton 35p
A guide to ships, harbours and customs of the sea. 'Will be of immense value' – PORT OF LONDON AUTHORITY. Illustrated.

**OLD DEVON** W. G. Hoskins 45p
'As perfect an account of the social, agricultural and industrial grassroots as one could hope to find' – THE FIELD. Illustrated.

**INTRODUCTION TO INN SIGNS**
Eric R. Delderfield 35p
This beautifully illustrated and fascinating guide will delight everyone who loves the British pub. Illustrated.

**THE CANAL AGE** Charles Hadfield 50p
A delightful look at the waterways of Britain, Europe and North America from 1760 to 1850. Illustrated.

**BUYING ANTIQUES** A. W. Coysh and J. King 45p
An invaluable guide to buying antiques for pleasure or profit. 'Packed with useful information' – QUEEN MAGAZINE. Illustrated.

**RAILWAY ADVENTURE** L. T. C. Rolt 35p
The remarkable story of the Talyllyn Railway from inception to the days when a band of local enthusiasts took over its running. Illustrated.

# A SELECTION OF POPULAR READING IN PAN

## FICTION

| | | |
|---|---|---|
| SILENCE ON MONTE SOLE | Jack Olsen | 35p |
| COLONEL SUN   A new James Bond novel by Robert Markham | | 25p |
| THE LOOKING-GLASS WAR | John le Carré | 25p |
| THE FAME GAME | Rona Jaffe | 40p |
| CATHERINE AND A TIME FOR LOVE Juliette Benzoni | | 35p |
| THE ASCENT OF D13 | Andrew Garve | 25p |
| THE FAR SANDS | Andrew Garve | 25p |
| AIRPORT | Arthur Hailey | 37½p |
| REQUIEM FOR A WREN | Nevil Shute | 30p |
| SYLVESTER | Georgette Heyer | 30p |
| ROSEMARY'S BABY | Ira Levin | 25p |
| HEIR TO FALCONHURST | Lance Horner | 40p |
| THE MURDER IN THE TOWER | Jean Plaidy | 30p |
| GAY LORD ROBERT | Jean Plaidy | 30p |
| A CASE OF NEED | Jeffery Hudson | 35p |
| THE ROSE AND THE SWORD | Sandra Paretti | 40p |

## NON-FICTION

| | | |
|---|---|---|
| THE SOMERSET & DORSET RAILWAY (illus.) Robin Atthill | | 35p |
| THE WEST HIGHLAND RAILWAY (illus.) John Thomas | | 35p |
| MY BEAVER COLONY (illus.) | Lars Wilsson | 25p |
| THE PETER PRINCIPLE   Dr. Laurence J. Peter and Raymond Hull | | 30p |
| THE ROOTS OF HEALTH | Leon Petulengro | 20p |

These and other advertised PAN Books are obtainable from all booksellers and newsagents. If you have any difficulty please send purchase price plus 5p postage to P.O. Box 11, Falmouth, Cornwall.

While every effort is made to keep prices low, it is sometimes necessary to increase prices at short notice. PAN Books reserve the right to show new retail prices on covers which may differ from those previously advertised in the text or elsewhere.